The United States of Empire

Sheaodunne 3@Aol.com

John 19:8-11
When Pilate heard this he was even more afraid and he went
back inside the palace. "Where do you come from?" he asked
Jesus, but Jesus gave him no answer. "Do you refuse to speak to
me?" Pilate said. Don't you realize I have power either to free
you or to crucify you?" Jesus answered, "You would have no
power over me if it were not given to you from above."
Holy Bible, New International Version

The United States of Empire

The passing of the mantle from the
United Kingdom to the United States.

James F. Dunn

2007

The United States of Empire

Chapters

Introduction
The Twentieth Century in Retrospect

At the beginning of the twentieth century, the United States was an also-ran in the global race for national preeminence. In 1906, President Theodore "Teddy" Roosevelt sent the "White Fleet" around the world. It sailed in an ostentatious attempt to flex American muscle and show the world that the United States was equal to any other nation. In spite of this, the United States was not taken seriously as a world power. How is it that in the "American Century" the United States came to rule the world?

The United States was a power only in its own hemisphere (except for a colonial excursion into the Philippines), as its army had ventured only 300 miles outside its own borders during the Mexican War in the 1840s or to Cuba in the 1890s. Just before the turn of the century, the United States successfully defeated a decrepit and dying empire during the short-lived Spanish-American War. Although the United States armed forces numbered 2.5 million men in arms during the American Civil War (accounting for both sides), this army had quickly dispersed following the war. This was owing to the lack of a significant armed threat against it, even considering the Indian Wars of the late 1800s. Compared to the armies and navies of Europe, the United States hardly ranked. As far as armies were concerned in the beginning of the twentieth century, Russia had the largest. Germany's was smaller but the most feared, and France came in a strong third. Great Britain's army was the smallest of the European forces, but very mobile and able to reach any spot on the globe quickly because of its navy. Considering the navies, Great Britain's was the largest and most feared. Germany, another young country flexing its muscles, grew to a close second. The United States could, however, revel in the fact that no European power could harm it; it was safely separated from them by the Atlantic Ocean. It remained protected from those imposing powers following two successful wars against the greatest sea power in the world, Great Britain. The former colony of Great Britain was now its commercial competitor, but offered no naval competition to the acknowledged ruler of the seas. It is interesting to note that during the Spanish-American War, the former mother country was on board ship with the United States, giving advice and consent to her offspring's first attempts at international power. Great Britain gladly sold colliers and supplies to Admiral George E. Dewey, before his attacks on the Philippines, and some of his ships carried British naval personnel. The Spanish-American War was a battle between an up-and-coming third-rank pugilist and an old, worn-out opponent, who no longer had any punching ability. It was hardly a sporting show, but necessary in the jungle warfare of power politics.

As 1899 became 1900, President McKinley was assassinated; Theodore Roosevelt became president of the United States and strengthened the Navy during his peacetime presidency, a practice that he had been engaged in since his brief assignment as the assistant secretary of the Navy. The first decade of the century was filled with invention, new technology in commerce and war machines, and a great arms race.

Germany and Great Britain were locked in a fierce competition to build bigger, faster, more heavily armed battleships called Dreadnoughts. Roosevelt was doing the same, but Great Britain did not take this as a direct threat. In fact, Roosevelt's Great White Fleet was editorialized as "a Godsend" in a newspaper in Melbourne, Australia, which was then still an essential part of the British Empire.

In 1914, well after Theodore Roosevelt was out of office, war broke out on the European Continent. At first, it was a war pitting Germany and Austria against France and Russia. Great Britain joined the French and the Russians in the battle for two main reasons. First, Germany's new fleet threatened the British High Seas Fleet. Second, a victorious Germany would be a major continental power. The coupling of this potential major power with a competitive naval fleet was not something that Great Britain would allow to exist; the resulting threat would be too great. The propaganda of the time promoted the thinking that Great Britain went to war to fight for democratic rule and the sovereignty of Belgium. However, this completely neglected the fact that Germany already had a parliamentary form of government akin to the British government, although not nearly as liberal. Also, when Chancellor Otto von Bismarck cobbled together the Germanic states with Prussia to form the modern state of Germany in the 1860s, he did so with the consent of the majority of its member states. They formed the *Reichstag*, a European-style parliament like the *Reichsrat* in Austria. Neither of these two parliaments was as powerful over its monarch as the British Parliament was over its own monarch, but that was due to the distinct history of England. In reality, the Entente's (British, French, and Russian) claim that World War I was a conflict between a warmongering monarch and freedom-loving democracies was purely the result of well-distributed Entente propaganda. This line of propaganda was so effective that it resonates to this day.

With Great Britain's entry the Great War was engaged. Almost all of Europe became engulfed in the conflict. France and Russia bore the heaviest tolls of death and destruction. France lost 1,400,000 men to the war, Russia, 1,800,000. Millions more were maimed or injured.[0] It was expected to be a short war, but it dragged on for four years. Russia was forced out first, in 1917, when losses on the front translated into the collapse of the Czarist Romanov government. German troops remained on the Russian front when successive Russian governments refused to give up the fight. It was not until the Germans sent a secret train into Russia carrying the Communist Vladimir Lenin, with fifteen million deutsche marks that the Russian troops withdrew from the battle. Lenin's Communists toppled the fledgling democracy and ended Russia's war effort. When this happened, almost one million German troops were released to go to the western front. These troops were unable to defeat the Entente forces in the west, something the German planners had been striving for years to accomplish. Buoyed by the declaration of war by the United States upon Germany, Entente troops dug in and fought doggedly. When the American troops arrived, they fought extremely well and they supplied support staff that enabled veteran European troops to go to the front.

The whole of the twentieth century turned on the outcome of this first major war. The war and the world could have turned quite differently for several reasons if Germany had prevailed. If the United States had not joined the fight, the Entente troops would not have received the morale boost from the promise of fresh armies. If the additional troops themselves had not arrived, then the Entente might not have had the will or ability to win. Without a steady supply of armaments and food from the United States, the war effort could not have been sustained. Most devastating of all, if the United States had done the unthinkable and forced Great Britain to end its blockade of the North Sea, then the German troops could have encirled the Entente armies and won the war.

Germany was defeated by the Entente forces but retained the dynamic and the will to be a great country. A leader with maniacal ambitions would soon harness that energy for evil. Adolf Hitler came to power in 1933 and seduced the German people back onto the battlefield in six short years following the end of World War I. He did more to unify the German-speaking people than German Chancellor Otto von Bismarck ever did. He united a Greater Germany (including Austria) in his *Lebensraum* (living space). Militarily he was more successful than Kaiser Wilhelm. He brought Paris to its knees in a matter of weeks at the beginning of World War II, and continued to occupy it until near the end of the war. But he also did more to destroy the German people than had occurred since the Thirty Years' War of the seventeenth century. Without the defeat of Germany in World War I, there would have been no abdication of Kaiser Wilhelm. Without the Kaiser's abdication, there would have been no power vacuum into which Hitler could walk. With a strong Kaiser in power, the Communists, who had been set up in Russia, would have had a strong German threat. It is unlikely that Russia, the Soviet Union, would have become the international enemy that it became if Germany had not been defeated.

Questions remain today. If Germany had been victorious in WWI, would it have turned its military might against the British Empire? Would it have attacked the United States or would it have been occupied by clashes in the east with the Communist government it had put in place in Russia? The German government had sent the Communists into Russia to hasten the end of the war in the east, so that troops could be sent to the western front and end the entire war. German plans were thwarted and German and Prussian dreams of empire were ended by the United States' entry into the war. Why the German high command failed to see the danger of bringing the United States into the war could fill many psychology books; it is also one of the underlying questions in this book. A Bismarck would have foreseen the dangers inherent in bringing a strong, young, healthy, and yet untested power into the fray. Frederick the Great, the warrior prince and founding father of the Prussians would also have recognized the danger. However, Kaiser Wilhelm was no Frederick. His prime ministers were no Bismarcks. General von Paul Hindenburg and General Erich Ludendorff had even less vision than the Kaiser did; victorious on the battlefield, their presence overpowered the crippled Kaiser, who had never been in action. Once the generals were assured of victory in the east, they did not fear the possibility of the United States entering the war. They assumed that the German troops would be lounging in Paris and the war would be over before the Americans could join the battle. They did not foresee setbacks, or the tenacity of the British Tommies. When swift victory did not occur for the Germans, nervous breakdowns, such as Ludendorff's, did. The failure of the leaders to lead in 1918, when the going got tough, brought about massive desertion by German troops. Suddenly, the unbeatable, victorious Teutonic army had been beaten. Defeat on the battlefield led to the abdication of the Kaiser, which led to a weak republic and then the rise of a great evil, the Nazis.

After the Great War was over and the Kaiser had left Germany to become a solitary citizen in the Netherlands, an allied-imposed democracy replaced the government. This German democracy was an induced birth of a government at best. The Kaiser was deposed, but the Entente would not negotiate with his son or with the military. So the Weimar Republic was born.

The chancellor had previously been a minister appointed by the emperor. Now, he was to be elected. Chancellor Phillip Scheidemann was about to be replaced by Friedrich Ebert. At the same time that Ebert was to become chancellor, adoring mobs carried the Communist Karl Liebknecht through Berlin, to take charge of Germany.

Although there had been a German Parliament—the Reichstag—it was subservient to the Kaiser and the chancellor.

Direct democracy was new to Germans. There had been democratic reformers around Germany throughout its young history. There were those who, in 1848, thought that the Frankfurt constitution would give birth to a liberal Prussia; however, Bismarck, no constitutionalist himself, revised it and power remained with the chancellor and the emperor, with minor checks by the Reichstag.

The imposed German democracy should not be compared to the English or American versions. German democracy in the 1920s lacked the depth and time needed for acceptance by the populous. English democracy can be traced to the Magna Carta of 1215, when English barons made demands upon King John. It can be seen in the many battles between the monarch and Parliament from the fifteenth century onward. The English Civil War put Oliver Cromwell in power as the Lord Protector of England's only republic from 1653-58. The monarchy was reinstated after Cromwell's death, but the king was never again as powerful as before Cromwell and certainly not as powerful as were the monarchs on the Continent. Although Henry VIII is popularly remembered for his many wives, he made the very insightful statement that the country was never as powerful as when king and Parliament stood together.

George I was brought over from Hanover, Germany, to be king of England, but could not speak any English. He was at the mercy of the Parliament. In fact, George III, whom the American colonists rebelled against, was only trying to exert the kind of power over his subjects—the colonists—that other monarchs of the time had exerted.

The American experience includes English history. American democracy grew from the time when the first pilgrims established permanent towns in Virginia and Massachusetts, to the Revolutionary War. The American colonists practiced 150 years of local democratic rule that mirrored the English government before the Revolution. All thirteen colonies had an assembly legistaure based upon the

Parliament style. The colonists considered themselves to be Englishmen, under the protection of the king.

For the United States or Great Britain to impose on Germany the kind of democracy that both nations had forged over centuries and expect it to work smoothly, was a gamble that was sure to lose—especially when one adds the bitterness of a defeat, which, given a few different decisions by the German leaders, could have been a glorious victory. When Hitler came along and appealed to the German people's remembrance of greatness and past glories, it was not empty rhetoric; it was based on their shared history. He recalled the Holy Roman Empire and the Teutonic Knights, and the German people gathered strength from it. American and English democracy did not fare well in the shadow of German folklore, of which it had no part. The reign of the strong warrior prince blessed by God or fate figured strongly in Germany's past. It was into this role that Hitler stepped.

In the 1930s, the Great Depression was a worldwide reality that was magnified in Germany, due to the ineptness of the Weimar Republic. Most students of history are familiar with the image of a German man with a wheelbarrow full of German marks, which amounted to virtually nothing. This, in the country that once produced the best steam locomotives in the world, the country of Krupp manufacturing, makers of the world's most feared cannons, the country that formerly dared to rival Great Britain on the high seas. Germany began to rebound by the mid-1930s. Since it had sunk lower economically than any other country, returning to the low levels of other Western nations was still an accomplishment. Once in power, Hitler could claim that Germany was benefiting from his leadership when, in reality, it had nowhere to go but up. There were benefits for those who were in Hitler's good graces. They benefited from the confiscation of land and property from Jews and Communists. Those who were in the military arms business profited from the rebuilding of

Germany's armed forces. When war broke out, Hitler and the German army looked invincible, once again.

When the German army, with its blitzkrieg, invaded Poland, the antiquated Polish army faced the confrontation by charging a mechanized army with a horse cavalry. It should be remembered that Prussia had extended through much of northern Poland. It is worth considering that many former Prussian *Junkers* (titled landowners) lived in Poland in 1939, and many Poles might have considered themselves to be German or Prussian. The French and British troops that came to aid the Poles were routed. The new British Prime Minister in 1940, Winston Churchill, promised to fight for Polish freedom; however, Poland would not see freedom until 1988. After Hitler's victory over Poland, he divided Poland between Germany and Stalinist Russia, a temporary neutral ally.

Once Poland was secured, Hitler turned to the west, to France. German troops were successful in the west for several reasons. They did not attack France's strong Maginot Line, where France was prepared to repel an attack. Instead, they sought a weak spot and went around the defensive line. They made excellent use of new technologies; the tank and the airplane, which they coupled with techniques, which had been developed and honed since the 1870s in the Franco-Prussian War. Hitler inherited a well-disciplined motivated army, which Europe, even with the British Empire's help, could not stop. That is why the United States was needed to bring an end to World War II.

Franklin Delano Roosevelt was well aware that the United States needed to enter World War II long before Pearl Harbor. The real question about the entry of the United States into WWII was not "if" but "when?" Some have claimed that FDR allowed Pearl Harbor to be attacked in order to get the United States involved in the war. This book will show that there is strong evidence that he was well aware that the attack was imminent days, if not months, before it happened. The evidence is weighty that a Machiavellian president did what he had to do to attain the goals that he determined were best for him and his country. It is clear, judging by the outcome of World War I, that Germany would have been the victor if the United States had not tipped the balance of power in the Great War. In WWII, it is inconceivable that Great Britain and the French forces under Charles de Gaulle could have been successful, even after Russia became a combatant, if the United States had not joined the war effort.

By the outset of WWII, the Germans had determined that the tank should be at the forefront of any troop movement. They had come to realize the importance of the tank since the First World War. Tanks had helped to turn the tide for the Allies in the first conflict, and this was not lost on the German planners. The failure of the Germans to supply a sufficient number of tanks to their troops in WWI greatly damaged their last attempts at victory. The British put the tank to work, and this helped to turn German victories in 1918 to German losses.

In WWII, the Germans ended the scourge of the First World War, the blockade, by taking Norway. In WWI, Great Britain commanded the North Sea by stationing its fleet in the Scottish Firth of Forth near Edinburgh. From there, they could close off any incoming shipping from any country because it would have to pass between Scotland and Norway. Hitler circumvented that problem by taking Norway early in the second war.

After these successes, Hitler began to feel invincible in his battle decisions. It was in the spring of 1940 when he began planning his attack on Russia. This had always been his objective. He believed that Germany's strength lay in going to the east and developing *Lebensraum* there, in contrast to the Kaiser's belief that Germany's strength lay to the west or on the seas. At first, Hitler was pragmatic enough to sign a peace treaty (or nonaggression pact) with Russia; however, he foolishly did not abide by it. In fact, he was still fighting British and French forces in North Africa at the time of the attack on Russia. It was Hitler who opened up a war on two fronts, something the Kaiser had dreaded. This predicament was what almost destroyed the brilliant Emperor Frederick, in the 18th century, as he fought the various alliances of the French, Austrians, and Russians. Hitler's attack on Russia was his ultimate doom. Most of his generals argued against it. They asserted that Germany could attack Russia in its soft underbelly, at some later time, without repeating the mistakes of Napoleon Bonaparte, or duplicating his ignominious defeat. Hitler, however, did not pay heed to his advisors, and on July 31, 1940, he announced to his generals his desire to conquer Russia.

Hitler exceeded his limits in a number of ways. He overextended his reach by pushing his troops too far to the east. The path that brought the United States into the war could have easily been avoided had Hitler worked to limit his potential enemies. Instead, he made Russia a combatant rather than keeping them on the sideline. He failed to remove the smaller targets of Britain and de Gaulle's troops in Africa and the Middle East. As a direct consequence of this failure, he was unable to secure control of the rich oil fields of Arabia. Because of this failure, Great Britain, the Netherlands, and the United States were able to continue pressuring Germany and Japan, whose own lack of natural resources in oil greatly hindered them. With control of Middle Eastern oil, Germany could have supplied Japan's and its own military machines' need for oil and assured Japan's control of South Asia. Without the oil, Japan needed to attack Pearl Harbor to ease America's oil embargo. Without this attack, the United States might never have entered the war, but this attack ensured it. Prior to the attack on Pearl Harbor, Gallop polls showed that seventy-five percent of Americans were against participating in a war in Europe or the Pacific. FDR had even campaigned, in 1940, promising American parents that he would not send their sons into another foreign war. Pearl Harbor changed the tenor of sentiments in the United States; this was no longer a foreign war but one that had been brought to America's shores and its very real threat must be brought to an end.

In one sense, Germany's fate was sealed when the United States entered the war. This is not to say that the effort was a simple one, nor can the memory of the tens of thousands who died to defeat Nazism be swept away. The war could have gone wrong for the Allies. The war would have ended differently had the Germans been allowed to retreat from Stalingrad. Hitler was firmly convinced that the real attack on D-Day was going to come to Calais, and so the German tanks sat there, while the Allies breached the defenses at Omaha.

Hitler was no military genius. He became drunk with his early successes and saw himself as invincible. He was blind to his failures and determined to have control over every aspect of his campaign for *Lebensraum*. He was committed to fight to the death and this commitment included all of Germany. Some of his generals came to see through this charade as the invincible leader of the Germans and saw a lunatic who would destroy the nation. Unfortunately for the German people, no one in Germany could stop him. He survived many assassination attempts but finally took his own life, using cyanide pills and a gun, when his utter failure finally became apparent to him. His body was being burned as the Soviet troops moved through the streets of Berlin.

The destruction of Germany opened the door to the next great confrontation, the Cold War. Both British Prime Minister Winston Churchill and President Roosevelt put aside their political differences, distaste and distrust of the Communist Josef Stalin, Lenin's successor, and made him a full partner in their effort to defeat the Nazis. When the war was won, Germany was split into four sections, one for each of the four victorious powers: Great Britain, France, the United States, and the Soviet Union. However, soon after the Nazis were defeated, the old distrust and enmity resurfaced and the Cold War was born. The city of Berlin was in the middle of the Soviet Union's sector, but it had been declared an international zone. Stalin threatened to cut it off from the west and to starve it. President Truman ordered an airlift of food, medicine, and fuel to be flown into the city to keep it free. The airlift lasted almost a year before Stalin backed down and opened the highways and railroads. The Berlin Airlift created high tensions between the Soviet Union and the West. Tensions continued to rise as the Soviet Union forced communist forms of governments on all the Eastern European countries it had freed from Nazi occupation.

A huge breakdown occurred in the balance of powers in Europe after WWII. For centuries, there had been a Western power on the Continent, France. There had always been a central Germanic power, most recently Germany, before that the Austrian Empire, and prior to that, the Holy Roman Empire. In the East, the great power was Russia, dominated for 300 years by the Romanovs, but now under Communist rule. Germany had now been utterly defeated and divided. The Austrian Empire was long gone. France was a power in name only, having piggybacked its way into the European power structure carried by Great Britain and the United States. Now there was no continental power to stop the Soviet Union from engulfing all of Western Europe to the Atlantic. Great Britain was the last remaining military force in Europe, but it was weakened and deeply in debt following the two world wars. Its empire was in the process of being dismantled. After fighting two wars for freedom and democracy, it could hardly deny the same to its far-flung possessions. FDR, throughout the war, pushed for greater freedom for the former British colonial lands from India to Palestine. This left only one other world power to stand up to the Soviet Union, the United States of America. Although the United States had lost many men fighting WWII and had spent millions of dollars, the country was not physically touched (with the exception of Pearl Harbor) by the war. It had the economic strength, the will, and the resources to fight a decades-long battle for dominance in the world that would pit it against the Soviet

Union. It was capitalism versus communism, Anglo-Saxon democracy versus feudal overlords, and individualism versus collectivism, between a God-fearing country and one that denied the existence of God and put man above all.

There were shock waves that reverberated throughout the Western world when Mao Tse-tung drove the armies of Chiang Kai-shek out of China onto the island of Taiwan. From the Korean and Vietnam wars and the Cuban Missile Crisis to the conflicts of Africa and Central America, the underlying theme was democracy versus communism. Another aspect of this conflict was the race into space and to the moon, which was as much about developing greater technologies to enable one side or the other to ultimately win in any war as it was about exploring what lay beyond our world. The nuclear race was an armament race, reminiscent of the building of the Dreadnoughts at the beginning of the century. Though this cold war never heated up into a direct confrontation between the two main antagonists, it came close during the Cuban Missile Crisis. President John F. Kennedy was able to convince Nikita Khrushchev that the United States would go to war over the placement of nuclear missiles ninety miles to the south of Florida. Khrushchev recalled the ships that were to deliver the missiles to Cuba. The immediate crisis was averted, but the Cold War continued for another twenty years.

The ultimate end of the Cold War was rather anticlimactic. There was no great war between the two powers. Instead, President Ronald Reagan was able to convince Congress to outspend the Soviet Union in an arms race. He specifically wanted the United States to develop an antiballistic missile program that proposed shooting down incoming missiles. It was nicknamed "Star Wars" after a popular movie of the time, which pitted a star-based federation against an "Evil Empire." In fact, Reagan himself had flabbergasted many appeasement-type politicians by claiming that the Soviet Union itself was an Evil Empire. In the end, it was the greater economic engine of the United States that allowed it to defeat the Evil Empire.

The Soviet Union, the workers' paradise, could not keep up with the production level or the technological advances of the capitalistic United States.

When Premier Mikhail Gorbachev saw that the Soviet Union could not compete with the West, he was forced to enact reforms of the communist system. These reforms, or *Perestroika*, hastened the collapse of Communism rather than strengthen it. The old Iron Curtain, from the Baltic Sea to the Caspian Sea, became a porous sieve. People from Eastern Europe flooded into Western Europe. The Berlin Wall, erected in 1961 to keep East Berliners in, fell. Those who had been imprisoned by it joyfully smashed it to pieces with sledgehammers.

When the Iron Curtain was shredded in 1988, and the Berlin Wall fell in 1989, there was no doubting it. That great symbol of the division of Europe, with armed forces staring each other down, waiting for the first shot to be fired, was torn down. The Soviet Union had died. The United States had survived. The Evil Empire was dead. The United States now ruled. It was now the emperor of the world.

But the whole process began with WWI. If Germany had been diplomatically smart enough to keep the United States neutral, then Germany could have won. There would have been no abdication of the Kaiser, no room for Hitler to rise to power, no Nazis, no WWII. Without a prostrate Germany in the late forties, the Soviet Union could not have risen to the level of power that it did. There would have been no Cold War. Conceivably, the world would still be split among the British, German, and Japanese empires, with the United States in the middle of all these. It was WWI that set in motion all the significant events that led to the United States becoming an empire in its own right, even if the government refuses to call itself an empire.

By the time the Cold War ended in 1989, the United States was the only superpower left standing. It was the hammer. Germany was the anvil that the United States used to solidify its power, its empire. Today, the United States stands as the lone superpower, the last empire of the European countries. As the Empire, it must absorb the blows from those who seek to dethrone it. Challenges will come because the former British colony has now become The United States of Empire.

Chapter One
The Formation of Germany and the Franco-Prussian War

To understand the wars of the twentieth century and how the United States came to dominate the world during that time we must examine the roots of the two nations at the crux of both world wars, Germany and France. The formation of Germany is an interesting mixture of European history. We will review the history of the Holy Roman Empire, Austria, and France, and also briefly look at the French Revolution, English Parliamentarian democracy, the American Revolution, and the Seven Years' War/French and Indian War. Germany did not develop in a vacuum, but via a particular set of circumstances.

France traces its roots to the much-heralded monarch, Charlemagne, who, in the 800s AD, created an empire that stretched from the Atlantic coast of France through the western part of modern-day Germany. An amusing point to note about this first "French" king is that he hailed from a Germanic tribe known as the Franks. He had his capital in what is today the city of Aachen, on the German/Belgian border, and established a separate nation, a political entity that through the ages has become known as France. Today, the "Isle of France" remains recognizable as a "French" state.

France, as a nation, has seemingly existed forever. On the other hand, while the Germanic people seem ageless, their nation is relatively new. The Roman legions fought against Germania, but the German country did not exist as we know it today. In the 1860s, Germany was cobbled together by Otto von Bismarck, the great Prussian statesman. He formed Germany from Prussia and many smaller Germanic states that bordered France and Austria. The member states did so for protection from France. By the nineteenth century, the former Germanic power, Austria, the Holy Roman Empire, was dying a slow death. Austrian Habsburg rule was a shell of its former power and glory. In fact, it was Napoleon Bonaparte who forced the Habsburg monarchs to renounce the Holy Roman Empire, and thus their power. (The Holy Roman Empire was a loose confederation of kings and princes whose territories bordered Austria, Switzerland, and France, across the Alps to the North Sea. It included Austria and Prussia, as well.) Even after Napoleon's reign ended, his influence affected Europe. It was Napoleon's great power and imperial reach across Europe that gave the impetus for the German states to band together for their defense.

Prussia came to dominate the Germanic peoples for two reasons. One was Bismarck; the other was Napoleon III.

Bismarck, the chancellor to Wilhelm I was able to offer union to the other states because Prussia had proven its strength on the Continent. Prussia had been victorious against Napoleon in 1815 when they helped Great Britain defeat him at Waterloo. Prussia showed Europe that it was the more powerful of the two Germanic countries when they fought in 1866; the old power, Austria, lost, when the two countries went to war. Prussia's armaments were superior and they made use of modern technology, a theme that would recur for almost one hundred years.

Prussia's defeat of Austria in the summer of 1866 changed the balance of power in Europe. Until then, Prussia had been an important but not paramount nation while Austria had sprawled grandly across much of central and eastern Europe, seemingly impregnable. Louis (Napoleon III of France), like most other national leaders, was sure that Austria would easily win its unwanted war with Prussia. Even Bismarck himself had his doubts. "If we are beaten, I shall die in the last charge," he told Lord Augustus Loftus, the British Ambassador in Berlin. As it turned out, he had no need to worry.[12]

The origin of the state of Prussia goes back to the 1600s and the Thirty Years' War as well as to the person of its founding monarch, Frederick the Great. This war,

> ...although it had ended over sixty years before Frederick's birth, had marked the mind of every German. A war of religion between Catholic and Protestant princes, fought with merciless savagery, it had broadened to assume a dynastic rather than confessional character—had, indeed, largely lost its original motivation, however lamentable— and had seen the Catholic Bourbons of France (assisted in this by the Protestant Sweden of Gustavus Adolphus) ranged against the Catholic Habsburgs and those who followed them.[3]

Essentially, the Thirty Years' War (1618-1648) started as an attempt by the Austrian ruling family, the Habsburgs, to teach the northern Germans a lesson. Northern Germany, from Brandenburg to Worms, was the home of Martin Luther. His teachings helped begin the Reformation in the Roman Catholic Church, which led to the Protestant religions being established. Luther's Christian religion had taken hold on the northern people and their rulers, and one result was that these Protestants no longer needed or wanted anything to do with Rome and its pope, or anything connected to Rome. The problem for the Habsburgs was that, from the days of

Charlemagne, the emperor always took matters of faith as an important function of his role on earth. In fact, the emperors and popes constantly battled over who had control over the spiritual and terrestrial direction of the people of the realm. For instance, Charlemagne passed laws and ensured that his ecclesiastical leaders could read and write Latin, the language of the church and educated classes at that time.

> "What gave unity and direction to the empire was the activity of Charles himself and a small group of leading counselors...Under the guidance of such men as these Charles sought to make his kingdom an *imperium christianum,* a "Christian empire."[4]

Many kings and emperors, besides Charlemagne, sent out monks (sometimes armed) to win pagan enemies over to the Catholic religion and add territory to their realms. The promulgation of Christianity often went hand in hand with military conquest and pacification of newly acquired lands. Whether or not this was a Godly use of the Gospel of Christ is a question that is outside the scope of this book. It is, however, important to glean from a historical point of view that this was how kings and emperors thought and acted. A single religion in a single country renders a like-minded attitude toward civil and social affairs. There will be a basic agreement on rights and wrongs and this will facilitate proper order in the realm. Furthermore, if the king has final say over matters of a faith and the observation thereof, he has greater control over the people of his kingdom.

In light of the emperor viewing himself as the "defender of the faith and proper order," the Catholic Habsburg emperor saw the northern Germans as being caught up in Luther's heresy and attempted to bring them back into the Catholic fold. The fact that he failed to bring them back as faithful subjects speaks volumes to the depth of this new religion and the military strength of these northern provinces. This situation could also be seen as defining the limits of the power of the Holy Roman Empire. Although it was far from being in decline, it would no longer gain in power. This era also witnessed the emergence of the Mark of Brandenburg (an area in northeastern Germany, which today encompasses Berlin), which would one day become Prussia, and later, Germany. The Thirty Years' War put most of central Europe through a brutal and rapacious war that would end only with the exhaustion of all involved. Brandenburg emerged battered and bruised, but as a military and political force that was extremely wary of any outside power.

Out of these events Prussia was born. It has been said that Prussia was not a state that contained an army but an army that contained a state. Given its birth amid a devastating decades-long war, its religious independence and its placement in the middle of the North European Plain (which stretches from the Atlantic Ocean in the west, to the Ural Mountains well beyond Moscow in the east), Brandenburg had to have a strong defense. A long line of Zollern princes made certain that it remained strong and free.

The Hohenzollern name traces its lineage to Frederick, the Count of Zollern who ruled in Württemberg, southern Germany around 1145.[5]

By the mid seventeenth century, when the Elector Frederick William, who would be known as "The Great Elector," succeeded his father, his domains included Brandenburg itself (extending from the "Old Mark" west of the middle Elbe to the "New Mark" east of the lower Oder), the duchy of Cleve-Julich on the Lower Rhine, the counties of Mark and Ravensburg in Westphalia, and the province of East Prussia. To these, Eastern Pomerania was added soon afterwards. Germany in the seventeenth century was ravaged by the wars which followed the reformation. By the Peace of Augsburg in 1555 each German prince had decided the religion to be adopted in his realm. The electors of Brandenburg had embraced Lutheran doctrines in the mid sixteenth century and had welcomed Huguenot and other refugees, many of whose descendants played distinguished parts in Prussian history. The Great Elector managed, however, to preserve neutrality in the final years of the Thirty Years' War and to obtain the withdrawal of the Swedes (the great Protestant champion, Gustavus Adolphus of Sweden, had been his uncle) from most of his territory. By his dexterous conduct of international affairs and by the loyalty his wise rule and prudent financial management attracted domestically, the Great Elector—our prince's great-grandfather—transformed the destiny of Brandenburg. He also reorganized the army of the Electorate and made Brandenburg, small as it was, a significant military power. As a glorious denouement he drove the Swedes (who, as allies of Louis XIV of France, had returned to invade Pomerania) from his domains by the resounding victory of Fehrbellin in 1675.[6]

To understand German history, one must understand the relationship between Austria and Prussia. There existed a rivalry between the ruling Germanic elites, the House of Habsburg and the House of Hohenzollern. This was a conflict between the old idea, dating back to Charlemagne, of the Christian Empire and the enlightened idea of freedom of religion. This rivalry pitted the king, who controlled all, including the direction of religious instruction and propagation among his people and those whom he conquered, against the new thinking molded by the Reformation. It was a revolutionary idea, that people could reject the teachings of Rome and the emperor and still be Christians, expressed by "the principle of 'cujus regio, ejus religio'—that a man's domicile determined his religion in accordance with the Peace of Augsburg."[7] These were foreshadows of the enlightenment, in which freedom of thought was valued above doctrine or superstition. For those who wanted to control people's thinking, domestic tranquility was threatened.

In many ways, the Habsburgs symbolized the old ways of running an empire on the European Continent; Prussia hinted at the new. Add to their free-thinking ways, the fact that Prussia became a military power that Austria could not dominate, and one can see that there was a potential problem in the making. The Holy Roman Empire, which was ruled by the Habsburgs from Vienna, was not technically a kingdom. The rulers came to their office by election, from seven electors throughout the empire determined by the "Golden Bull" of 1356. This Golden Bull was an edict given by Charles IV, emperor of the Holy Roman Empire, which decreed that seven "electors" would choose who the succeeding emperors would be. This process ended the selection of the emperor by the pope. The Margrave of Brandenburg was one of the electors.

> The Habsburgs, Dukes of Austria, had occupied the imperial throne since 1438, giving the empire a continuity which was, or should have been, a welcome contrast to the chaos that had followed the end of the Hohenstaufen period. The rise of the Habsburg power had been among the most striking developments in the sixteenth century; Austria was a large but not uniquely large territory in southern Germany. Yet there were periodic grumblings among the German princes at Habsburg, attempts as they saw it, to treat the empire as if it were a hereditary kingdom, a Habsburg fief. On the contrary, they argued, it was an association of independent sovereigns, joined by general assent and electing a superior, with their independence (certainly since 1648) recognized as a legitimate fact of international life.[8]

The fact that these minor kings and sovereigns saw themselves as equals in that they put him in power exposes the fragility of the emperor's position. The experience of the Thirty Years' War underscored that fragility. The emperor tried to control one of its own and opened the Continent up to a war that devastated the land. Consequently, the emperor forced one of its own, Brandenburg, to look to itself for its own defense and prosperity, driving a wedge between the "independent sovereigns."

If the emperor had allowed the Northern provinces to follow their own religious patterns, the war would not have been engaged, the split between Brandenburg and Austria would not have occurred, and Brandenburg would not have felt isolated from the empire. This, of course, supposes an attitude that was not acceptable to the emperor in the seventeenth century; thus, religious differences split the German-speaking people. Brandenburg became the Kingdom of Prussia in 1701, with the emperor's consent.

The Brandenburg princes consistently showed attention to detail, in fiscal and military management, which allowed them to be able to fight battles larger than one would think they could handle. This was true of the Great Elector, as well as his son Frederick William I, and his grandson Karl Frederick, known as Frederick the Great. But if attention to money and the military have any drawbacks, they were highlighted in the life of Frederick William. His time was one when rapacious hordes could sweep in from the north, south, east, or west, by land or sea, and ravage a land. His tutors were battles won with a heavy price in men. He fought alongside Prince Eugene of Austria, one of the greatest military minds on the Continent at the time. Frederick William was on the field when Prince Eugene, together with the English Lord Marlborough, defeated the French at the Battle of Malplaquet. France lost 12,000 men that day. Marlborough and Eugene were victorious in the battle; however, the victory came at the cost of 24,000 men. He was "a violent-tempered autocrat; in the words of his son, 'a terrible man but a just man.'"[9] He violently beat his wife and his children, in private and in public, and demanded strict obedience. He thought that his oldest son, Frederick, was too effeminate to be a good ruler for Prussia, and tried to beat him into being a better son and heir.

The story of Frederick William and his son Karl Frederick is the age-old story of a father wanting a son of whom he could be proud, and to whom he could pass on the greatness of the family line. The son that he produced, however, thought independently from his father and did not share his father's enthusiasm for *ubermannliche*.

> Frederick William then discovered that he had bred a young man who seemed at all points the opposite of himself, and the opposite of what, in his view, the throne of Prussia needed. The young Frederick, despite prohibitions, learned Latin secretly—and all the more enthusiastically, although never proficient. He showed, when not forced to conceal, a passion for literature and the arts. He wrote with taste, delicacy and increasingly elegant skill; and like most of cultured Europe at that time, he wrote and evidently thought in French. He wrote poetry prolifically although seldom with memorable felicity. He never spoke or wrote German with fluency or style and showed his distaste for the language. He detested hunting—"to kill for pleasure is odious," he wrote. He grew his curled hair long and dressed as exotically as possible. He loved music, composed and played the flute as well. Within the rigid constraints of his court life he managed as he grew a little older, to incur debts. He seemed to go out of his way to infuriate his father. His personality as well as his tastes seemed to Frederick William perverse and inappropriate in one destined to rule Prussia.[10]

The generation gap that existed between Frederick William and his son, Karl Frederick, came to a head when the son tried to run away from his father. When Karl Frederick was eighteen, he tried to escape the terrible treatment from his father, along with three of his friends. At the time of the attempt, Frederick was a lieutenant colonel in the Prussian army, and his accomplices were in the military as well. Not only would they be defying the wishes of the king and father, but they would also be traitors and deserters. If caught, any penalty would be harsh. The plot to escape was found out. Two of Frederick's friends managed to escape to England with their lives; the other was caught with Frederick. The accomplice was beheaded in front of Frederick, despite the pleas for mercy from monarchs throughout Europe and the parents of the young friend, who came from a prominent military family. It is very likely that this incident scarred Frederick; he was said to have had nightmares about it for the remainder of his life.

Frederick grew up to become the leader of Prussia and led an accomplished life. He helped found a great nation, and he was a great warrior general, but there was a cold side to his persona, accentuated by a loveless marriage, no offspring and, even rarer, for a monarch, no mistresses or concubines. It is possible that his father's violent episodes can be blamed for this; however, we will never know with certainty. Frederick William felt he needed to toughen up a "soft" son to become a great leader. It is possible that what he failed to give through affection, he achieved by the cold, hard realities of battles won.

In the seventeenth and eighteenth centuries, the Prussian kings were rising up and developing a kingdom, within the Holy Roman Empire, that was fast becoming a force equal to the Austrian Habsburgs. Frederick, despite all the beatings from his father, became a child of the enlightenment, composing music and reciting poetry at length. He even became a patron of Voltaire, the leading light of the French enlightenment. He went into battle with Caesar's volumes about war and also wrote poetry himself. He studied military campaigns with Prince Eugene of Austria and later defeated him in battle. Frederick was able to beat Austria, France, and Russia, at separate times, and made peace with all three, as it fit Prussia's needs. Always, he was aware of the extreme vulnerability of his kingdom. He strengthened it and fought with all its abilities and then made peace with those whom he had defeated. Bismarck claimed that politics is the art of doing what is possible. Carl von Clausewitz, German military writer, in his book, On War,claimed that war is just politics taken to another degree. Frederick did what was possible with the art of war.

Frederick the Great established Prussia as a land and country that all of Europe would recognize as a powerful force on the Continent. King George II of England, originally from German Hanover, may have referred to Frederick the Great as a "bad neighbor, a bad relation and a bad sovereign,"[11] but he had to deal with him on Frederick's terms. Frederick carved out Prussia from Austria and France. From Austria, he took the Province of Silesia, along the Oder River. He did not take any lands from the French, but he won the allegiance of many of the states bordering France and Prussia. The situation with France and Austria was very similar. Each nation had been around long enough to have built up a reputation and an expectation of greatness.

Monarchs, however, do not always rise up to their expectations; neither do their armies. When the expectation is greater than that which the monarchy can deliver, that monarch's rule is in trouble. That is why the failure of the Habsburg Empire to truly bring Brandenburg into line in the Thirty Years' War spelled trouble. Similarly, when France could not easily handle Frederick the Great in their own wars, it was a clarion call for France that it would have to make major changes.

> [In France] at the level of common consensus the King-as-Father-of-the-Patrie had three basic duties: to see that his people had bread, that his realm was victorious in battle and that it was supplied with heirs. In the years following his (Louis XVI) succession there were already doubts on the first two scores but it was in the last matter that his failure provoked the most comment.[12]

All of Europe spoke or wrote in French. In fact, Frederick the Great hated the German language when he was young and found ways to study French, which certainly would have earned a beating from his father if he had known of it. Often, however, the glory of a country still shines even when the reasons for the luster are gone.

The eighteenth century was not a favorable one for France in wars of conquest. In fact, throughout the century, the French kings could not provide victory in battle. Combinations of Austria and Prussia, and Prussia and Britain, had thwarted France's push eastward. At the same time that France was maintaining its continental force, it was building a worldwide maritime force, which was rivaling that of Great Britain. Frederick the Great saw this as folly. No other continental power was trying to do both, and Frederick thought that this would bring financial ruin on France. He was adamant that Prussia should neither build a navy, nor develop water-borne colonies. Frederick's main concern and worry was Austria, just as Prussia was Austria's main concern. Austria could not regain her control over the empire as long as the northern tribe was an independent force. The two countries fought more than once over the Silesian territory, which bordered both countries.

> Silesia was populous—about equally divided between Catholic and Protestant. Silesia was potentially rich; there were minerals (later to be the source of huge wealth), textiles, and a flourishing linen industry. And Silesia had rebelled against Habsburg rule in the Thirty Years War.[13]

When the weak Emperor Charles VI needed support from Prussia, the Prussian king reopened the Silesian question. Charles VI needed internal and international support for his daughter, Maria Teresa, to succeed him to the throne. According to the Salic law that governed Austria, the throne could pass only to a male heir. Charles had no male heir, and so he enacted the "Pragmatic Sanction" to allow Maria to receive the crown. This change in the law needed widespread support inside and outside of the empire, so that there would be no challenge to her reign. In return for supporting the Pragmatic

Sanction, Frederick William asked that the emperor look favorably on the Hohenzollern claims to the land in Silesia. Dominion over this land had been in dispute since the middle of the fifteenth century; Prussia claimed that the territory should return to Prussian ownership. Prussian officials had thought that Charles gave them the region, but Maria reneged on the deal.

In the first Silesian War, Prussia was able to hold off the old empire. This drove Austria into the arms of France, looking for aid in defeating the Prussians. The next time Prussia and Austria fought, Frederick the Great went to war when he decided that Prussia had the best chance to win, attacking Austria preemptively. This war, the second Silesian War, was known as the Seven Years' War, on the Continent. The blame for starting the Seven Years' War falls squarely upon his shoulders; however, he was convinced that Austria, France, and Russia were ganging up to destroy Prussia. Prussia found itself being pressured by Austria to the south, Russia to the east, and France to the west. He proceeded to make an ally out of France's old enemy and Austria's usual ally, England. England became involved because it was already fighting the French on the North American continent (in what is better known in the United States as the French and Indian War). The Seven Years' War/French and Indian War would change the world and establish Prussia and England as the major winners, although, at the outset, it did not appear that either of these two powers would be the victors.

For years, the French and English empires had been growing on the North American continent. England had concentrated colonies along the North Atlantic coast, from Georgia to the Saint Lawrence Seaway, and stretching into the Ohio Valley. The French had territory north of the seaway, along the five Great Lakes, down the Mississippi River, to the Gulf of Mexico, and extending to the Rocky Mountains. France's territory was a huge area that was sparsely populated, except at fortified towns and at the natural confluences such as Montreal or New Orleans. The native Indians of the area traded and allied themselves to either the French or the English. The Iroquois decimated other tribes in *inter se* warfare in order to control trade with the white settlers. The French had some success against the British and the colonists in the beginning of the war, and the Indians chose to side with the French in the coming battles. Then the British sent in extra troops, and Prime Minister Penn made some concessions to the colonists that increased their volunteers. The French eventually lost the war and all its North American holdings; all of Canada went to the British, and the territory west of the Mississippi went to Spain to prevent British control.

Meanwhile, on the Continent, Frederick the Great was marching throughout the German territory outflanking almost every army he met. First, he drove the Austrians out of Saxony—though he lost dramatically at the Battle of Kolin. Next, he routed the French. The Prussian General Lehwaldt fought the Russians to a bloody standoff at Gross Jagersdorf, from which the Russians limped back eastward to lick their wounds. The tiny German state of Prussia had defeated the European giants that had tried to snuff out its life.

France and Austria were the big losers in the Seven Years' War/French and Indian War. Austria would never regain her former glory, although its continental empire remained intact. France lost heavily and incurred great debt as a result of the war. After the war, various French finance ministers came and went, under the reigns of Louis XV and Louis XVI. Their policies tended to contradict and negate any positive effects that the previous minister had accomplished. Nothing was fixed, and the state debt remained high; France had a financial problem and a political one also—the monarchy was not doing well. It had not produced a victory in war in nearly a century. It lost huge possessions in Canada to bitter enemies, the British. It had to relinquish other North American territories to Spain to keep them out of British hands. And they lost on the Continent to Prussia. Things were going poorly for them until their enemy across the channel, Britain, had problems with their colonists. When the American Revolution broke out, France sat on the sidelines, happy to watch the conflict. It was a war in which Louis XVI at first had little interest in joining despite the fact that Benjamin Franklin had been sent to Paris as an ambassador for the Americans to win the aid of France. But after the Americans had won a significant battle in Saratoga, New York, Louis changed his mind and rendered aid to the rebellious colonists. Louis then recognized that he had a chance to win a war at the expense of the enemy, Britain.

The Marquis de Lafayette was a military aide to General George Washington in the American Revolution and later became an important figure in the French Revolution that broke out in 1789. He saw the American Revolution as an opportunity for personal and national revenge; his father had died at the hands of British forces in the War of Polish Succession, another one of France's losing efforts. Lafayette was not alone in his thinking.

> We were tired of the *longueur* of the peace that had lasted ten years," wrote Lafayette's fellow volunteer the Comte de Segur, "and each of us burned with a desire to repair the affronts of the last wars, to fight the English and to fly to help the American cause.[14]

France scored a victory after helping the Americans gain their independence. France lost part of its empire after the Seven Years' War/French and Indian War. Britain lost its American colonies, through France's aid to the colonists' cause. Furthermore, for France, the war opened up greater trade with the Americans and the Caribbean islands, but these would be short-lived gains. France was going broke from maintaining both a continental army and a naval empire; Britain had its naval empire, but no continental army. Prussia and Austria had only their armies. Russia had its army and a navy, but no seaborne empire. France was trying to have it all, which was driving them into bankruptcy.

England had a great advantage over France, even after it lost territory in the American Revolution. It was able to raise revenue through Parliament without fear of political upheaval, because if the policies of the government were too onerous, the British people could raise objections and complain to their representatives for redress of grievances. France's system of raising taxes and listening to people's complaints was antiquated and needed changing, as France's monarchy also needed to be changed, but how? That was the question that would eventually lead to the French Revolution. The French would soon throw out the monarchy and establish a republic that would fall to the dictator.

The question of why democracy succeeded in the United States but failed in France is important. The American Revolution was a great example for the French, especially for soldiers like Lafayette, who came to America to fight. France tried to establish enlightened democracy, without having experienced its mechanics and was as enamored of these ideas as any other country in Europe at the time. But France, after 1789, became the political failure that many in Europe had predicted the United States would become. French failure here would lay the foundation for the history of Europe for the next 150 years—after all, the wars of the twentieth century were fought on the pretext that either Britain or the United States, or both, were fighting to protect democracy. France became a revolutionary anarchy and would have order imposed on it by a military dictator—Napoleon Bonaparte. The French Revolution would reverberate throughout Europe as an example of everything that was wrong with democracy; thus, monarchs would cling to power more tightly, rather than risk regicide and anarchy. They were protecting themselves and their people by protecting monarchical rule.

Democracy worked in the United States because, during the 150 years before the American Revolution, English colonists had practiced English democracy. Each of the thirteen American colonies had a legislature modeled on the Parliament in London—with a few modifications here and there. They practiced capitalism, just like Britain; they were as English as any Londoner, except that they lived 3,000 miles away and therefore were able to take the English experience and make use of it as if it was their own. The Magna Carta, the English Civil War, the Glorious Revolution, the growth of Parliament's power over the monarch, all formed and influenced democracy in the United States. The English experience was the American experience.

France could not make this claim, nor did they want to do so; pride would not allow them to look across the channel and see a mixture of monarchy and democracy, and then import it. France's experiences were too different to simply transplant English democracy. The many wars between France and England alone gave many Frenchmen reason to hate everything that was English. Honore Gabriel Riqueti Mirabeau had a Genevan friend "translate Romilly's account of parliamentary rules—an initiative that brought down on him a storm of indignation for being enslaved to antique, foreign customs."[15]

> Nor—for better or worse—had this moment been reached through sage deliberations on workable government in the manner of the American Constitutional Convention. To wish that it had is to mistake the process by which politics unfolded in France—a process that was always intensely theatrical and histrionic…"The people of Paris," observed Etienne Dumont, "were filled with inflammable gas like a balloon."[16]

So, instead of democracy that worked on hammered-out compromises, France had a government that thrived on spectacular oratory, political grandstanding and, most of all, obstructionism. During revolutionary times, nothing brought a politician more acclaim in Paris than to bottle up much-needed reforms. However, obstructionism does nothing to solve current problems, which are merely left to fester.

The wound of the French government did, in fact, fester until it exploded with revolution, anarchy, and blood running in the streets. The French Revolution, unlike its counterpart in the United States, brought failure. The French Revolution was truly revolutionary and revolting; it swept out the existing order of government, killing many, leaving in its wake anarchy and then a dictator. The American Revolution had been a conservative revolution. It established (actually reestablished) English democracy on the American continent, without the mother country interfering anymore. The young American nation could look to its Anglo-Saxon parentage and borrow and copy and call it its own. France could not.

> France would, instead, incorporate the politics of "virtue." This had two faces. One was "the secular religion of Sensibility," in part imported from England, with its emphasis on emotional truth, candor, naturalness, which had received its definitive form in Rousseau's sentimental writings in the early 1760s. One of the many important consequences of this revolution in moral taste was the purification of egotism. With the ascendancy of Romanticism, sentimental personality cults became possible. Paradoxically, the more apparently self-effacing and modest the subject, the more potent his celebrity. And in this formula patriotism and parenthood were inextricably mixed.[17]
>
> The other was "Roman Patriotism." This was a yearning for the past glories and virtues of the Roman Republic. "Roman Patriotism...shared some of the virtues of the cult of Sensibility, but in other respects it was differently accented. For one thing, it was less inclined to marinate in the lachrymose, but instead exalted stoical self-possession over emotional outpouring. It was, quite self-consciously, a 'virile' or masculine culture: austere, muscular and inflexible, rather than tender, sensitive and compassionate."[18]

Here were two competing, yet very compatible, trends of moral thought. Both had excellent aspects but, taken to extremes, could shut down a fledgling democracy. Being sentimental and having heroes is fine, but the personality cult may become a false god to lead one astray, a la Adolf Hitler or Benito Mussolini. On the other hand, being too austere, too muscular, too inflexible can also bring a fledgling democracy to its knees. Ideologues can bring their rhetoric to the conference room, but without compromise, politicians will make grandstands, speaking eloquently, winning support among their faithful followers, but no positive results will be produced. The American Constitutional Convention can be seen as a success of compromise in action. In 1787, a mere four years after the end of the American Revolution, the new country faced a huge dilemma: the federal government under the initial constitution, the Articles of Confederation, was weak; it couldn't collect enough taxes to pay its debts and it had no power over the states, which were beginning to drift apart. If this continued, the new nation would become prey to the major European powers and become recolonized. As a result, in the city of Philadelphia, in the middle of the summer heat, delegates from the thirteen states spent weeks behind locked doors, with the windows closed (remember, air-conditioning was yet to be invented), barring the press, and hammered out a workable constitution through argument, debate and, finally, compromise.

It was that spirit of compromise that helped forge the Constitution of the United States. The lack of compromise in the French government doomed it to a bloody revolution, which the revolutionaries themselves could not control. The leaders of the revolution did not truly have full command of the revolution; many of the most ardent revolutionaries fell prey to the guillotine. Maximilien de Robespierre was one such leader who literally lost his head. Because of the uncontrollable anarchy in the streets of Paris and elsewhere, France needed a military presence to restore order. An outside power might have taken France if the Prussians had been able to claim Paris. In 1792 the Prussians, led by the Duke of Brunswick, marched into France to save the monarchy—this was the first time that German troops marched into France, but it certainly was not the last. Even with the anarchy in Paris and the confusion throughout the nation, French generals Charles Demouriez and Francois-Christophe Kellerman still fielded an army sufficiently strong enough to repel the Prussians—they cut the Prussians' line of supplies. With their supplies dwindling, hunger and sickness drove the Prussians out of France. When Goethe, a leader of the enlightenment traveling with the Prussians, was asked for his opinion after the Prussians had been outflanked and forced to leave France, he gave cold comfort to the Prussian troops. "From this place and this time forth commences a new era in world history and you can all say that you were present at its birth."[19] Curiously, Britain did not interfere in France's convulsions, though Britain did become a refuge for those fleeing the guillotine. The ensuing anarchy left the door open for a young, brilliant artillery captain to step into the gap and control the revolution, none other than Napoleon Bonaparte, who would rule France and conquer all of Europe. Under Napoleon, France's continental power extended from Spain, all the way to Moscow. He would also reacquire lands in North America, which he then sold to Thomas Jefferson to help finance his European wars. Despite his own short stature, he brought France to great heights of power and glory; however, his rule ended in defeat.

Napoleon carried some of the better aspects of the revolution to Europe. He ended serfdom, codified laws, and introduced the metric system throughout Europe. He also ended the Holy Roman Empire, forcing Emperor Francis II to abdicate his power and role, but the nations that Napoleon conquered would rebel against him. His short-lived reign began in 1798 and ended in 1815 at Waterloo. There, the combined British and Prussian forces defeated and captured him. He was sent to the desolate Saint Helena Island, in the middle of the South Atlantic Ocean, never to escape. This left a power vacuum in Europe, into which the Germanic states began talking about uniting. They conferred about their common needs for defense and secure, duty-free travel and trade within their own lands. They discussed a Greater Germany: Prussia, Austria, and all the smaller Germanic states, from Hanover to Bavaria, but they also discussed the possibility of a Lesser Germany: Prussia and the smaller states, minus Austria—the Habsburgs still did not trust the Hohenzollerns enough to combine with them as one state. In the early 1860s, Otto von Bismarck made the modern state of Germany a reality.

Thus, the Habsburgs and Napoleon helped to forge Germany through the process of fighting in a multitude of religious and territorial wars. A military power and a people were born. France, Austria, and Russia pressed on the lump of coal that was Prussia and created a diamond, Germany. By the dawn of 1900, France and Austria were descending in power. The young, strong, prosperous Germany was ascending. It was only logical that this new country would aggravate the old powers, and this did occur when, in 1870, France and Germany argued over whom should succeed to the throne of Spain. The Hohenzollerns gave their support to a member of the Habsburg family, Prince Leopold, to take the position. Louis Napoleon Bonaparte III, a vainglorious nephew of the original Napoleon, was emperor of France at the time—he had helped tear down the Republic, which had replaced the reinstated monarchy, which had replaced Napoleon's reign. Napoleon III used back-channel diplomacy to force Wilhelm I of Prussia to withdraw his nominee for the throne. When the deal was nearly complete, Napoleon's wife, Eugenie and war-hungry French politicians butted into the affair, demanding that Napoleon III make an open show of these upstart Germans. They desired the Kaiser to publicly promise that he would never again submit Prince Leopold for the throne of Spain, something that the Kaiser could not and would never do.

> When that evening Emile Ollivier announced the news of Prince Leopold's withdrawal to the Legislative Body, it was not greeted with cheers. On the contrary, most of the deputies—like most of the French nation—were certain of the superiority of the French army over all others in Europe and they angrily bellowed their war-lust.[20]

Napoleon III submitted to political pressure and his wife's demands and informed Comte Vincent Benedetti, the French ambassador in Berlin, that he should press the Kaiser for a public disclaimer of Leopold. The Comte planned to do so and set up an appointment with the Kaiser in the German spa town of Ems. The appointment was set for late in the morning, after the Kaiser's "promenade in the park." But Benedetti was so pressured by telegrams from Paris demanding that the Kaiser never support Leopold again, that he interrupted the Kaiser during his promenade. Wilhelm was a little indignant about the interruption and the attempt to pressure him into making a public statement that he had no intention of making. As far as he was concerned, it was a dead issue and should remain buried. The Kaiser sent a telegram to Bismarck to inform him of the encounter. He wrote:

> Count Benedetti spoke to me on the promenade, in order to demand from me finally, in a very importunate manner, that I should authorize him to telegraph at once that I had bound myself for all future time never again to give my consent if the Hohenzollern should renew their candidature. (I refused at last somewhat sternly, it is neither right nor possible to undertake engagements of this kind *a tout jamais*. Naturally I told him that I had yet received no news, and he was earlier informed about Paris and Madrid than myself, he could clearly see that my Government once more had no hand in the matter, His Majesty has since received a letter from the

Prince.) His Majesty (having told Count Benedetti that he was awaiting news from the Prince) has decided (with reference to the above demand) not to receive Count Benedetti again, but only to let him be informed through an aide-de-camp that his Majesty (had received from the Prince confirmation of the news which Benedetti had already received from Paris and) had nothing further to say to the ambassador. (His Majesty leaves it to your Excellency whether Benedetti's fresh demand and its rejection should not be at once communicated both to our ambassadors and the press.)[21]

The form that Bismarck released to the press excluded all the information in parentheses above, and read:

Count Benedetti spoke to me on the promenade, in order to demand from me finally, in a very importunate manner, that I should authorize him to telegraph at once that I had bound myself for all future time never again to give my consent if the Hohenzollerns should renew their candidature. His Majesty has decided not to receive Count Benedetti again, but only to let him be informed through an aide-de-camp that His Majesty had nothing further to say to the ambassador.[22]

When the French press received Bismarck's truncated telegram, it had the effect he hoped it would have. It infuriated the already inflamed French populous and they clamored for war. On July 15, at one o'clock, Emile Ollivier, Napoleon's most senior cabinet member, informed the legislative body, and Duc Antoine de Grammont reported to the senate the cabinet's decision to go to war. The decision was greeted with wild applause.

A week earlier, Napoleon III had asked Marshall Edmond Le Boeuf, the war minister, if the French army was ready for war against Prussia. "His reply has become famous as one of the most stupid comments in European history: 'If the war were to last for one year, we would not need to

buy one gaiter-button!' This totally unfounded assurance
soon became public knowledge and fanned the agitation
for war into a blaze."[23]

The truth was they were far from ready, they needed
extensive training for battle. Thus began the Franco-Prussian
War. It became a disaster because of Napoleon III's poor
battlefield management and it lasted for ten long months
before Germany finally won it. It could have been over in
just two, but Germany demanded the annexation of Alsace-
Lorraine, on the border between Germany and France.
This territory had traded hands many times before, usually
between France and Austria, but Bismarck did so, he claimed,
to defend against any further French aggression. It did not
hurt Germany that it was rich in coal and iron.

Germany's defeat of France astounded the world. Before
this war, France was still looked upon as being the greatest
European military power. This is part of the reason that
France flew into the war unprepared; they believed in their
own former glory. The Franco-Prussian War established
Germany as the preeminent power for which there was no
match on the European Continent at the turn of the twentieth
century. Here, at last, we have the volatile brew of the history
leading to the First World War. Without this background,
this war makes no sense. Why did these Christian European
nations slaughter each other for four years? Germany wanted
to continue to expand and establish an empire similar to
what France and Britain had. France wanted Alsace-Lorraine
back, and its former glory. What good did it bring them? Very
little. But why did the United States join the war? Who was the
ultimate victor?

Chapter Two
The Last War of Empire Building: The Boer War

It may seem strange to look at Great Britain's fight in the Boer War while trying to get a greater understanding of World War I and its aftermath, but the Boer War is a setup in many ways for the Great War. First, as the title states, this was the final war in which Britain engaged in policies of enlarging the empire. In contrast, World War I was a defensive war protecting the status quo of the empire. Germany began to threaten Britain's dominance on the high seas with the construction of its High Seas Fleet—the Boer War was instrumental in fueling this construction. If Britain's sea power had been watered down, then there was potential for Germany to alter the British Empire. The Boer War showed Germany's impotence on the seas to the admirals and other decision makers back in Berlin. This impotence prevented them from aiding the Boers, which meant that Great Britain could eventually win a war of attrition in Southern Africa. This impotence fueled Germany's desire for a naval fleet that could rival the one Great Britain had.

Ever since the English and the Scottish kingdoms united to form Great Britain, the island kingdom had been growing in power, that is, until the twentieth century. There were rivalries with France, Spain, and the Netherlands in which Great Britain usually came out on top. The Dutch are sometimes overlooked, but they had many colonies in the New World as well as in Africa and Asia.

In the New World, America, the Dutch colony was named New Amsterdam. In 1674, the English ended the Dutch rule and promptly renamed the colony New York, for Prince James, Duke of York. The Dutch colony in Africa was the Cape of Good Hope, founded in 1652. It was a small peninsula on the southwestern tip of Africa, along the trade route from Europe to India, a most important stop on the Spice Trade route. Arid and none too prosperous, the colony never became heavily populated while the Dutch maintained possession.

> After fifty years there were fewer than two thousand white settlers. And from the beginning these were outnumbered by their coloured servants (including imported slaves) on whom the Europeans depended for their manual labor. These settlers were mainly Dutch Calvinists, with a leavening of German Protestants and French Huguenot refugees. To Africa these Pilgrim Fathers brought a tradition of dissent and a legacy of resentment against Europe. They called themselves "Afrikaners" or "Afrikanders" (the people of Africa) and spoke a common language, a variant of Dutch that came to be called "Afrikaans." The poorest and most independent of them were the *trekboers* (alias Boers); the wandering farmers whose search for new grazing land brought them progressively deeper into African territory.[24]

These people were fiercely independent but could not hold off the great European powers. During the Napoleonic wars, the British took control of the colony and, in 1834, ended slavery throughout their empire. The Dutch descendants, however, were not so liberally-minded and refused to end their enslavement of the black Africans. They retreated from the imperial reach of the British, into ever deeper parts of

Africa and formed their own nations of the Transvaal and the Orange Free State. Unfortunately for these people, the British Empire kept following them, particularly when diamonds were found on Kimberly, 300 miles inland, and then gold was discovered in the Boers' territory. This sparsely populated area of southern Africa suddenly drew tens of thousands of prospectors.

These prospectors, *Uitlanders* (outlanders), changed the dynamic of the situation. The Boers established a republic and they had strict voting franchise rules; only white males voted, and the Uitlanders had to have lived seven years in the Republic of Transvaal or the Free Orange State to qualify to vote. Needless to say, those who came to strike it rich in the gold or diamond fields probably had no intentions of living there for seven years before moving back home or on to better prospects. So these men, some of them British, became the pawns used to bring in the strength of the British Empire to "ensure" their rights.

The British started to press for greater voting rights for their British citizens in the Boer territories. What right did the British Empire have to influence the voting patterns inside another country? Beginning in the nineteenth and continuing through the twentieth century, spreading Anglo-Saxon democracy had been one of the underlying reasons for the many wars that were fought. One of the battle cries for both world wars was to make the world safe for democracy. But just as there were other reasons for Britain going to war in World War I (fear of German military superiority on the Continent and a refusal to allow any continental power to be its equal on the high seas) gold and diamonds fueled the Boer War. The claim remained that Britain was fighting to secure the voting rights of Britons. The governor in South Africa, Sir Alfred Milner, and the "gold-bugs," Cecil Rhodes and Alfred Beit, manipulated the British press and government so that Britain would use its power to annex the entire southern portion of Africa. By doing so, Rhodes and Beit (already significantly wealthy) would become even richer, and Milner could be a king in his portion of the world. Milner, in spite of his belief that the British Empire was already in decline, pursued a course of ubernationalism. He desired Great Britain's control of southern Africa, (including Transvaal and the Orange Free State), as it would ensure his continuing power as its provincial governor.

> But were these new black colonies to be the source of either wealth or power? Until they were developed, no one could say. In Milner's eyes, as indeed the eyes of all the more sophisticated imperialists, Britain's main concern was not with adding to or even developing the black Empire. It was with reasserting her power in the white Empire. Could the empire now be made into a reality as a federal Greater Britain? Could it become the supreme world-state, with defense and trade controlled by a single grand imperial parliament? Or was the white Empire doomed to dissolve into a medley of nation-states, no closer to Britain than the first great ex-colony, America?[25]

The problem in Milner's view was that Britain had in recent years grown rich and powerful as an empire without the expense in blood and treasure of being a conquering force. Free trade had allowed Britain to operate throughout the world—in Europe, the Americas, and Asia. Britain ruled the seas. Most cargo traveled on British ships, protected by the British navy; in this way Britain was able to exploit markets where they had no political control. Why should Parliament pay for an empire, with armies and wars of conquest, when they were reaping the benefits of empire and profiting without firing a shot?

How to bring Britain back to its greatness? This was the dilemma Milner faced. The answer was simple. Be bold, be aggressive, take South Africa, the gold and the diamonds, for the greater glory of himself, but more importantly, the empire. All Milner had to do was exploit the Boers' natural distrust for Britain and provoke a fight. The influx of thousands of British prospectors, who were being kept out of the political process in the republics of Transvaal and the Orange Free State, gave the pretext for this situation.

Milner was not the first to try to provoke the Boers into an all-out war with Britain. Another British adventurer had made things quite simple through his involvement in a major blunder, the Jameson Raid. Dr. James Jameson, the administrator of the Chartered Company in Rhodesia, led the Jameson Raid of 1895. His purpose was to march into the Transvaal Republic and start an uprising of Uitlanders to overthrow the Boer government. The Boer president, Paul Kruger, knew of the raid...news of Jameson's intentions had been broadcast through the Transvaal by the press. As Kruger waited to trap him, Jameson carried on.

This was a huge gamble, but Jameson was a gambler.

> Clive would have done it, Jameson told a friend. He was sure of that. If Jameson gambled and won—if they could rush Johannesburg into a rising and forcibly take over the Transvaal—they would be forgiven the illegality. If they gambled and lost—well, the usual penalty was death. Death but not necessarily defeat. It was one of the lessons of history that it needed a disaster to make the British interested in their Empire.[26]

Jameson threw the dice and they came up snake eyes. The Uitlanders of Johannesburg were not ripe for revolution. There was no British majority; it was, instead, a British, French, American, and German amalgam; none of these foreign prospectors really wanted to give their lives for the greater glory of the British Empire. Jameson considered it a betrayal, and he and his band pushed onward to Johannesburg, only to have the stragglers of his company shot and killed. Then outside of Johannesburg, at a *kopje* (small hill) named Doornkop, Jameson and his men made a last stand, at which the Boers killed sixty-five out of Jameson's six hundred men and lost only one of their own. Jameson and his raiders were stopped.

Back in London, Joseph Chamberlain, the head of the Colonial Office, had a problem. He was fully aware of what it was that Jameson was trying to achieve, but he wanted to stay disconnected from any action, unless of course, it was successful. It was not, and there were telegrams that showed that Chamberlain knew and approved of the raid. Kruger, to his credit, did not hang the leaders of the raid, nor put them on a show trial in the Transvaal, but sent them to London to be put on trial there. This was a political *coup d'etat* that could have won Kruger accolades for himself and his fledgling country, except for one thing—Kaiser Wilhelm of Germany had sent Kruger a telegram congratulating him on his victory. This telegram infuriated the British public and turned a public embarrassment into a patriotic stand. Thanks to the Kaiser, Jameson spent only fifteen months in jail, his reputation transformed from bungling conspirator to patriotic hero of the first degree.

In 1899, the door was open for the newly appointed governor of the Cape Colony, Alfred Milner, to provoke an all-out battle for the annexation of the Transvaal and the Orange Free State. The Boers had been victorious—for now. It would be left up to Milner to change the situation and bring in the full force of the British Empire on these backward clod-busters and prospectors. The animosities and grievances were there, if they could only be stoked into a white-hot fire. The larger question was how to win the support of the British public.

The Boers' seven-year waiting period was the point on which Milner would push the war, stating that he would accept nothing more than five-year enfranchisement.

It may seem odd that one country could hold sway over the internal actions of another country, but the Transvaal and Free Orange Republic were not entirely free countries. Britain, at one point in the early 1850s, was on the verge of annexing most of what is now South Africa. A change of governments (elections in England), with newly elected Prime Minister William E. Gladstone at the helm, changed the political direction. Instead of annexing all of southern African, two new republics were formed north of the Cape Colony. They were the Transvaal and the Orange Free State. Again, in the 1880s, British troops marched into the Transvaal and suffered three shocking losses at the hand of Paul Kruger, culminating in the battle of Majuba. Gladstone, who again became the prime minister at this point, put a halt to additional troops on their way to put down Kruger. He drew up a compromise in which the countries were free, but in matters of foreign affairs, they had to bow to British wishes. The British would retain control over their foreign affairs so they were only semi-free states.

There was nothing new to Britain's interference—for better or for worse—in the Boer's politics. This added to the distrust that Kruger had for any kind of compromise that was struck with London. Kruger signed the treaties, the Convention of Pretoria in 1881, and again in the Convention of London in 1884, which solidified the deal between the countries, but he openly claimed that he did so under protest. It was politically expedient and necessary at the time, but he made it clear that he would work to change the treaties at his first opportunity. Hence, Kruger was naturally suspicious of any treaty with Britain. Now, Milner was pressing for a five-year waiting period for the enfranchisement of the Uitlanders—in some ways, this made him appear to be a patient advocate for voting rights. Kruger saw a trick to somehow annex the two republics.

> The simple fact is that Kruger rejected the chance of compromise because he did not realize that it existed. He refused to make further concessions because he thought they would have been futile. Chamberlain, he thought, had set a trap—a trap to humiliate the volk, before he destroyed them...Kruger himself cabled, "With God

before our eyes we feel that we cannot go further without endangering our independence."[27]

He was right, it was a trap. Milner was betting that Kruger would sense that there was a trap to eventually get pro-British men elected, thereby weakening the Boers' say in political matters. Actually, Milner was not that patient. He wanted to press Kruger into rejecting out of hand the whole enfranchisement deal, thereby challenging British authority. If Britain were challenged in this fashion, it would have to resort to war to force its will on the republics. Milner bet his money that Kruger would be so distrustful of British intentions that he would choose war over compromise. He did. But the coming war would be no cakewalk for the British, as Milner thought.

> In money and lives, no British war since 1815 had been so prodigal. That tea-time war, Milner's little "Armageddon," which was expected to be over by Christmas 1899, had cost the British taxpayer 200 million pounds. The cost in blood was equally high. The war office reckoned that 400,364 horses, mules and donkeys were expended in the war. There were over a hundred thousand casualties of all kinds among the 365,693 imperial and 82,742 colonial soldiers who had fought in the war. Twenty-two thousand of them found a grave in South Africa; 5,774 were killed by enemy action (or incident) and shoveled into the veldt, often where they fell, 16,168 died of wounds or were killed by the action of disease (or the inaction of army doctors).
> On the Boer side, the cost of the war, measured in suffering, was perhaps absolutely as high; relatively much higher. It was estimated that there were over 7,000 deaths among the 87,365 Boers—including 2,120 foreign volunteers and 13,000 Afrikaners from the Cape and Natal who served in the commandos of the two republics. No one knows how many Boers—men women and children—died in the concentration camps. Official estimates vary between 18,000 and 28,000.[28]

This war was fought to satisfy the desires of Governor Milner, who wanted to be king of South Africa, and a few adventurous goldbugs, but this war was just a prelude to the wars of the twentieth century, for Britain went into it fighting the set-piece battles of Napoleon's era. Open with cannons, then have the infantry charge, and follow up with a cavalry sweep. The Boers did not play the European set-piece game, neither did they opt for the mass-horde onslaught, into the ferocious Maxim guns (machine guns), which had given Britain such easy victories in Egypt and India. Instead, the Boers used new technology, smokeless guns. These were both cannon and rifles that shot cleanly, with gunpowder that did not leave the telltale puff of smoke that the old gunpowder did. This allowed marksmen to hide better when shooting, enabling them to fire on enemy troops without giving away their position. Also, the Boers made use of trenches where they would hide and wait to ambush the British as they marched forward in parade-day fashion, into a wall of flying lead. Lastly, all the Boers were mobile. A whole infantry unit, if it could be called that, would keep their horses nearby, so that they could mount up and leave whenever the situation called for it. The British were up against a fast, hidden, mobile, smart enemy that made the best of their home environment. They were immensely lucky to come out of this war victorious.

The war was a classic case of sending too few troops with generals who were fighting the current war with the last war's tactics. When Sir Redvers Buller, commander in chief of the operations, finally learned from his mistakes, another general, Lord Roberts, replaced him and repeated his mistakes. The early losses of the war were blamed on Buller, but Roberts also had much to learn. Many other British generals went into this war with a high-minded arrogance that got repaid in reversals and defeats.

> To some extent he (General White) was merely expressing the conventional British general's ignorance of the

realities of large-scale war. For half a century Britain had fought small wars against disunited and ill-armed tribesmen of India and Africa. Often these wars had started with shattering reverses; small bodies of men, surrounded by savages who gave no quarter, fighting to the last cartridge. In due course, the main British army would come on the scene and inflict a crushing and permanent defeat on the enemy.[29]

The crushing blow never came in South Africa. Rather, the war drew long, and the greater population of the empire and its deeper resources won out.

There is one biographical note that must be added to the account of the Boer War—that is, the rising star who would rise and fall with the actions of the empire over the next fifty years. This man, a future member of Parliament, future lord of the admiralty, future prime minister, future world leader, was none other than Winston Churchill. He was on the same boat heading to the Cape Colony as Sir Redvers Buller. If, as Alfred Milner had said, the British Empire was in decline, Churchill would become its last great leader, but for now, he was doing his job as a correspondent. He was going there as a dispatch reporter for the *Morning Post*, a position that he had held before. Churchill, age 25, had been a war correspondent and an active member of the military on several different occasions. His connections through his family name, that of his deceased father, Lord Randolph Churchill, and his mother's current connections, helped get him placed in the front line actions in India and Egypt. It is singularly impressive that Churchill did not use his pull to avoid action, but to put himself in the heat of the conflict. For this he would be labeled a grandstander and a self-promoter. Though Churchill loved the limelight, he performed there as well as anyone.

> "When he sailed on October 11th (the day that war was declared was October 11, 1899) he could not guess that he was embarking on a voyage which was to shape his whole future," wrote Violet Bonham Carter. She was the

daughter of Prime Minister H.H. Asquith, and was a close personal friend, confidant, and devotee of Churchill's. "It was to make him within six months a national figure, to instill in him the imaginative sympathy and compassion he never lost for prisoners and captives, and with it to improve their lot whenever he had the power to do so. It increased the chivalrous respect he had always felt for gallant enemies. Above all it was to confirm his belief in his own star and the conviction that he was specially protected and persevered by Fate for the fulfillment of some unknown purpose."[30]

It did indeed seem like Churchill led a star-crossed life. Much of his life reads as though it Hollywood had scripted it for an action picture filled with blood and guts, things blowing up, and the quest for greatness. There were the all-important evil agents, and the good-hearted foes that he would fight against; the former were to be destroyed, the latter, befriended, after being defeated. But then art imitates life. And if there are blockbuster heroes in the movies it is because there are some star-crossed, God-blessed men, who rise above their own limitations to conquer great heights. Churchill was one of those men. His quest to be at the forefront of the action, at all times, would eventually thrust him into the position of the most influential man in British politics in the twentieth century.

At the start of the war, Churchill was just a correspondent with connections. He and his compatriots were concerned that the war would be over before they arrived, and many thought that it would all be over by Christmas. The first news they had heard, while sailing to the Cape Colony, was of three Boer defeats, which reinforced their fears that they would miss out on the action. They had no need to fear, the war would last for three years.

Churchill's plan of action after they put into port was to go to the township of Ladysmith; however, it was captured and sealed off before he arrived. Then he was told that he could ride along in an armored train that was going to bring supplies to British troops who were expecting some heavy resistance. Although he knew that it could be a dangerous ride, Churchill could not resist going along.

> "An armored train!" wrote Churchill. "The very name sounds strange; a locomotive disguised as a knight errant; the agent of civilization in the habiliments of chivalry. Mr. Morely attired as Sir Lancelot would scarcely seem more incongruous." He was well aware that nothing looks more formidable and impressive than an armored train; but nothing is in fact more vulnerable and helpless.[31]

Helpless, indeed, it was. The Boers allowed the train to pass their outpost and then attacked it on its way back. An explosion on the track derailed part of the locomotive and bullets rained down on the train and its passengers, from the Boers' rifles and Maxim guns.

> With bullets whistling overhead which "rang and splattered on the steel plates like a hail storm" Winston Churchill ran along the line and called for volunteers to free the engine. The driver, his face cut open by a splinter and streaming with blood, vowed that he would not stay another minute and ran for shelter. Winston assured him that no man is ever hit twice on the same day and that a wounded man who continues to do his duty is invariably rewarded for his gallantry. "On this he pulled himself together, wiped the blood off his face, climbed back into the cab of his engine and thereafter obeyed every order that I gave him." Thanks to the coolness, courage and resource of Winston Churchill's leadership the men were rallied and steadied and the engine freed.[32]

A civilian correspondent for a newspaper took control of the situation, and while under fire, calmed the engineer, rallied the troops, freed the engine, got it going, and put the wounded on the railcar. When the engine was safely out of range of the Boers, Churchill went back to fight with the other men. This real-life scenario took another twist, however, when Churchill and the other soldiers were captured, as the engine raced off, carrying the wounded away from the action to safety.

Churchill became a prisoner of the Boers who were aware that they had someone of importance. They recognized the red-haired son of Lord Randolph Churchill. He tried to get his release as a non-combatant, but when his role in freeing the train became known to his captors, they refused to free him. He immediately began planning his escape. Although he was a prisoner, he had some freedom because he was able to "cash a check and buy a suit of tweeds…He planned his escape with two officers, one who spoke Dutch and Kaffir,"[33] but only he made it out of their jail. Captain Haldane, Regimental Sergeant-Major Brokie, and Churchill had picked one corner of the prison where the latrine was located and thought they had found a dead spot in the sentry post. They milled about there one night before going to dinner. Somehow, Churchill was separated from the other two and, as the guard became distracted, he saw his chance to jump the fence. He claimed that he waited about an hour and a half until they signaled him that he had to go alone. Later publications of the event by Captain Haldane bore out Churchill's position, but that did not stop him from being attacked for abandoning his friends—they did not make it over the fence. Churchill did.

Churchill had only some chocolate in his pocket for the long trek across hundreds of miles of open veldt filled with Boers looking for him, trying to get to British-held territory. He walked, staggered, jumped on and off trains like an American hobo, and when hunger finally overcame him, he took a chance on one particular house, hoping against hope the people there would not turn him over to the Boers. He agonized over the decision.

> He had heard it said that in the mining district of Middleburg there were a few English residents who had been allowed to remain to keep the mine working.

Had he been led to one of these? He resolved to stake all on this chance. "With faltering steps...I walked out of the shimmering gloom of the veldt into the light of furnace fires, advanced towards the silent house, and struck with my fist upon the door. A light sprang up and an upper window opened. 'Wer ist da?' (German for "Who is there?") cried a man's voice. I felt the shock of disappointment and consternation to my fingers. 'I want help...I have had an accident,' I replied. The door was opened abruptly and a tall man with a pale face and a dark mustache stood before him. 'What do you want?' he said, this time in English."[34]

Upon entering the house, Churchill first tried to tell a story about having an accident. Finally, he confessed to his armed host blurting out his identity. As he recounted the story, the man then bolted the door, giving a further sinking feeling to Churchill, who thought that he might well be recaptured. Then, to his surprise, the mustached man declared:

"Thank God you have come here. It is the only house for twenty miles where you would not have been handed over. But we are all British here, and we will see you through." Describing the "spasm of relief" which swept over him Winston Churchill wrote: "I felt like a drowning man pulled out of the water and informed that he won the Derby."[35]

Churchill's adventure was not over yet; he had to hide in mine shafts until he could be secreted out of the country. The Boers were still looking for him and he was now a wanted man, dead or alive. While in the mines he had white rats for company, and he scared off local workers who stumbled in on him by acting like a ghost. He was then transported in wool bales on a railroad car that brought him to the Witbank station on the Pretoria Lourenco Marques (Portuguese East Africa) line. Charles Burnham, an English shopkeeper and shipping agent, accompanied the delivery to help divert prying eyes and to bribe those who could not be diverted. Burnham was separated from his cargo before finally entering Portuguese territory, but he had accomplished his task. Churchill arrived in neutral territory in one piece. When he peeked through the bales and realized that he had crossed the border into freedom, he extricated himself from the wool bales, started singing, and fired his revolver in celebration.

The news of Churchill's escape became a propaganda windfall for the British. After weeks of reverses and defeats, the fall of Ladysmith, the fall of Kimberly, the daring exploits of one British man, against all of the Boers, was eaten up by the press and public. It reaffirmed the British people's belief in themselves and sent Churchill's fame shooting high in the sky, like grand fireworks. Churchill lost no time capitalizing on this newly found fame. He soon left South Africa, but not before riding with the army again. Then he ended his stint with the *Morning Post* and entered politics. He was elected to Parliament in the Khaki Election (it was called this for the color of the British army uniforms and the way the pro-war faction wrapped themselves in the flag of patriotism); Churchill was on his way to greatness as the troops were on their way to battle.

Once the war was engaged by the British Empire, it had to be won. Since the British ruled the seas, they did not need to worry about European interference. The Dutch, who were the forbearers of the Boers, had become impotent as a fighting force long before this war, and the French and Russians were not interested enough to join the fight. The Kaiser in Germany was very torn over the fight. He wanted very much to emulate the British Empire, especially on the seas and, in many ways, he was very pro-British. His mother was Queen Victoria's daughter, and some of his fondest memories were spent in British harbors, but he was Prussian, he was German, and he would not have minded seeing the British brought down a notch. Yet he could not help the Boers. In fact, three

German merchant ships, the Bundesrat, the Herzog, and the General, had been interned by the British as they sailed to German South Africa (today's Namibia). These ships were suspected of carrying weapons to the Boers, though none were found on board. Nevertheless, this internment infuriated the German public giving sufficient grounds for Admiral Alfred von Tirpitz to pass one of his naval bills in the Reichstag, to increase the money spent on the German Navy. His argument was that this internment could happen only because the German navy was weak and impotent compared to the British navy. He argued that if the German empire was ever to be taken seriously, it would need a strong navy; then the empire would not have to suffer the humiliation of having its merchant marine fleet interned by the will of any other power, even Britain.

So Great Britain was able to seal the seas off from any outside source bringing material to the Boers. They also had the Boers enclosed on the south. Europe could not and did not interfere with the war. This, however, did not stop the European press from howling about the British and how unfair the war was.

This was a must-win for the British. Their role as the world's superpower would have been greatly damaged if they had been beaten by this tiny young country.

Similarities can be and were drawn between the Boer War and the American Revolution, as in both instances there was a colonial, or semi-colonial, part of the British Empire wanting to break away from Great Britain. Both were founded by European religious separatists. But the American colonies had built strong commercial ties with European rivals to Britain (France for one). Also, the American colonies grew greatly from the rich soil and 1,500 miles of coastline that they had; the Boers did not enjoy this, and France, in 1899, did not want to anger Great Britain. That did not stop many Americans from sympathizing with the Boers. This sympathy is exemplified in Churchill's first lecture tour in the United States.

It was a year to the day since he had escaped from the prisoner-of-war camp in Pretoria. He was introduced by Mark Twain, who declared, "Mr. Churchill by his father is an Englishman, by his mother he is an American, no doubt a blend that makes him a perfect man." Twain stressed that he approved neither of Britain's war in South Africa nor America's conquest of the Philippines two years earlier. "England and America; we are kin," he said. "And now that we are also kin in sin, there is nothing more to be desired. The harmony is perfect—like Mr. Churchill himself, whom I now have the honor to present to you."[36]

Other American audiences who were not quite as eloquent as Twain, cheered enthusiastically at pictures of Boer soldiers. But Churchill was well received by these same audiences as he praised the valor of the Boer warrior while at the same time extolling the British Empire.

The British Empire was all alone here in this war. It needed to win. Since Great Britain was the top dog, the Kaiser was not the only one who would not have minded if Britain was knocked down a notch or two.

Kitchener added, somewhat ominously, "If it (the war) fails neither I nor the Field Marshall can tell what the result on the Empire may be." He stressed the word "Empire." [37]

The Boers had some successes, capturing the towns of Ladysmith and Kimberly. Cecil Rhodes himself was caught in Kimberly and he made a noisy captive, constantly complaining, through notes snuck out to the British, that if he and the town were not rescued, he would surrender the town and its inhabitants, including a handful of British soldiers, to the Boers. This would have been a dramatic propaganda win for the Boers, but it never happened. It was, most likely, because Rhodes was making empty threats in an attempt to get his way.

Since the Boer army was soon outnumbered, they decided to fight a war of attrition against the British. Their forces were too small to engage the British in force, so they used hit-and-run tactics with the occasional large-scale attack when they could muster the forces in favorable situations. The Boers also developed a tactic that would become common in the First World War, the use of artillery in a creeping barrage.

> The artillery's role was being revolutionized; instead of merely supplying the first act in a three-act drama, the gunners would be in demand, day after day, throwing a creeping barrage ahead of the advancing infantry.[38]

In the "creeping barrage" the artillery would fire in ever-increasing ranges, which would drive the British forces back and give cover to the Boers as they advanced toward the British lines. When the barrage was ended, the enemy troops would be right on top of the British while they were still recovering from the artillery shell attack. The British, on the other hand, had the problem of containing the mobile Boers so that they could attempt to wipe out their armies.

The British army had a similar problem in Boer country as they had in the American Colonies.

> He (General Buller) compared the present task with the one set Generals Howe, Clinton, and Cornwallis in the American War of Independence. It was no good capturing the capitals as they had captured New York, Philadelphia, and Charlestown, unless they subdued the territory between. As soon as the enemy re-emerged, the population would revert to its earlier allegiance— understandably, unless they could be protected from intimidation. The real task was to beat every man in the field.[39]

The British, after a slow start, were able to relieve the captives in Ladysmith and Kimberly, but it could not pin down the mobile Boers; as long as they kept moving, they could attack the British at will, and then disappear into the veldt. They could be commando one day and farmer the next. The countryside was filled with farmers who could supply fresh horses or food for the Boer raiders. Kitchener tried two things to stop these raiders. One was a system of blockhouses, with barbed wire strung between them. This was intended to stop the Boers, at which juncture the blockhouse could send word to the British forces to come and attack the Boers. The veldt proved to be too expansive for this tactic to work. The other method was the most barbaric and effective aspect of this war, the concentration camp. The farms on the veldt, especially if it could be determined that they belonged to a Boer commando, were burned to the ground. Then the women, children, and servants were rounded up and sent into makeshift camps. This also had two aspects to it. One was the psychological aspect that the Boer women and children were not safe while the men were out fighting the war. In contrast, the British families were safely at home thousands of miles away and could not be touched. Beyond that, it also had an immediate effect upon the Boer army—they were losing their source of supply in this two-pronged attack on the minds and the stomachs of the Boers in the field.

Needless to say, life in the concentration camps was harsh. Food was scarce and medicine even more so. Many women and children died. The situation became fodder for the liberal wing of the British government. Those who decried this war as an unjust war of annexation used the horrific treatment of the prisoners as proof that the war was evil and wrong. However, these arguments had very little impact on the war effort, except for meager attempts to relieve the plight of the prisoners.

In the long run this barbaric "Spanish" treatment of nonbelligerents did the nasty deed it was designed to do. (Concentration Camps were used extensively against Cuban rebels by Spain and they were excoriated for it in the American press.) Without fresh horses and food, and worried about the fate of their families, the Boers lost the will to fight. The British and Milner got what they wanted—not the decisive knock-out victory but a fight won on points. Great Britain, the ruler of the seas with an empire stretching across the whole globe, took three years and 22,000 lives to conquer a land defended by 80,000 determined farmers and prospectors. In the meantime, they had sullied their image in a barbaric slugfest. The Boer War helped prove to the Germans that if they were going to be influential in the world, their country needed a better naval fleet. It proved that, at the start, Britain was not up to the fight, though when it was obvious that the position of the British Empire depended upon victory, the entire empire from Australia to New Zealand to Scotland joined together to ensure victory. It also showed that Britain had the stomach to do what was uncivilized and unjustified (except, of course, in wartime). They incarcerated women and children. Think for a moment what the outcome might have been if they had not gone down that barbaric path. The Boers could have gone on fighting for years. They would have slowly picked off a few British troops here, a handful there. Remember that, in the American Revolution, George Washington did not win many battles. There was the defeat of the Hessians at Trenton, New Jersey, a propaganda victory, which allowed him to pick up badly needed recruits. He had his major victory when he defeated Cornwallis at Yorktown, but mostly he led the British on an eight-year trek through the woods and swamps of the East Coast of the United States. What could the Boers have done with another five years? And they had a resource, which the American colonists had been in dire need of, money. The Boers had diamonds and gold to buy arms. Imagine what WWI would have been like if Britain was still engaged in on-again, off-again battles in South Africa. They would not have been able to consolidate their fleet in the North Sea to blockade Germany if a sufficient force was needed to patrol the coasts of Africa. Nor would they have been able to field a significant army in France if their forces were split between

South Africa and Europe. How things would have turned out differently! But that did not happen. The British ruthlessly subdued the Boers by imprisoning their families and brought an end to the war.

The fact remains, however, that Britain fought a war of annexation. As poorly as the Boers treated the human rights of the people they conquered, Britain's trumped-up reasons for engaging the fight were weak indeed. This was the last war of empire building for Britain.

Great Britain did gain some lands after WWI, but to the victor goes the spoils. Britain did not enter World War I for gain but had to fight tooth and nail to retain its empire. It began the war with a barbaric tool; it did not wait until near the end of the war as it did in the Boer War. It imposed a naval blockade, preventing all forms of war material, including food, from reaching Germany. Many women and children died of starvation in Germany because of the blockade.

The empire made no effort to expand further after the annexations of the Boer War. Maybe, as Milner had lamented, the empire had climaxed, had reached its zenith. But there remains an interesting fact. The empire, the mother country, was saved by its many former colonies—the Australian, New Zealand, Indian, and Canadian forces fought bravely in South Africa. They had come of age and were able to help the mother country. They also left their marks on the battlefields of Europe in the two world wars. In the wars of the twentieth century, it would be the eldest of the colonies, the breakaway colony of the United States, which would take the lead once Great Britain could no longer head an empire of free trade and democracy.

Throughout the whole Boer War, the entire world was watching. Britons were lucky just to maintain what they had of their empire. France had more reason to wish the British well than to try to foul up British standing; the French foreign minister was trying to build a rapprochement with Britain to gain an ally against Germany. The Kaiser was on one hand praising the brave British soldiers, and on the other hand telling the Danish queen that she would have to wait for the day when there was a German navy strong enough to challenge the British Empire in the far reaches of the world. Russia was not interested in this spot on the globe. The United States was embroiled with its own recent attempt at colonization in the Philippines and was in no mood for a fight. So, this was Britain's last war for empire building, and, had any of these European countries been able to interfere, it could have changed the outcome. They did not. Yet in Germany, Admiral Tirpitz was able to use this example of unhindered imperial expansion as a reason to build a formidable navy for Germany.

Chapter Three
Location, Location, Location

In Chapter One, we looked at the growth of the German nation, which was meteoric. It inspired awe, it inspired fear. Its designing genius, Chancellor Otto von Bismarck, was a man of ruthless ambition and daring maneuvers that forged the loosely confederated German states into one nation in 1862. First they beat the Danes in battle, then Austria-Hungry, then France. Denmark was not a first-rate power, but Austria-Hungry and France were. By beating both of them, Bismarck transformed Prussia into a larger, more powerful Germany and, as a new nation; it took its place among the most powerful nations in Europe. (The proof of the strength of his work is that even after two disastrous world wars, after being split up during the cold war, the German nation is still together. This speaks volumes for the endurance of his work.) But the Germans, the Teutonic people, were always known for their armies. What changed in the twentieth century was that they expanded their land mass, their population, their economic wealth, and built a navy.

Germany, and especially Prussia, had always had a problem with its neighbors: they fought wars with Austria to the south, France to the west, and Russia to the east. There were also raids that came in from Scandinavia to the north, but that was less of a problem. It seems that being on the Northern European Plain, with no natural borders from the Atlantic Ocean in the west to the Ural Mountains in the east, anyone in the middle was open to attacks from any side. If Germany was to become a strong nation, it had to become a natural border of its own; hence, there is the saying that Prussia was not a state that contained an army, but an army that contained a state. It became a natural state of being that Prussia/Germany should have a strong military.

A similar situation can be said about the British Isles, but instead of a strong army, they needed a strong navy. In ancient days, England did not have a navy, relying instead upon the distance over the waters to separate itself from marauding hordes. They remained safe until their enemies built ships to come from Europe or Scandinavia and invade the island nation. Julius Caesar had done so, the Vikings had done so, and William the Conqueror had done so. When England had built its navy sufficiently, as it had in Henry VIII's time, it was able to prevent an invasion of the island by any European country. So it was as natural for England (later Great Britain when it combined with Scotland and Wales) to build and maintain its great fleet as it was for Germany to house and march great armies. Ideally, the two should never have to meet; as long as Germany stayed on the Continent and Britain remained on its island and enjoyed its empire across the oceans, the two should have been able to live in harmony. Nothing is ever that easy.

Britain had one major problem with continental powers. Britain had always concerned itself with the balance of power on the Continent. Normally, they allied with the weaker powers on the Continent to diminish the power of the greater nation: Britain and Holland fought off Spain, the British and the Austrians fought against Louis XIV's France, the British and the Prussians defeated Napoleon at Waterloo, yet the British stood aside in 1870 when the Prussians/ Germans soundly beat the French in the Franco-Prussian War. Europe was changed by that war, a war that everyone thought France would win, they lost. Its emperor, Napoleon III, was forced out of power, and the weak French Republic took his place. When they lost the war, they lost the provinces of Alsace and Lorraine, and they lost status. Germany was victorious in all three. It was then that they became the most formidable force on the European Continent.

It is a curious fact that once Bismarck had gained the power he was seeking, he ended his wars and became a man of peace. It was a lesson that those who followed him would fail to grasp. He helped to broker a peace treaty between Russia and Turkey and helped to bring about the peace treaty for the Crimean War.

In the decades that followed the Franco-Prussian War, Britain had great admiration and close ties to Germany. Victoria, daughter of Queen Victoria and Prince Albert, married the prince and heir to the emperor of Germany, Frederick Hohenzollern, for whom the British had high hopes once he ascended the throne. He alone, among the German princes, embraced liberal democratic ideas for Germany, which brought even more hope that, together, Germany and Britain could forge a new world. There was talk of a joint Teutonic-Anglo-Saxon sharing of world responsibilities. Joseph Chamberlain, the minister of the Colonial Office during the Boer War held such pro-German views.

> In reaching out to Germany Chamberlain ignored the centuries old precept of English history: to survive and prosper, England must always ally herself with the weaker power or powers in Europe. Otherwise, allied to the strongest power, England finds herself in a subordinate role, her interests and independence subject to the dictates of the strongest power. Only by rallying the weaker states into a coalition to oppose the strongest power can England prevent Continental hegemony and preserve her own security.[40]

The German emperor, Wilhelm I, finally died at the age of ninety-one. The idealist, democracy-minded war hero, Frederick, came to the throne, delighting everyone across the North Sea in Britain. He was, however, infected with some sort of throat cancer. At his wife's urging, he ignored the pleas of his German doctors for immediate surgery and opted for a more holistic English doctor's cure, giving the cancer more time to spread. He died during his first year on the throne.

In his stead rose Wilhelm, his eldest son. He had a crippled arm from birth that seems to have been preventable. His birth was a breach and the doctors damaged Wilhelm's arm at that time. Wilhelm was very aggressive, boisterous, and had a habit of saying things that he should not, especially as the emperor. What could pass for barroom bravado at a beer hall or a pub did not become an emperor; he embarrassed himself and his country more than once because of his conduct. The chancellor had trained him to disdain anything that had to do with democracy. He did so because, given Wilhelm I's long life, it was likely that Frederick would live a long time also, and Bismarck wanted a counterbalance to the emperor's democratic leanings, supposing a long reign by Frederick. What Bismarck received instead was a headstrong emperor, Wilhelm, who soon had no need of his chancellor. For many years, Bismarck was the true power behind the crown, but the chancellor served at the wishes of the emperor. Even though Bismarck wielded greater political power than the emperor, the latter could remove the minister at his will. It was a Frankenstein monster that Bismarck had created. He filled Wilhelm with the idea of an all-powerful monarch. When Wilhelm came to the throne and there was a clash between the two, Wilhelm had little problem jettisoning his chancellor and putting in men to his liking. Unfortunately, Bismarck's replacements were no match for the old creative genius.

From the beginning, Prussia—pressed on all sides, fought doggedly to carve out a kingdom for itself—became Germany, the main force on the Continent, and in doing so also became the enemy of Britain. There was one major factor that helped to push Britain over the edge—Germany dared to challenge Britain at its strength, its navy.

The British might have been able to live peaceably with a powerful Germany if they had taken a few things to heart; first, war would commence between the two if there was an invasion of Holland or Belgium, second, Britain could not allow France to be further humiliated or weakened after the Franco-Prussian War.

> "An English attack would only be thinkable if we found ourselves at war with both Russia and France or if we did anything so utterly absurd as to fall upon Holland or Belgium or block the Baltic by blocking the Sound," said Bismarck.[41]

Yet the Schlieffen Plan (the German invasion plan used at the start of WWI) called for invading Belgium while fighting both Russia and France; it should have come as no secret to Germany where Britain would side if Germany had to fight a two-front war. Some in Germany held out the hope that Britain would remain neutral in a possible continental war. This was wishful thinking. Others, one being General Helmuth von Moltke (the Younger), figured this into their war calculations and were not concerned about a British involvement.

Before we go further, one must look at a map of Europe. The great seaports of the Lowlands of Belgium and the Netherlands are about 100 to 150 miles away from the south of England. In about a five-to-eight hour sail, a battleship could be bombarding and invading Britain from these ports.

> Since the sixteenth century, England had been unwilling to see the Low Countries in the hands of a Great Power. To keep the channel coasts out of threatening hands, England had fought Philip II of Spain, Louis XIV, and the Emperor Napoleon Bonaparte. The nation of Belgium had risen from the ashes of Napoleon's empire, and in

1839 its perpetual neutrality had been guaranteed by France, Britain, Austria, and Prussia.[42]

Britain, like Germany, was a guarantor of the neutrality of Belgium and had been since the foundation of that small kingdom in 1831. But more than national honor was at stake. British strategy could not tolerate the threat of a strident and overarmed Germany solidly positioned on the Channel coast and master of its greatest port, Antwerp, and its largest industrial complex. Belgium, grafted on to Germany, meant menace unlimited.[43]

This desire by Britain was twofold. It kept economically powerful industrial areas and seaports out of the hands of any great power on the Continent, but more importantly, it was a buffer zone that protected Britain. Britain could not push France out of Normandy, but it was not going to allow France, Austria, or Germany to stage an attack from the Lowlands. If an attack started from there, it might be too late to prevent great harm from befalling London or other southern ports, before Britain could effectively repel the attack. To draw the line in the Lowlands, Britain was protecting the little guy while at the same time protecting Britain. It assured that before there would be an invasion of Britain, there must first be an invasion of the Lowlands, and once these lands were taken, a belligerent nation could look across the English Channel and make plans for invading the British Isles. Now it did not matter that there was no plan in the German General staff to attack Britain—they would not wait for the attack to be planned and staged before they would act. In essence, an attack on the Lowlands would instigate a preemptive war, a case of self-preservation. It was well within Britain's self-interest to involve itself in a war in Belgium, Holland, or France, which would keep the war confined to the Continent. The civilian death and destruction would occur on the Continent, not Britain. (Of course, the airplane changed that idea and Britain received devastating blows at the hands of the German Luftwaffe in WWII.) But there has been no invasion of Britain since the Glorious Revolution in 1688, when William of Orange was invited to become Britain's king, by Parliament. The same cannot be said of France, Germany, Austria, Poland, Russia, or any continental country. The Glorious Revolution was glorious, hence the name. William of Orange sailed up the Thames River with an army ready to do battle with King James II, Louis XIV's ally on the British throne. It was called the "Glorious Revolution" because of the swiftness of its success and its bloodlessness—quite a sight to behold.

> In the words of Thomas Macauley, "More than six hundred vessels, with canvass spread to within a favorable wind, followed in his train...his fleet spread to within a league of Dover on the North and of Calais on the South. The men of war on the extreme right and left saluted both fortresses at once. The troops appeared under arms on the decks. The flourish of trumpets, the clash of cymbals and the rolling of drums was heard at once on the English and French shores." Once ashore, the Protestant army, assembled from half a dozen nations, astounded the country people of Devon with the many faces of England's Protestant deliverance. Parading into Exeter, black colonial soldiers from the Dutch West Indies in embroidered white caps topped by white feathered plumes were followed by the King of Sweden's Finnish cavalry in black armor and bearskin cloaks. One wonders what the reaction must have been in James' army, because within weeks, it was melting away.[44]

This Glorious Revolution is very instructive. At that time, it was the Dutch who helped out the parliamentarians in England by sending William of Orange and his "Protestant army" with him to force the Catholic King James II out of England. The religious aspect of this war cannot be denied. France was as strongly Catholic then as it is now secular. The Catholic kings of Europe wanted to conquer England and convert it, by sword if necessary, back to Catholicism. This was part of the motivation of Spain and France with whom England battled ferociously through the centuries. The world wars do not take on an aura of a religious war, but rather a war for dominance in Europe and the world, albeit, behind the religious aspect was the will for dominance. If Britain could be conquered and converted, its navy and its wealth could be used for the benefit of the conquering nation as well as money and land for the pope.

In WWI, Britain could no more turn its back on Belgium than the Dutch could have done to England during the Glorious Revolution. The same logic that applied to England in 1914 applied to the Dutch in 1688. They could not allow a hostile foreign enemy to have the ports in southern England to use as a staging area to attack Holland. If England had fallen under the influence of France during the reign of King James II, then Holland would have potential hostile forces on its western and southern borders. If they teamed up with England, deposed the king, and set a favorable monarch there, then it would have only one enemy to the south and a willing ally to the west. The armies could be consolidated and the navies put to sea in unison, which would form mighty fighting forces. It was the obverse of Britain's strategic position in 1914.

In WWI, Britain claimed that it was going to war to protect democratic Belgium. This is nonsense. Belgium was no more democratic than Germany; in fact, its ruler, King Leopold, was guilty of allowing real atrocities to occur in the Belgium Congo against the African natives in the first decade of the new century. Africans were hacked and mutilated by the scores under Belgium's watch, which was reported widely in newspapers across the world. Germany was accused of similar actions during World War I, but reporters from the field during the war and afterward found no evidence of these occurrences. These atrocious acts did not matter in 1914 when the war started. It would not have mattered if Belgium was a dictatorship, a monarchy, or an oligarchy. Britain was not going to allow Germany to sit in the port of Antwerp.

Some in Germany saw the folly of the Schlieffen plan. They understood that any attack on the Lowlands would immediately bring Britain into the war. But Moltke made a claim that sounds similar to what Governor Milner had said about annexing South Africa: "Success alone justifies war."[45] In fact, Moltke was so confident of success that he did not ask Admiral Tirpitz to send any ships to block the transport of British troops or supplies going to Belgium at the start of the war. The Germans almost achieved their goal of reaching Paris in six weeks, then the fight bogged down into the infamous trench warfare for which WWI is remembered.

There was a cold, hard logic in the Schlieffen Plan.

> Observing the principle of concentration of forces, Count Alfred von Schlieffen, Chief of German General Staff from 1891 to 1906, decreed that in a two front war, "The whole of Germany must throw itself upon one enemy, the strongest, most powerful, most dangerous enemy, and that can only be France."[46]

The Russian army was looked upon as being weaker and therefore would take fewer divisions to hold off. Seven-eighths of the German army went to the west; one-eighth went to the east. Another reason why the German army did not concentrate its forces on the east at first was their fear that the Russian army could continually give ground over the massive Russian landmass as the Germans moved forward. "Russia could always frustrate victory by retreating, as Kutuzov had done when facing Napoleon."[47] So the Germans could lose a war in the east even if they won all the battles. Instead, they concentrated their forces to defeat the French forces as they had in 1870.

Why Moltke did not demand that the kaiser send the newly minted German navy to block transport across the English Channel is a huge question. Mainly, the Germans did not really fear the British army and did not think that they would make much of a difference in the battle.

> The size of the British Expeditionary Force—four or six divisions—is well known; should the English choose to place these men in the path of the German juggernaut, they would be ground under along with any Frenchmen or Belgians who got in the way. "The more English the better," Moltke said to Tirpitz.[48]

This bravado in hindsight was just one of the many blunders that prevented the Germans from winning. Moltke was convinced that the army could win this without any help from the navy; thus he failed to destroy the French and British forces in six weeks, and the war bogged down. What would have been the situation on the ground if Germany had sent out its navy to block the British in the first few weeks? Would the Germans have scored a major naval victory? Would the British ships have annihilated the Germans? Would the German navy have been able delay the British Expeditionary Force long enough for Moltke's army to defeat the French forces? These are all questions without answers because of Moltke's bravado. It would not be the last time the Germans would fall prey to their own boasting; at times, it was as if they believed their own myths about the invincible Teutonic warrior.

Two causes brought Britain into WWI: first, Germany built a navy to rival Britain's, and second, Germany invaded France through Belgium.

Geography played a huge part in the buildup to WWI. Britain did not feel threatened by the fact that the United States was building a huge navy, yet they did feel threatened by the German navy. Britain was not concerned when the United States acquired the land and built the Panama Canal, while the completion of the Kiel Canal linking the Baltic Sea with the North Sea through German territory did worry Britain. Nor did they feel threatened over the United States' victory in the Spanish-American War. British observers were on American ships as Commodore George E. Dewey fought his battles in the Philippines; yet, again, Britain was threatened by German shipbuilding in the North Sea. There was no fear that the United States would come steaming across the Atlantic to invade the British Isles. There had, however, always been great fears of a European invasion. British pulp press novels throughout the 1800s once decried an invasion by sneaky Frenchmen who were depicted as saboteurs and spies in England, working service jobs by day and sending messages to the invaders by night. These novels were replaced in the first decade of 1900 by novels about the sneaky Germans lying in wait in the midst of an unsuspecting London setting.

These fears were not just the peddling of paranoid trash for a pound. The British Isles had known periods of invasion. The term *Danegeld* is a medieval term for tax. It originates from tribute money paid to Danish invaders so that they would not sack and burn a village—extortion money. The term literally means Dane's gold or gold for the Danes. When England had built a strong navy, it could prevent these marauders from attacking their villages, or go one step further and attack the enemy before they had a chance to attack them.

Geography played against the German naval aspirations. It goes without saying that, in order to have a great navy, Germany needed access to the ocean; Britain had blocked Germany's access to the Atlantic. Britain's previous naval competitor, France, has a western border on the Atlantic, so nothing blocks France's access to the ocean. Because of this, it was much harder for the British to pin down the French fleets than it was to corner the German ships in the North Sea. In the First World War, Britain imposed a naval blockade on Germany, although it was not a close blockade of Germany's ports, which is what the Germans had expected. They were planning to use their torpedo boats and destroyers in the shallow waters with aid from shoreline batteries to thwart a British blockade. Britain's first sea lord during the first decade of twentieth century, Jackie Fisher, foresaw this and feared the possible disastrous results. He devised a long-distance blockade, closing Germany's access to the Atlantic Ocean and locking the German fleet in home confinement in the North Sea. This was possible because new technologies made the ships faster and more powerful than previous warships. Steam had replaced sails and even during the First World War, diesel was replacing steam. The guns were more deadly at longer ranges (three to ten miles), which made it possible for Britain to close the passage of the North Sea between the Firth of Forth near Edinburgh, Scotland, and the Norwegian Coast. This would have been a near impossibility during the era of the Napoleonic wars, but quite achievable at the turn of the century.

The British stopped all ships going into the North Sea and seized all ships or material they considered to be contraband heading toward Germany. This aggravated many countries that bordered the North Sea that were not involved in the war. These "Northern Neutrals" as they were known (Norway, Sweden, Denmark, and the Netherlands) also suffered due to the blockade. If Britain thought the material would find its way to the German front, it was confiscated. Any material that could be used in the production of weapons, any food, any clothing, soon fell under the blockade impositions. Most of this was being done illegally according to international treaty. Germany, however, was not getting much of a sympathetic ear in world opinion. Again, their blindness to the importance of the propaganda war cost them dearly in dealing with the blockade. The Northern Neutrals complained bitterly to United States President Woodrow Wilson about the blockade, but he did little to aid their plight.

The propaganda machine that Britain had developed early in the war was continuing to paint the Germans as the evil, barbaric Huns destroying thousands of years of civilization. This was being said while Britain slowly starved men, women, and children in Germany and put the Northern Neutrals in dire situations. The German population as a whole endorsed the unrestricted U-boat warfare against the Entente powers. They saw it as a legitimate weapon to be used to break the blockade and bring food to the table and the war to a close. The outside world saw the U-boats the way the Entente wanted it to see them, as the barbaric attack on women, children, and unsuspecting sailors perpetrated by the cold-hearted Huns. Germany's pleas to President Wilson to help break the blockade paled in comparison to the list of dead passengers from the Lusitania. The Lusitania, a Cunard Line Ocean Cruiser was sunk by a U-boat on May 7, 1915. The Germans claimed that it was carrying war material on board, making it a legitimate target according to international laws. That was a moot point, although it has since been proven to be correct. It was just one of the points used to make the British propaganda look true at the time. The "evil Huns" were doing it again—if they were doing it on the open seas, then the stories about the Belgium atrocities must be valid. Never mind that there was highly explosive material on board. Never mind that civilian ships were not supposed to transport war material, according to international law. Never mind that the United States was obligated to confiscate any ship that was illegally transporting war material together with civilian passengers. Never mind that President Wilson had been told of its illegal cargo. Never mind that the explosive cargo caused a secondary explosion after the torpedo hit, causing the boat to sink faster. Never mind that more people could have been rescued if the ship had not been carrying explosives. Never mind that the Lusitania had been fitted with "high power naval rifles in conformity with England's new policy of arming passenger boats."[49] Never mind that these guns made it an armed merchant ship, and therefore a legitimate target. Never mind that the British Admiralty had already commandeered space on the Cunard Line ships for transporting war material or troops throughout the duration of the war.[50] Never mind that the Germans had attempted to warn people to stay off of ships that contained contraband, and particularly, had warned people to stay off this ship.

Germany torpedoed and sank an ocean liner with innocent people on board—that was all that mattered. Germany was forced to stop the use of unrestricted submarine warfare due to an outraged world reaction, mainly from the United States. (This would have been the wise position from the start. Why Germany didn't make better use of the submarines against warships is examined in subsequent chapters of this book.) When Germany reinstated the unrestricted submarine warfare in early 1917, the United States soon joined the war. On the other hand, Britain was never forced to give up the blockade of the North Sea; nor would they, even if the United States had joined the war on the German side. Britain had the power of the navy and they were going to use it no matter what anyone said. It was that blockade that starved Germany's will to continue the fight. If it was a war of attrition on the western front, it was also a war of attrition on the home front. The German women and children who died of malnutrition never made it to the official tallies of the war dead.

To be fair to the British side, there was no reason for them to want to admit how war material was being shipped to the European theatre. Their best bet was to hide it wherever they could, even on civilian liners. The Germans had given their enemies a propaganda coup when the Kaiser had compared his forces to the Huns in 1900 during the Chinese Boxer Rebellion. The Germans could have used their submarines only against military targets to break the blockade. They would have had more submarines sunk, but a battle of warship to warship would not have angered the United States citizenry to the point that would bring them into the war.

Even though the naval buildup was one of the reasons for the start of the war, the Kaiser was very reluctant to use his navy, especially the surface ships. They were sitting in port waiting for the attack that never came. They were expecting a close blockade and expecting the British navy to sail past the

Helgoland Island, just north of the German coast, and to sail up the Elbe into the Nord Ostsee Kanal. That was not going to happen. The British Admiralty was not going to subject the British fleet to a close-quarter sea battle in enemy territory where the monstrous Dreadnoughts would be torn apart with torpedoes and land-based artillery

Germany was stuck in their corner of the North Sea, blocked from access to the ocean by the most powerful navy in the world. There would be only one great sea battle in this war, the Battle of Jutland, and that would prove to be a draw. Germany never broke the blockade. They were cut off from the outside world, could not receive the supplies they desperately needed, and were not able to get their side of the story out to the world.

> "The geographic position of a country may not only favor the concentration of its forces, but give the further strategic advantage of a central position and a good base for hostile operations against its probable enemies,"[51] stated Captain A.T. Mahan, a United States naval expert and president of the Naval War College in Newport, Rhode Island.
>
> "Nations, like men, however strong, decay when cut off from external activities and resources which at once draw out and support their internal powers. A nation, as we have already shown, cannot live indefinitely of itself, and the easiest way by which it can communicate with other peoples and renew its own strength is the sea," Mahan wrote.[52]

The Great War proved much of Mahan's book to be correct. Great Britian was in a central position to block Germany's access to the sea, which hurt Germany's war effort and its population, making a war of attrition more favorable to the Entente powers. Even if Britain or France were not winning on the battlefield, they could bleed Germany dry by the duration of the war. Hence, Germany was made even more desperate in seeking the one last battle or in believing that unrestricted submarine warfare would end the war. This war of attrition should have also made the German generals and the admirals very reluctant about bringing in any of the neutrals on the side of their enemies. They lost this concern about the possibility of defeat when they thought they had victory in their grasp.

The Germans never really understood the concepts that underlay naval strategy. They thought about the navy as if it was not another part of the army, a rather poor stepson of the army, nor did they grasp its finer points and pursued a naval strategy that fell in line with the British strategy. Britain's naval strategy was a defensive one: they had the dominant geographical position; the English Isles blocked German access to the Atlantic Ocean; the English Channel was twenty miles wide and easily defended. When Moltke had advised von Tirpitz not to use his ships to block the British Expeditionary Force from going to France, Germany lost its one best chance to affect the war with a naval battle in the Channel. The opening of the North Sea, sailing between Norway and Scotland, was a different story but still defensible in the age of steam- and diesel-powered engines. Some people in England clamored for another Trafalgar, a Nelsonian-like attack on Germany's naval base. This is what the Germans planned for. The Germans were prepared for this battle with shore batteries, mines, submarines, and torpedo boats to tear apart any British attack. British Admiral John Jellicoe was not about to run his ships on a suicidal mission into enemy territory; he did not need to. Britain maintained the superior position by cutting off Germany's supply lines to the outside world because of the blockade it enforced on the North Sea. Britain had the stranglehold that Germany needed to break. As long as the German fleet sat in its corner of the North Sea, it posed no threat to Great Britain's position. Great Britain did not need to go on the offensive, Germany did.

> "The English fleet might have been three times stronger or half as strong as it actually was," claimed Vice Admiral

Wolfgang Wegener. "The proportion of forces between us might have been exactly reversed: the English operations would have remained the same, always defensive, because the primary purpose of the English fleet consisted of defense of England's strategic position, from which she controlled the important commercial arteries in the Atlantic.[53]

"Without access to trade routes a waterway is without strategic significance. Hence there is no reason for the enemy to attack. The North Sea around the Helgoland Bight was and is, and remains a dead angle in a dead sea."[54]

It was up to the Germans to change the situation, not for Britain to risk its fleet in whole or part by raiding German territory. Germany would have to find a way to break through the blockade or draw Great Britain out into battle, which it did at the battle of Jutland, which is looked at in detail in Chapter Six.

If Germany had been able to reach the world markets through the North Sea or through the Northern Neutrals, it would have had many more supplies for troops. One of the reasons given for Germany's failure to defeat the Entente forces in 1918 was that many of their famished troops were looting stores of food and liquor as they proceeded. They were amazed at the abundance of food, enticed by the liquor, and demoralized when they learned firsthand that the submarine attacks were not starving the Entente powers into submission. If these foodstuffs, and even the liquor, had been commonplace for the German trooper, then there would not have been a temptation to forego his mission, and the Entente forces might have been defeated before the Americans had arrived in mass. This was part of the strategy of the naval blockade—to deny the enemy troops basic necessities so that they could not perform their duties in the field. No one could state that it could ever have had this specific effect, but in retrospect, this is one of the factors of the blockade.

"We could have obtained the keys to the Baltic as the result of a political agreement with Denmark. We could have covered the Sound and the belts from the north and thus secured the Baltic from England's clutches," Wegener claimed. "Furthermore the northern trade route would have devolved to us, and without the means of exercising pressure on the northern kingdoms (Northern Neutrals) an increase of power [in terms of] political influence and prestige. Finally our position in the Kattegatt, after the fleet would have been stationed there would have constituted a threat to the English position and would, as a further result, have opened up perspectives in the Atlantic."[55]

Hence, Great Britain's geographic positioning blocking Germany's access to the sea prevented Germany from benefiting from their High Seas Fleet. Great Britain, being a naval power for centuries, understood better the strategic value of the seas that were hidden from the novice. The Germans suffered the long-term effects of the blockade because they did not know that they had the means in their hands to break the blockade. They need not attack the British fleet in force and could have set up diplomatic and commercial relations with the Northern Neutrals, gotten needed materials, and changed the dynamics of the Northern Sea. If they were getting materials from Norway or Sweden through Denmark or the Baltic Sea, this would have forced Britain to go on the attack. The choices would be to attack the neutrals, an option they probably would avoid, or attack Germany; then, and only then, would Jellico have ventured into German territory. But as long as Britain was maintaining the blockade from a distance, there was no need at all to endanger the fleet. In this category, the British reigned supreme because of centuries of knowledge of warfare on the high seas.

Chapter Four
Dreadnought: The Gospel According to Mahan

Mutually Assured Destruction (MAD) was the Cold War name given to the defensive strategy where either the United States or the Soviet Union could annihilate the other with atomic weapons. The theory stated that this mutual ability to take the other out prevented either from making the first strike; this was the result of the arms race in nuclear weapons. Yet, arms races go back beyond the Cold War, even beyond the ancient Greeks and Persians. The Judean King Uzziah (of the Davidic line) is reported to have "engines, invented by cunning men, to be on the towers and upon the bulwarks, to shoot arrows and great stones withal."[56] So throughout the ages there has been warfare and the desire to make bigger and better weapons than the foe. Now, looking at the early twentieth century, Great Britain and Germany were locked into a classic arms race, building huge and heavily armed, thickly armored steel floating fortresses called Dreadnoughts.

> The first Dreadnought, a vessel of four hundred tons carrying 200 men, was launched in 1573 and sailed against the Spanish Armada. Queen Elizabeth I chose its

name "to infuse her own dauntless spirit into the hearts of her subjects and to show...Europe...how little she dreaded and how little such a people could dread, the mightiest armaments of their enemies."[57]

The Dreadnought class of ships was built to be the biggest, most heavily armed, fastest ships that the world had ever seen, and at the turn of the century, they were. All of the European powers built them, as did the United States. It was the building plans of the British and Germans that was a major cause for the precipitation of WWI.

As was shown in the chapter about the Boer War, Germany felt impotent because of its inability to come to the aid of the Boers. There was no rail connection running down into Africa; the closest thing was a Berlin-to-Baghdad rail line that was being planned. The only way to get supplies and troops down there was by ship. The British had already shown that they would stop any foreign ship they suspected of carrying arms to the Boers, which stoppage fell right into line with ideas put forward in a book by naval war historian United States naval captain, Alfred Thayer Mahan, in *The Influence of Sea Power Upon History 1660-1773*. This book influenced all of those who wanted to be admirals or command naval powers, from Europe, to the United States, to Japan. Theodore Roosevelt, Franklin Delano Roosevelt, Kaiser Wilhelm, Admiral Tirpitz, and many others devoured this historical tome that explained why Britain was the greatest power of the day. Mahan said it was because they controlled the seas. He stated that there were two important aspects of sea power.

It is the union of commerce and protection and the power of a sea force that brings a country world power. The sea power of England therefore was not merely in the great navy, with which we too commonly and exclusively associate with it; France had such a navy in 1688, and it shriveled away like a leaf in a fire. Neither was it in a prosperous commerce alone; a few years after the date at which we have arrived, the commerce of France took

on fair proportions, but the first blast of war swept it off
the seas as the navy of Cromwell had once swept that of
Holland. It was the union of the two, carefully fostered,
that England made the gain of sea power over and beyond
all other states...[58]

According to Mahan, a great country needs water-borne
international commerce to become even greater. It also
needs a navy that will protect the sea routes upon which
the commerce travels. He stated that all great empires from
Rome, to Spain, to Great Britain had become great because
they had growing sea commerce. To Germany and the United
States, this book was a "how to" book on becoming a great
nation. To Britain, it was a pat on the back showcasing their
job well done. The Kaiser and everyone in the German naval
fleet took Mahan's book to heart, creating a dilemma for
Britain. They warily eyed Germany's aspirations for national
greatness and to become equal with Britain on the sea. If
Germany were ever to be equal with Britain, Britain would
no longer be the sole ruler of the oceans; it would have to
look over its shoulder and see what Germany was doing or
saying. Again, the Boer War is illustrative. Britain was able to
send whatever it needed, when needed, and did not concern
itself with what anyone on the Continent thought. They even
interned three German ships, not fearing any retaliation for
this national humiliation. If Germany had had a navy equal
to Britain's, Britain would not have dared stop the German
ships for fear of bringing Germany into the war. Considering
that the Boers were giving the British troops a good fight,
and they had plenty of gold and diamonds with which to buy
arms, the war would have been quite different if Germany
could have aided the Boers. Therefore, Britain could, under
no circumstances, allow Germany to seek parity on the sea. It
would mean the unraveling of the empire.

Another aspect of Mahan's book is that this naval power
is to be used ruthlessly. A rising power is not to be given a
chance to compete evenly with a major power. The growth of

the German navy was a threat to Britain, as was the power of the British navy a hindrance to Germany's growth as a world power. If Germany had wanted to aid the Boers, they would have had to send arms and men by ship to German West Africa. There they could debark and make their way across the Bechuanaland to the Transvaal and help the Boers. They would need armed ships powerful enough to defeat the British in open water. Also, they would need ships that could run a blockade that Britain might inflict upon their ports. Germany did not have this kind of navy. Since they did not have it, they had to bow to British pressure when their ships were interned. It did not matter how much they screamed or yelled at the illegality of the internment. Britain was going to do what Britain had to do to win the war. No one was able to tell them otherwise.

This goes to the heart of Mahan's point. Because Britain had the power, it could protect its interests to the detriment of the Boers. It was also to the detriment of Germany, because they could not ally themselves with the Boers. The Boers were landlocked, hence they had no navy; in fact, it is because their antecessors were swept off the naval stages that the Boers had to recede farther and farther into Africa. As stated earlier, the Cape Colony of South Africa had once been a Dutch territory until Britain had annexed it, and the Boers tried in vain to escape British rule.

As Mahan states in his book, the superior power does not allow a weaker navy to grow to be an equal. He shows the example of how the English dealt with the Spanish navy in 1718.

> He (Admiral George Byng) had before him a disorderly force, much inferior both in numbers and discipline. His merit seems to lie rather in the readiness to assume a responsibility from which a more scrupulous man might have shrunk; but in this and throughout the campaign he rendered good service to England, whose sea power was again strengthened by the destruction not of an actual

but a possible rival, and his services were rewarded by a peerage.[59]

Here Byng attacked a weaker enemy and with it thwarted attempts by Spain to threaten British dominance in future years, which assured Britain of maintaining its role as the supreme power on the seas.

Germany could have rendered a significant blow to the British Empire and would have had a possible rich ally for future wars if they had had the ability to send ships with arms and soldiers to aid the Boers. This could have been done in a foreign war where Germany could have claimed the higher moral ground saying that they were only aiding the weaker nation against a stronger bullying nation. But they were not able to do this because Britain's sea power was so overwhelming. Thus, Germany was reduced to being a spectator in the conflict.

> To the young Queen Wilhelmina of Holland, who appealed to the Kaiser to do something to save the crumbling Boers, William presented another face. (He was currently praising the valor of the British troops to his relatives in Britain.) He declined Wilhelmina's entreaties grandiloquently, "Yet whoever believes in God the Lord as Supreme Judge of world-order knows that he overlooks nothing and that he punishes injustice with relentless severity...Therefore it is in the interest of world peace as well as the Dutch-Frisian race on the Continent that a mighty (German) fleet shall be on the sea...Till then silence and work."[60]

Admiral Tirpitz saw this problem and used it to increase the amount of money that the Reichstag was considering for approval for naval construction. Of course, this is well within a nation's prerogative to do so. It is quite appropriate for the legislature of a given state to provide money to build ships for its navy. The shipbuilding program in Germany had the support of a broad part of the populous, including the

German press who howled at the abuse of their merchant ships by Britain. But even the building of ships posed a problem for the British. If Germany built a navy equal to its own, then they would be able to interfere with British battles both inside and outside of the empire, i.e., the Boer War. Any movement of troops by Britain could be thwarted by a German intervention—even the shipbuilding program that Tirpitz had started was a threat to Britain. This is the eventual reason why Britain had to become involved in WWI. They could not allow the Germans to pull even. If they did, the empire was threatened, even if Germany had no intention of invading the island nation.

Britain saw itself as a power for good to the world. A man will never fear his own strength, but view it as his natural God-given virility. He may, on the other hand, feel threatened by a young up-and-coming man who is shaking up the old man's established order. These are the roles that Britain (the old man) and Germany (the young tough) filled at the turn of the twentieth century. Ever since Britain had annihilated the French and Spanish fleet at Trafalgar in 1805, they ruled the seas. When Britain declared an end to the slave trade in 1834, it came to an end (except on pirate ships). When Britain yielded to President Lincoln's request and decided not to send blockade-busting ships to the Confederate states in America's Civil War, there was nobody the South could turn to for help. In fact, Winston Churchill claimed that the United States actually benefited from this sole ownership of the sea's highways.

> Here democracy (in America) shielded by the oceans and the Royal Navy from European dangers, founded upon English institutions and the Common Law, stimulated by the impulse of the French Revolution, seemed at last to have achieved prosperity and power.[61]

Of course, Churchill was not one to demur from self-promotion or the promotion of the empire, but there is a point to be made. International trade was an important part of the British Empire, and an idea upon which the empire was founded. The empire benefited from much of the worldwide trade because it was British ships that were deemed the safe passage. Britain was to be feared if a country attacked one of her citizens or vessels and revenged slights with overwhelming odds. A pirate, or what may be termed a terrorist in today's language, might avoid an attack on a British ship and go for an easier target. For the most part, when they laid down international law that settled it. They abolished the slave trade from the high seas when Parliament declared it so. Slavery still existed in the world, including in the United States, though the slaves were native born, or shall we say that they were American slaves, but that is another story.

The claim that Churchill made about the United States being protected by the Royal Navy goes to the heart of this book. The British Empire was built upon the navy that saw itself as the master of the ocean and thought of itself as master for the good of mankind. The British believed in their own benevolence. Those outside of the empire could look upon their empire with awe, with jealousy, but they were not likely to share in the benevolent nature. From the outside, Britain did what Britain wanted because it could. In layman's terms, "Where does an 800-pound gorilla sleep? Wherever he feels like." So it was with the British navy. If they wanted to abolish slavery, they could; if they wanted to take land from the Boers, they could—there was no one to stop them. If they decided that the Confederate states were not to get blockade-busting ships, there was nowhere for the Southern states to turn. Not the French, their navy was defeated by the British in 1805 and their army in 1815. Not the Germans prior to 1910. Not the Austrians, not the Russians. So the threat from the Germans was unexpected.

The German Navy, like the German Empire, appeared late in the history of Europe. Fifteenth century Germans had gone to sea in fighting ships; the Hanseatic League once set out against Scandinavia in a war fleet of 260

> vessels. But the Thirty Years' War, which killed half of
> the population of Germany in the seventeenth century,
> eroded the power of the great Hansa ports, Hamburg,
> Bremen, Lubeck, and Rostock, and for two hundred
> years, there were no German warships.[62]

The Thirty Years' War lasted from 1618 to 1648 and left deep scars upon Prussia. This war would shape the house of Hohenzollern for centuries. This line of German princes, from whom Kaiser Wilhelm was descended, had ruled in the city of Brandenburg and then Prussia since the fifteenth century. The Hohenzollerns became determined that Prussia would never again be ravaged as they were in the Thirty Years' War. They developed the fearsome army for which they became famous. Prussia gave up the sea in order to build its land power. Frederick the Great, who could be called the Founding Father of Prussia, saw no need to build a naval fleet. He scoffed at France's attempts at becoming both a continental power and a sea power, seeing France as being fiscally foolish. He set the pattern of Prussia's warrior successes by defeating the Russians, Austrians, and the French.

Frederick set the pattern that Wilhelm broke. It had been 200 years since Germanic warships were a force to be reckoned with on the seas. In the early 1800s, German warships were treated as pirates. The change in the status quo is what upset the old man of the sea, Britain, who could watch from the sidelines as the German army knocked France out of the ring on the Continent. They were a little dismayed at Germany's bombardment of Paris in the Franco-Prussian War; France, in 1870, was still seen as Britain's greatest enemy.

After the Franco-Prussian War, Bismarck was quite satisfied with his work and became a man of peace. It seems he understood what his successors did not: there was a limit to which a country could push the political boundaries in Europe before everyone else would gang up on it; that warfare was the last resort, not the first in expanding a country's power, and how to keep allies and friends.

"I will not live to see the world war," Bismarck said to Ernst Ballin in 1891, "but you will. And it will start in the East."[63]

These prophetic words came from a man who understood European politics quite well serving Germany as its chancellor for twenty-eight years from 1862-1890. But in 1890 the young Kaiser Wilhelm forced Bismarck out, pushing for an expanding Germany; a Germany with a Mahanian concept of what it was to be a great power. Where Bismarck was content with the empire that he had carved out of the European landscape, Wilhelm wanted to go out onto the oceans—to be more like his British cousins, though he disdained their liberal parliamentary democracy. He had been brought up under the shadow of the British navy. He summered in Portsmouth as a youth, recounting that some of his fondest memories were times that he had spent in England around the racing yachts and warships of his relatives. He wanted a seaborne enterprise of his own, like his cousins. He aspired to have an empire like Britain's, and he had the abilities at his disposal to get it.

Maybe Wilhelm was trying to overcompensate for his crippled arm. He claimed in his memoirs:

with sang-froid that his arm "had received an injury unnoticed at the time, which proved permanent and impeded its free movement." Even when he was an adult it remained about six inches shorter than the right. Adorned with heavy rings, the hand was perfectly formed and looked healthy apart from an ugly brown mole, but it was too weak to grip or hold anything heavier than a piece of paper. It would just go into his coat pocket, where he would keep it out of sight. Throughout his life, few photographs showed his left arm clearly, let alone the hand: from an early age, the art of concealing it from the camera lens became second nature to him. The injuries were not confined to an undeveloped hand. His neck had also been damaged at birth—as the arm and hand muscles and nerves were torn from the vertebral column in the neck during the final stages of delivery; his head was tilted abnormally to the left, and the cervical nerve plexus was subsequently damaged. The hearing labyrinth of the left ear was defective, resulting in partial deafness from childhood and lifelong problems with balance, probably as a result of damage to part of the brain closest to the inner ear. Throughout adolescence and early manhood he suffered from alarming growths and inflammations of the inner ear, and at the age of forty-seven he underwent a major operation which left him deaf in the right ear as well.[64]

As a result of having one bad arm, the right one was very strong. He would often use its vice-like strength to bring winces from those with whom he shook hands.

Wilhelm's birth was a breach birth ordeal that lasted thirty-six hours that almost ended in the death of the mother and the child. The obstetrician who was supposed to attend the birth was not informed about the princess' condition for almost the whole thirty-six-hour period. When he got there, the woman was almost dead; it was not uncommon then for women to die in childbirth. The year that Wilhelm was born, 98 percent of the children born in the breach position were stillborn.[65]

So Wilhelm was born with a crippled arm and inner ear problems that affected his balance. Yet he learned to become an avid seaman and loved to rival his cousins. He looked forward every year to sailing at Cowes, England, although his relatives did not welcome his presence as much as he enjoyed being there. He tried hard to win, was overly aggressive, his jokes rude and boisterous, and he loved playing pranks and practical jokes on anyone who came aboard his ship. His English cousins resented that he took the fun out of Cowes because of his aggressiveness, especially the Crown Prince Albert, "Bertie." He became king in 1901 and reigned until his early death in 1910. Bertie was a very sociable and affable man. Where his parents had been stuffy and aloof, he was friendly and outgoing. His parents had disdained London society as below them. Bertie was not a good student, nor did he take an interest in the things about which his mother thought a future king of a worldwide empire should know, like geography, politics, and history. His father had died in 1861. He disappointed his mother in his studies, became a socialite, a man about town, a dandy. His house became the place to be for actresses, actors, and the socially connected people of London, and he loved the Parisian lifestyle. The German military attitude and "preachiness" were something that turned him cold. These two men, Bertie being the older, could not have been further apart.

It is quite easy to look back and see a family rivalry being played out here that would extend to a competition between two nations. It is also easy to assume that Wilhelm's striving to be accepted in British yachting society fueled his desire to be as English as the English, only better, because he was a German, Prussian on top of that. No one competed or fought better than a Prussian. And then there was Bertie, the social dandy who could not be bothered with his German cousin. It would be easy to boil the British-German animosities down to a family feud.

All that would be too simple. The rivalry between these two nations went much deeper than any family competition or quarrel, though it did add a human element to the story that cannot be ignored.

Germany in the late 1800s was growing in every aspect that was important to a country; its population was rising (even as millions emigrated to the United States); its factory production and wealth were increasing; Germany was either catching up to or passing Britain and France in every economic measurement there was. They were producing more steel, the backbone of the industrial revolution. The Hamburg to America Line was beating the British Cunard Lines across the ocean and attracting more passengers. As a result, the economy was generating increased tax revenues for the government to spend. Much of this money went to building armaments for the army and the newly born navy.

> But the German population soared to 56 million in 1900 and 65 million in 1910. The comparison to France is even more stark: between 1891 and 1910 while the Reich's population was swelling from 49 million to 65 million, the French population rose from 37 to 39 million. Coal and steel production were equally dramatic. In 1871, British coal dominated the world's markets with production of 112 million tons a year; Germany, the second-largest producer of coal, was half of Britain's; by 1913 it was equal. Steel production, an essential component of heavy industry and war offered still more striking contrasts. In 1890, Britain produced 3.6 million tons of steel a year, Germany two thirds of that. In 1896 German steel production first exceeded Great Britain's. In 1914, Germany (14 million tons) produced more than twice as much steel as Britain (6.5 million tons).[66]

One man, Alfred von Tirpitz, the father of the German navy, helped to bring Germany onto the world stage as a naval power. He was helped by progressives in the Reichstag who saw the naval program as a part of Germany's economic growth. Those in the middle class were swayed because of the jobs it provided them and the prestige it gave to the country. Britain's Boer War showed them how woefully lacking Germany was on the high seas; this naval embarrassment gave Tirpitz a more convincing argument to be made to the Reichstag for building up the navy. If the German nation could increase its naval program, it would never again be shoved around on the high seas like a ninety-nine pound weakling, nor would Britain be able to dictate where or when Germany would sail. Britain would have no say in whom Germany could aid in a time of war. Germany would determine its own course, which was the right of a mature nation, and Germany was growing and maturing. The problem was that Britain stood in its way, blocking Germany's access to the ocean, thus blocking Germany's progress to becoming a great nation. The friction between these two countries was inevitable because they were two great nations in the same corner of the world.

What is interesting is that Tirpitz ignored two Mahanian concepts when he argued for an increased navy. First, he claimed that Germany's economic growth, not its naval buildup, threatened Britain; second, he seemed to ignore the fact that the British Isles physically blocked Germany's access to the sea. In pure Mahanian terms, Germany's naval buildup would threaten Britain's status as master of the sea, and Britain's geographical location would impede Germany's expansion to the ocean. War was inevitable if the naval buildup continued, and continue it did.

Again in Mahanian terms, Germans would need friendly ports leading out of the North Sea. They had nothing along the western British side, and they never secured friendly ports along the Norwegian coast. As a consequence, Britain was able to blockade the Germans by patrolling between the Orkney Islands, north of Scotland, and the Norwegian coast. In WWII, Hitler bypassed this problem by invading Norway, giving him the whole Norwegian coast to use for his navy. Germany in WWI did not have this option and was locked up in the North Sea.

One man who was not going to sit by idly as the German navy grew in size and power was British Admiral John Arbuthnot (Jackie) Fisher. He served as the first sea lord of the Admiralty from 1904 to 1909. (There were four sea lords, all naval officers, who administered the navy.)

> The Fourth Sea Lord was responsible for supplying the fleet, the Third Sea Lord was responsible for the design and construction of the ships, the Second Sea Lord was responsible for manning them with officers and men, and the First Sea Lord was responsible for directing naval operations in peace and war. The First Lord, a politician and a member of the cabinet, was responsible

to the Prime Minister and to Parliament for the navy as a branch of the government.[67]

Technically, it was the third sea lord who was responsible for the design of the new ships, the Dreadnoughts. But Jackie Fisher was not about to allow another country, whether Germany or France, to supersede Britain's power on the sea, nor was he going to allow a subordinate to direct the shipbuilding program. Fisher was the first of eleven children born to a twenty-one-year-old Englishwomen and Captain William Fisher, aide de camp of the governor of Ceylon. He was sent from his birthplace in Rambodde, Ceylon, to England at the age of six after his father left military service. His father went broke trying to become a coffee farmer and could not afford to feed his family. The young Fisher was sent to his maternal grandfather in London, who did no better at being a wine merchant than his father had been a farmer. His living was meager and, at the age of thirteen, Jackie Fisher joined the navy. He was tested and became a cadet on Admiral Horatio Nelson's flagship, HMS Victory.

> The test was simple; "I wrote out the Lord's Prayer and the doctor made me jump over a chair naked and I was given a glass of sherry." He was certified "Free from defect of speech, vision, rupture or any other physical disability," and was accepted.[68]

The next sixty years in which Fisher would serve his country would see the greatest changes in sailing that had occurred since man first harnessed the wind to power a ship. The ships changed from wind power to coal to oil. Sails came down for good, replaced by paddle wheels, turbines, and propellers. The ships that had been made out of wood changed to steel. The efficient captain was no longer the one who stood upon the deck and could read the wind and the stars. The efficient captain was now a mechanic, one who knew steam engines and pressure gauges and had grease under his fingernails. As in any moment of great changes, those who could be flexible survived the evolution from wood to steel. Those who wanted to hold onto romantic ideals of sailing and riding the winds were tossed aside. Fisher was very much on the cutting edge of the technology of his times. He did not yearn for the old days and valued the new weapons as they came out, including the submarine and the torpedo. If the British navy was going to remain the preeminent sea power, it would have to stay on top of changes as they came along. Fisher quickly moved up the ladder in the navy because he studied the new technologies. When he came to being in positions of decision making, he made enemies because he did not care much for seniority and tradition, he cared for efficiency.

> He brought to the fight an exceptional inventory of qualities: Herculean energy, burning ambition, towering ego and self-confidence, and fervent patriotism. He was bold, quick-witted, and original, and in everything he did he was passionately involved: for or against, yea or nay.[69]

One of the changes that Fisher was quick to recognize was fundamental to British thinking and the upcoming war; France was no longer the great enemy that Britain would have to do battle with; it would soon be Germany.

As the German navy laws ground inexorably forward and new battleships slid one after the other into the water, Fisher was convinced that only he could prevent a naval defeat of England with consequent starvation or invasion of the homeland and ruination of the empire.[70]

To Fisher, it was his sworn duty to make sure that the Germans did not surpass the British in naval capability. As far as he was concerned the fate of the empire rested in his hands, and he was not going to drop it.

> On the British fleet rest the empire, he said, and only a congenital idiot with criminal tendencies would

permit any tampering with the maintenance of our sea superiority.[71]

Fisher was not going to wait for a war to break out to test Britain's abilities with its new challenger. He was going to stay ahead of Germany in peacetime as well as in war. During the early years of his admiralty, Fisher had a difficult time convincing the Parliament of the need to build his expensive super battleships. Ironically, Winston Churchill was one of his opponents in the first decade of the new century. He had switched from being a Tory to the Liberals' side of the aisle. The Tories, under the party leadership of Joseph Chamberlain, had abandoned what Churchill saw as a cherished fundamental idea of the empire, the concept of free trade. Churchill crossed over party lines to preserve the economic policy that he credited for giving rise to Britain's wealth. He and his new party argued for economizing the government and spending money on social needs rather than military ones. Of course, Churchill was no slouch when it came to the defense of the empire. He was first elected in the Khaki Election of 1900 and had seen battle many times, including in the Boer War, where he had been a hero. He was, however, a latecomer to the Dreadnought building war between Germany and Britain.

The arguments against the Dreadnoughts were numerous, mainly revolving around economy of size and money. Some admirals argued that Britain could build a greater number of smaller ships for less cost. The advantage that this could give Britain, they stated, was that Britain could send out more ships against an enemy and even if the country lost one in battle, the cost in lives and money would be less. It was also argued that the British navy was twice as large as the next largest navy; so what need was there to build these monstrosities? Fisher countered that the bigger ships would enable the navy to add armor and bigger guns that shot heavier projectiles. The larger ships being built by Italy, Germany, the United States, and Japan would be able to outgun the smaller, more lightly armored ships. The smaller class of ships would render the British navy an old relic at the bottom of the sea. Besides, Fisher claimed that the amount of material needed to build the Dreadnought class was only an additional 1,500 tons and a 10 percent increase in money per ship. At least that was the situation at the beginning of the arms race in 1905. The Dreadnought completed in 1906 weighed 17,900 tons and had a speed of 20.9 knots with 12-inch guns. The Queen Elizabeth class of Dreadnought, completed in 1913, weighed 27,500 tons with a speed of 25 knots, with eight 15-inch guns and fourteen 6-inch guns. Obviously, the additional size, material, and technology would increase the price tag way beyond Fisher's original 1905 estimates.

In 1909, Britain began hearing rumors of a secret acceleration of Germany's ship building program. Churchill and the liberals did not believe it. They wanted to continue to economize on naval building to pay for social programs. The ships were huge and expensive, and they were a favorite target for the liberals.

> In 1907, 136 M.P.'s (Members of Parliament) had petitioned Campbell-Bannerman (the Prime Minister) to reduce the spending on armaments; in 1908, a similar petition was signed by 144 M.P.s.[72]

At the end of 1909, there came alarming reports to First Lord Robert McKenna, who had replaced Fisher. He was told that the Germans were accelerating their building programs and were acquiring large amounts of material for building ships, amounts beyond what was needed for the current rate of production. They had been told by an Argentine naval mission, who had visited the Krupp of Essen company and some of the German shipyards, that they were stockpiling guns, turrets, and armor. Also, it was reported that they were laying down keels before the ships had been voted on in the Reichstag. If the German government were doing this, then it would be illegal, according to the German constitution; one of the few real powers that the Reichstag had was power of the purse over military disbursements.

According to the German Naval Law, the Germans planned to build thirteen Dreadnought-class ships to Britain's sixteen. This alone was alarming; Britain wanted to maintain a 10 percent numerical superiority over the next two sea powers. Germany's building program would obliterate that idea. (The next great sea power was the United States, but there was no one in the British government who feared that the United States would fight against Britain.) When McKenna heard that Germany was accelerating its building program, he went to Parliament to ask for more ships. At this point, Britain was building two ships per year—now McKenna, backed ferociously by Fisher, asked for six.

At the same time, diplomatic gestures were made to Germany to find out if this information was true. The German naval attaché in London, Captain Widemann, was called to McKenna's office and asked about the material. He denied it.

> "Indeed," he said, "he was shocked that the First Lord would attribute such obviously unconstitutional behavior to the State Secretary Tirpitz." McKenna, believing his own information, not Widemann, did not consult the naval attaché again.[73]

The German ambassador in London, Paul Wolff-Metternich, was asked about this issue as well and said that there was no acceleration in the building program. He was being kept in the dark by Tirpitz, when actually, the companies doing business with the navy were building material in anticipation of the Reichstag bills, but it was not being done at the government's bidding, according to Tirpitz. The companies were taking it upon themselves to prepare the material, keep the cost down, and ensure winning the contracts. Wolff-Metternich had to admit that he was wrong. Indeed, there was material being stored in advance of approval by the Reichstag, but it was not being done by the government; ergo there was no violation of the constitution.

The other sticking point for McKenna was that he asked for trading naval attachés to visit each other's shipyards and view the building processes. Wolff-Metternich claimed that both the Kaiser and Tirpitz were dead set against this idea. When asked on a third occasion why Germany would not trade attachés, he bluntly stated, "Impossible. Other governments would want to also. Besides, something might be seen which we might want to keep secret."[74]

The other thing alarming the Britons was that the German shipbuilding yards were increasing in number. In 1909 there were seven German shipyards that could build a Dreadnought—in theory they could build seven ships a year.

McKenna and Fisher, with all this evidence behind them, argued strenuously for more Dreadnoughts. In fact, they upped the ante, asking Parliament for eight new ships. Churchill and some liberals still opposed the measure, that is until Austria and Italy announced plans to build three or four Dreadnoughts apiece. They were both part of a triple alliance with Germany which meant that Britain could face a cumulative foe with twenty-one Dreadnoughts to their sixteen. Liberal Prime Minister H.H. Asquith, looking at the facts before him, including a recent by-election, in which the liberal candidate was overwhelmingly beaten, conceded to the first lord.

> The resolution was painful for a Liberal government which had taken office pledging to reduce the armaments burden. For three years, the government had met this pledge. Now within twelve months it had ordered eight costly ships.[75]
> "In the end a curious and characteristic solution was reached," Churchill stated. "The Admiralty had demanded six; the economists offered four; and we finally compromised on eight."[76]

Later on, when Churchill became the first lord of the Admiralty, he changed his tune slightly. He claimed that he and Asquith were right when they claimed that the navy needed only four ships, but he was very glad to have the extra ones.

Chapter Five
The War to End All Wars!

Now that we have looked at the previous four chapters, the First World War makes much more sense. If you did not know that Germany was only fifty-two years old as a nation, that it had been formed in defense against French invasions and Austrian domination, the First World War would remain a bizarre war with no meaning. Again, if you did not know that Austria was a crumbling power reeling from a long line of tragedies and reversals of fortune, the First World War remains lost in the fog of war. The same Prussia that had pushed Austria out of the German Diet in Frankfurt, that had defeated Austria at the battle of Koniggratz, and had gained supremacy over the German-speaking peoples in the mid 1800s, now needed the old crumbling empire.

At the turn of the 20th century, Germany did not have many allies, certainly not France. Germany had defeated and humiliated France when they fought in the Franco-Prussian War, plus it had annexed the province of Alsace-Lorraine as a buffer zone against any future French military actions. Russia, an ancient adversary, was a weak nation with internal strife tearing the country apart. The Czar vacillated between strength and weakness, making concessions one minute, unleashing the troops on the people the next. They lost a humiliating naval battle at the Battle of Tsushima Straight when the Japanese Navy attacked, which started the Japanese-Russo War which Russia lost. It was a surprise attack, much like the attack on Pearl Harbor in 1941. In 1904, the Japanese Navy was new on the scene, a modern one with state of the art armor and guns. The Russian Navy was annihilated, and the Czar looked weak and ineffectual both within and outside of his country—they needed an ally in the global scheme of things. Previous to this war Bismarck had tried to keep relations smooth with Russia, but the Balkans was a tinderbox even during his days. (The Balkan area is south of the Danube River, bordered by the Adriatic, Ionian, and Black seas. It includes the states of Croatia, Bosnia, and Herzegovina, Montenegro, Albania, Yugoslavia, Macedonia, Greece, and Bulgaria. Part of it was in the Ottoman Empire, part was in the Austro-Hungarian Empire, and part of it was independent. Its population was largely Slavic, descendents of Slavic Russia.) In 1877, there was war between Russia and Turkey. Germany stayed out of the conflict, not wanting to have to choose sides between Austria and Russia, who both had conflicting vital interests in the Balkans. Britain and Austria then pressured Russia to the bargaining table with the threat of joining the war if Russia did not retreat. Russia came to the negotiating table in Berlin to mediate the truce; Russia came out the loser in the negotiations, though it had been the victor on the battlefield. Russians and the Slavs in the Balkans were furious at the outcome and the bitterness turned on Germany because Bismarck had mediated the Congress of Berlin.

After this, Bismarck allied with Austria, made possible because the truce in the 1866 war between Austria and Prussia had been generous. There was no annexing of territory as with the French. The Germans needed an ally and the Austrians were German-speaking people. If there was ever a war with

Russia, the German-Austrian alliance would be a Teutonic alliance against the Slavs. This also protected Germany's southern flank—the Austrians needed their upstart northern neighbor. Their power had been diminishing ever since the Napoleonic wars and they needed help if Russia ever declared war on them. Italy was added later on to this alliance, which became known as the Triple Alliance. Now it was Russia who was isolated and weakened; Russia initiated talks with France about an alliance, which became known as the Dual Alliance. Britain, for most of the 1800s, remained outside of these alliances. There were several reasons for this: one was that Parliament would never abide by a peacetime alliance that could drag them into a war simply because their ally decided to battle another country; another reason was the British tradition to ally themselves with the weaker nation(s) to prevent the Continent from being dominated by any one country. In the Napoleonic Wars, that meant allying with the Prussians against France. In WWI, it meant allying with France against the Germans (Prussians). In 1877, they were willing to go to war with Russia; in 1914, they were allies. Britain did not want any permanent alliances that would dictate their actions. In the early 1900s, Germany threatened to dominate the Continent. And, of course, as stated in the chapter about Dreadnoughts, Germany was threatening Britain's empire by daring to seek parity on the oceans.

The Balkan States were in flames because the Ottoman Empire was disintegrating, as was the Austro-Hungarian Empire. Together they had dominated the Balkans for centuries—now nationalist groups all over the Balkans were flexing their muscles trying to form new states.

In 1914, the Emperor of the Austro-Hungarian Empire was the eighty-four-year-old Franz Josef who had reigned for sixty-six years. He had witnessed the diminishing of his empire's power firsthand. When he was a youth, Lombardy and Venice broke away from the empire. It was no longer the dominant Germanic power after losing the Austro-Prussian war, and it now had to lean on the Prussians for help. The recently independent Kingdom of Serbia was drawing away the allegiance of the Slavs in the empire; especially vulnerable were Austria's southern provinces of Bosnia, Herzegovina, and Montenegro. Serbia was a magnet for Nationalist Slavs, filling them with ideas of breaking away from Austria and joining a Greater Serbia. Either the octogenarian or his nephew, Archduke Franz Ferdinand, would have to deal with the issue.

Emperor Franz Josef had experienced many personal traumas in his life. His brother, the liberal-minded Maximilian, had been persuaded by Emperor Napoleon III to go to Mexico and become emperor there; he was executed on a hillside when the French-backed empire failed. His own son, Crown Price Rudolf, killed himself and his mistress in a suicide pact; his wife, the beautiful Empress Elizabeth, left him after six years of marriage. She wandered about Europe until an anarchist cut her throat. Add to these personal calamities the loss of power by the empire.

Enter Archduke Franz Ferdinand, the heir apparent to the throne. He also must have been a disappointment to Franz Josef. He married a woman below his station in life; his children were disinherited from the throne. Ferdinand's solution to the Slavic issue was to include them in a triple-sided government. At that time, the government was run by the Germanic Austrians and the Magyar Hungarians, but there was no room in the government for the Slavs (Poles, Czechs, Slovaks, Serbs, Bosnians, and Montenegrins), though they made up three-fifths of the population. That meant that even Ferdinand's compromise was no solution to extremists who wanted a purely Slavic kingdom. These Slav extremists wanted a separation, a further disintegration of the empire.

Ferdinand came to Sarajevo on June 28. He proposed that the armed troops that usually lined the street for an imperial procession were to be removed in a display of good will. He drove off through the city; as his car approached the city hall, the alert driver noticed something coming toward the car. The driver pressed the accelerator and a bomb, which would have landed in the Empress Sophia's lap, landed instead under the wheels of the next car in line. The royal couple's lives had been saved. Inside the city hall, Ferdinand was furious; the archduke's men demanded that a military guard be arranged. The provincial governor replied, "Do you think that Sarajevo is filled with assassins?"[77] Obviously the answer was yes, but the governor's words assuaged Ferdinand. The motorcade proceeded again, but on a different route. Somehow, the driver of the lead car forgot that the route had been changed, and he turned onto one of the streets preplanned for the motorcade to travel.

> An official shouted "That's the wrong way." So he turned the car around putting the royal couple just a few feet away from Gavrilo Princip. Princip, a slim nineteen year old member of the Black Hand Society, a clandestine guerrilla group, stepped forward aimed a pistol into the car, and fired twice. Sophie sank forward into her husband's chest. Franz Ferdinand remained sitting upright and for a moment no one noticed that that he had been hit. Then the governor, sitting in the front, heard him murmur, "Sophie! Sophie! Don't die! Don't die! Stay alive for our children." His body slumped and blood from the severed jugular vein in his neck spurted across his uniform. He died almost immediately. Sophie, the Duchess of Hohenberg, died soon after.[78]

All of Europe was shocked at the assassinations. It was obvious that Austria would seek some sort of revenge, and everyone throughout the Continent thought that it was called for. Austria blamed the Serbs for being behind the murders.

> The assassin, Gavrilo Princip, was a native of Bosnia, who, on trial, declared that he had acted to "kill an enemy of the South Slavs" and also because the archduke was an "energetic man who as ruler would have carried through

ideas and reforms which stood in our way." Princip was part of a team of youthful assassins, all of whom were Bosnians and thus Austro-Hungarian subjects, belonging to a revolutionary movement whose object was to detach Bosnia and other Slav provinces from the Habsburg monarchy and incorporate them into a Kingdom of Greater Serbia. They had been provided with six pistols and six bombs taken from the Serbian State Arsenal and smuggled with Serbian help across the frontier.[79]

This group of Bosnians feared that Ferdinand would actually succeed in strengthening the empire with his ideas; therefore, they killed the heir apparent. Austria now wanted its revenge. For a long time, the hard-liners in the empire had wanted to crush the Slavs in the south, including the Kingdom of Serbia—now they had the chance.

The odd thing about the assassination of Ferdinand was that nobody seemed to like him. Obviously, not only did the extremist Serbs hate him, but even those in the Dual Monarchy did not like him. His proposals to share power with the Slavic people probably did not win him any accolades from those who wanted to keep the status quo. Not even the emperor liked his nephew, the heir apparent.

The truth of the matter was that, with the possible exception of (the foreign Minister of Austria-Hungary Count Leopold von Berchtold), few in Austria-Hungary were sorry that Franz Ferdinand had been removed from the scene. True, the leaders of the dual monarchy deplored the killing of royalty, but if someone of the blood had to be sacrificed, the Archduke was everybody's choice to be the one.[80]

People were gathering around the bandstand, listening to some announcement. Stephen Zweig joined them. The crowd was receiving the news of the assassinations in Sarajevo. These were Austrians, hearing of the death of their leader-to-be. Yet, Zweig wrote later, there was no particular shock or dismay to be seen on their faces; for the heir apparent was not at all well liked...He was never

seen to smile, and no photographs showed him relaxed.
He had no sense for music, and no sense of humor, and
his wife was equally unfriendly...[81]

The distaste for the prince and his wife was so transparent
that other royals in Europe were asked not to attend the funeral
(with the exception of Wilhelm who was one of Ferdinand's
few friends). The other royals had no problem not attending.
Wilhelm wanted to go, but was dissuaded from it by his ministers
who feared that he may be the next to be attacked.

The Balkans had been erupting in wars for the preceding
two years. The years 1912 and 1913 saw no fewer than three
wars in the Balkans as the Ottoman Empire fell apart. It had
already lost the provinces of "Cyprus in 1878, Tunisia in 1881,
Egypt 1882, Bosnia and Herzegovina in 1908 and Tripoli
in 1911."[82] Now the small Christian Balkan States saw their
chance to break away. The Turkish army had collapsed as
the Bulgarian army was outside the walls of Constantinople;
these little wars, however, did not escalate into larger ones
because the major countries stayed outside of the fighting.
They came close, but there was no major war over it. Austria
had mobilized an army of 900,000 when the Serbs took the
port of Durazzo on the Adriatic Sea and demanded that they
withdraw. Russia would have entered the war to aid the Serbs
if the Austrians had attacked. Britain's foreign Minister, Sir
Edward Grey, proposed a conference of the Great Powers in
order to negotiate an end to the conflicts.

> For Europe, the significance of the Balkan Wars lay less
> in the backstabbing between allies or the subsequent
> shifts of territory than in the Great Power decision that
> little wars should not be allowed to spread.[83]

Serbia was eventually convinced to allow Durazzo to
become the independent state of Albania. Although the
conference settled the disputes at hand, it did not change the
winds of war that were swirling about. Grey had noted:

> [I]n 1912-13 the current of European affairs was setting
> towards war. In agreeing to a Conference…it was as if we
> all put out our anchors to prevent us from being swept
> away. The anchors held. Then the current seemed to
> slacken and the anchors were pulled up. The conference
> was allowed to dissolve. We seemed to be safe. In reality
> it was not so; the set of the current was the same, and in a
> year's time we were all swept into the cataract of war.[84]

This time things were different, the murder in Sarajevo
was an attack upon the Austro-Hungarian Empire. Not
only was this an attack against a high representative of the
government, it killed the heir apparent, the successor to the
throne, disrupting the continuity of the empire. This could
mean the end of the Habsburg rule in Austria. They had
ruled Austria for centuries, but the emperor was an old man,
his only son dead, his nephew, the heir apparent, assassinated,
his children morganatically disinherited from the throne.
This last act was just another insult on top of a life filled with
insults. In the world of real politic, this was an attack that had
to be answered swiftly and forcefully; if it were not, it would be
seen as a capitulation by the older, larger state to the younger
Serbian state. There must be a reprisal; everyone, including
the Slavs' cousins, the Russians, accepted this fact. There was
calm throughout Europe despite the horrified reaction most
had to the assassination. Backstabbing, intrigue, and war had
plagued the Balkans for years, thus nobody really thought
that a war involving the major powers of Europe would
proceed out of this event. Even the Austrians thought that
Russia would back down from interfering with their plans for
retribution. They did plan revenge—they not only wanted
to teach the Serbs a lesson, they wanted to destroy the tiny
nation to the south.

Austria had wanted to destroy Serbia for a long time and
then bring the province back into the empire. Ferdinand's
death did two things. First, it gave the Austrians the pretext
for going on the offensive. Second, since Ferdinand was

the one who wanted to extend power-sharing rights with the Serbs, now that he was gone, this foolishness died with him and the empire could have its way—that is, of course, if Austria-Hungary acted quickly before the memory of the assassination had gone cold. Even the Czar could not go to war to protect regicides. The shabby treatment of Ferdinand and his wife during their funerals, the sloppy investigations that could have proved an actual Serbian government link, showed to Europe that the retaliation inflicted upon Serbia was not the red hot reactionary move by a hurt populous, but something more sinister, something deep and more premeditated.

Austria was sure that Russia would back down once they were put on notice that Germany was backing them. Of course, if Germany went to war with Russia, then France, according to its alliance with Russia, was to come into the war against Germany to help Russia. If Russia and France were at war with Germany, Britain would have to decide whether to join the fight.

On July 7th the Council of Ministers of the Dual Monarchy met to decide if there would be war or peace. The council voted for war, all except the Hungarian premier Count Istvan Tisza, who wanted the last vestiges of diplomacy to be played out. They decided to send an ultimatum.

> All present hold the belief that a purely diplomatic success, even if it ended with a glaring humiliation of Serbia, would be worthless and that therefore such a stringent demand must be addressed to Serbia that will make refusal almost certain, so that the road to a radical solution by means of military action should be open.[85]

So read the minutes of the council meeting.

It took another two weeks to draft the ultimatum. Germany was chomping at the bit for Austria to go on the attack—the German generals were furious when they found out that the Austrian emperor was going to wait until the ultimatum was delivered and responded to before mobilizing his troops. That would take another sixteen days once the ultimatum was given. Things were going painfully slow for the Germans. Most of the important Foreign Service men, General Moltke and Kaiser Wilhelm, went on vacation to give the appearance of normalcy. They did not want to alarm the rest of Europe, nor tip its hand that it knew exactly what Austria had in mind. Emperor Josef and his war minister went on vacations as well; most of the important people were kept informed of what was happening, except the Kaiser. He was in the Norwegian Fjords and had to find out about the details of the ultimatum through local newspapers. When the ultimatum was ready, it was delayed a couple more days. It was timed to be released after the French president, Raymond Poincare, and the Russian ambassador to Paris, Alexander Isvolsky, ended their visit with the Russian Czar and while they were heading back to France. (Isvolsky was especially warmongering since the last time when the Czar had backed away from fighting.) Both were in Moscow from July 20th to the 23rd. The ultimatum was delivered to Serbia after the departure of Poincare and Isvolsky so that they would not influence the Czar.

It was so severe that it stunned even the Serbians in Belgrade who were expecting severely humiliating demands. It had ten points, all of which infringed upon Serbia's sovereignty in some way.

> All Serbian publications critical of Austria-Hungary must be suppressed. All schoolbooks presenting "propaganda against Austria-Hungary" must be withdrawn. All Serbian government officials, army officers, and schoolteachers holding these views must be dismissed; specific officials and officers named in the note must be arrested. These changes must be monitored inside Serbia by Austrian officials.[86]

It read like the ultimatum given to a country after its defeat in a war. Serbia reached out for help, and the other European nations counseled Austria for moderation, but finally Serbia capitulated to all but one of the demands. That was the one demanding that Austrian officials participate in the judicial process inquiring into the plot. This was against the Serbian constitution and against their laws.

> Wherever the reply was read, in Europe and in the United States it was regarded as a remarkable concession to overbearing demands. The Serbs enhanced their submission by offering, if the Austrians agreed, to submit the entire issue either to the Great Powers for arbitration or to the International Court at The Hague. Serbian accommodation, of course, was the last thing desired by Vienna and Berlin.[87]

When the Kaiser had heard about the response from Serbia, he set sail to return to Germany. On hearing the news about Serbia's capitulation, he was ecstatic, claiming that it was a great moral victory for Vienna and that war could now be diverted. It seems that he forgot that the ultimatum was just a pretense, a "nicety" to give cover for the decision for war by both the Austrians and the Germans.

> Wilhelm ordered the State Secretary to initiate immediate mediation between Austria and Serbia, with Belgrade as a temporary hostage to ensure good behavior. Bethmann and Jagow (his Chancellor Theobald von Bethmann-Hollweg and Secretary of State Gottlieb von Jagow) were shocked by this imperial command. Had their master not realized that the purpose of the ultimatum was to ensure rejection and provide grounds for war? Vienna was not interested in a 'great moral victory;' she meant to reduce Serbia to vassalage.[88]

The emperor was simply ignored. On July 29, 1914, Austrian artillery crossed the Danube and started firing on Belgrade. The First World War had begun.

There was still time for the governments to back down and

not mobilize their troops, but that did not happen. Germany did wait for a declaration from Russia before they declared and mobilized, but the strange thing is that Germany and Russia declared war against each other before Russia and Austria did. Russia was entering the war to back up the Serbs, and Germany declared war to back up the Austrians. Now Austria had to declare war against Russia. Germany sent another ultimatum to France.

> Berlin demanded to know whether France would remain neutral in the coming Russo-German war. If the answer was yes, Germany demanded that France hand over the fortress of Toul and Verdun as security on her pledge of neutrality. Paris was given eighteen hours to reply.[89]

France did not reply. The German Ambassador Baron von Schoen went to the Quai d'Orsay to find out France's reply.

> He was told coldly, "France would act in accordance with her own interests." At three-forty P.M. the French Army and Navy were mobilized. Germany understood there would be no French neutrality...[90]

Germany mobilized on their western front.

There were now four major powers at war, Austria, Russia, Germany, and France. The last question to be answered was where Britain stood. The Foreign Secretary had already informed Germany's ambassador that it would not be able to sit idly by as the rest of Europe was at war. They did not want to see France reduced as a continental force; they were fearful of the power of the German fleet, and there were secret unofficial assurances to France that Britain would help if France went to war. In fact, the assurances went so far as an unprecedented exchange of naval responsibilities in the Mediterranean. Britain did not give up any of its bases to the French, but they pulled out most of the ships there so that they could be amassed in the North Sea to fight the Germans. (This was another idea of Fisher's.) This also meant that Britain would have to guard France's western Atlantic seaboard. Since Germany would either have to sail through the English Channel, or go up around the Orkneys at the northernmost part of the British Isles, they would have to get past the British fleet first. So the French Atlantic Seaboard was safe, if Britain joined the war. There were also plans to send a 100,000-strong British Expeditionary Force into the Lowlands where the German attack was expected, if Britain joined the fight. There were assurances from Grey and Prime Minister Asquith that they would aid France. But if Parliament was against going to war, especially on the side of their ancient foe, the French, then that could bring down the Asquith government. It would also dash any assurances given to France, and they would have to face the German forces alone. There was one thing that would mobilize the British population—if Germany dared to trespass on Belgium neutrality. As stated in Chapter Three, Britain would fight to the last man to prevent a major continental power from invading or annexing either Holland or Belgium (together they are the Lowlands.) Many in Britain did not believe, nor wanted to believe that Germany would run roughshod over Belgium, which had been the plan ever since the Schlieffen Plan was first adopted.

> Belgium neutrality was the single issue which created a Cabinet majority, but Germany had not yet directly threatened Belgium. Further, Britain could not be sure that the Belgians would resist a German invasion. Britain could not compel Belgium to fight; neither could Britain go to war to defend a passive Belgium. Indeed it was the position of the peace group in the British Cabinet that a "simple traverse" of Belgium territory by German troops would not be a cause for British intervention.[91]

On August 9th, there was a huge peace rally planned in London. Before the meeting could take place, the British people learned of the ultimatum given by Germany to Belgium.

> Then came the news of the threatened German invasion of Belgium. A wave of indignation rolled over the nation, sweeping up the mass of Britons who, reluctant to fight for France, sprang to the side of neutral Belgium. The Trafalgar Square demonstration evaporated, and on Sunday afternoon, crowds shouting for war with Germany poured into Whitehall, jamming Downing Street.[92]

The cabinet put itself on war footing. Those who still rejected the idea of joining the fight quit the cabinet: they were Sir John Simon and Lord Beauchamp, joining two others who had previously resigned over the infighting that had been taking place in the Cabinet for months. But these were the last of the resignations. Everyone else was likeminded about the coming war. All that was left was to convince Parliament to declare war; that responsibility was left to the Foreign Secretary, Sir Edward Grey.

> Just before three, Grey left the foreign office to walk to the House of Parliament. The Crowd in Whitehall was so dense that police had to open a path. Grey found the House of Commons overflowing: the green benches packed with members, shoulder to shoulder; other members sitting in rows of chairs placed four abreast in the Gangway. In the Peer's Gallery, Lord Lansdowne was wedged next to the Archbishop of Canterbury; Lord Curzon, unable to find a seat, stood behind in a doorway. Every seat in the diplomatic Gallery was taken except two, which attracted attention as if they were painted orange; they belonged to the German and Austrian ambassadors. Despite the packed hall, the crowd was silent and members were startled when the Chaplain, backing away from the Speaker, stumbled noisily over chairs unexpectedly placed in the isle behind him.[93]

This was the atmosphere, filled with solemn anticipation of what was to come. There was no doubt that Grey was going to ask for a declaration of war. While he sat waiting to be called he was nervous. He was not a practiced, eloquent speech maker like Churchill, nor was he the fiery combative type, like the First Sea Lord Fisher was. He was a diplomat. When he did speak, "his words were 'grave,' 'dignified,' 'clear,' and unadorned,' although behind the quiet voice, correspondents noted 'suppressed fire' and 'a certain terrible indignation.'"[94]

He told the packed Parliament House that, up to a week before, he had been working for the peace of Europe. That peace was broken now; Britain had to look at the conflagration in what were the best interests of Britain. He informed the Parliament of the assurances that were given to France, but admitted that there was nothing forcing Britain's hand to commit to the war. He told the assembly of the exchange of fleets, the French to the Mediterranean and the British to the North Sea, and how France's Atlantic seaboard was now open.

> "Nevertheless," he said, "my own feeling is that if a foreign fleet, engaged in a war which France had not sought and in which she had not been the aggressor, came down the English Channel and bombarded and battered the unprotected coasts of France, we could not stand aside [cheers broke out in the House] and see the thing going on practically within sight of our eyes, with our arms folded [the cheering mounted in volume,] looking on dispassionately, doing nothing." Grey clenched his right fist, raised it, and at the word "nothing," slammed it down on the Dispatch Box. The House observing this unique display of emotion by the Foreign Secretary exploded with a roar. When the noise subsided, Grey added quietly, "and I believe that would be the feeling of this country."[95]

He continued speaking, making the case for going to war. He spoke about the neutrality of the Lowlands, the defense of the island nation, and preservation of peace in Europe. His speech won the day, but of course that had already been won when Germany invaded Belgium. All that was left was to be convinced that this was the right fight, and Grey did this. England declared war on Germany and Austria.

At dusk that evening Grey stood with a friend at his window in the Foreign Office, looking down at the lamps being lit in St. James Park. It was then that the unpoetic Sir Edward Grey uttered the lines which memorably signaled the coming of the First World War. "The lamps are going out all over Europe," he said. "We shall not see them lit again in our lifetime."[96]

Chapter Six
The Battle of Jutland

The sinking of the Lusitania, a British Cunard Lines cruise ship, on May 7, 1915, did not bring the United States into WWI. That was despite the fact that 1,201 people died in this attack, of whom thirty-five were babies. There were 128 Americans on board who died, including the bachelor millionaire, Alfred Gwynne Vanderbilt. Former presidents Theodore Roosevelt and William Taft thought that this provocation was great enough to send the United States into the war against Germany. Colonel Edward House, President Woodrow Wilson's special envoy to England, thought that America would be going to war within a month of the sinking. Wilson saw it differently; he did not want to see Germany win the war, but neither did he rush headlong into the fight when others would have. The political slogan he ran on in the 1916 presidential election was that the United States was "too proud to fight." Roosevelt sneered at this statement lambasting the current president for being too weak and afraid.

It must be remembered that the United States had fought wars declared and undeclared over freedom of the seas. The War of 1812 was engaged in primarily over British impressments of American sailors. The second president, John Adams, fought an undeclared war with France in 1798 that was instigated by French pirating. Although there was no declaration of war (Adams could have easily gotten it from the Congress), there was a peace treaty that exonerated the United States from its Revolutionary War debt to France. There was, therefore, precedent for the United States going to war to preserve its right to sail freely on the open seas, but Wilson did not press for it, and Congress, in 1915, may not have given him a declaration of war over the sinking of the Lusitania. After all, it was a British ship, not an American one. There was no doubt in anyone's mind that sailing to Europe at this time was a dangerous proposition. A warning notice had been prepared by the Imperial German Embassy, reluctantly published by American newspapers (many of which were decidedly anti-German), prior to the sailing of the Lusitania. It stated the dangers of traveling on the high seas during this time of war.

> **Notice! Travelers intending to embark on the Atlantic voyage are reminded that a state of war exists between Germany and her allies and Great Britain and her allies; that the zone of war includes the waters adjacent to the British Isles; that in accordance with formal notice given by the Imperial German Government, vessels flying the flag of Great Britain, or any of her allies are liable to destruction in those waters and that travelers sailing in those war zone on the ships of Great Britain do so at their own risk...**
> **Imperial German Embassy**
> **Washington D.C. April 22, 1915**[97]

Though the sinking of the Lusitania did not bring the United States into the war, much political pressure was brought upon Germany to stop its unrestricted submarine warfare. The German ambassador to the United States, Count Johann Bernstorff, worked tirelessly to get the Kaiser and the German military personnel to see the danger of antagonizing the United States. For a while, the generals agreed with him, that is, until Russia had been taken out of the war in 1917. Then they thought that the ultimate goal of defeating the Entente armies was within their grasp and they did not fear the possibility of the United States entering the war. The admirals, on the other hand, were furious at having their hands tied by the politicians; they thought that the U-boat warfare was the ultimate weapon that would bring Britain to its knees and to the peace table. Both commanders in chief of the German navy, Hugo von Pohl and later his replacement, Reinhard Scheer, called all their U-boats back into port when they had been forced by the Kaiser to strictly obey the internationally accepted cruiser rules of engagement when confronting a prize ship. This put the submarines in a very vulnerable spot. They would have to surface and order the crew and passengers to abandon the ship and then sink it after everyone had disembarked. A surface ship had much thicker armor and more guns than a submarine; the submarine's strength was its stealth and secrecy, not overt force. The surface ships, on the other hand, had the choice of towing the captured ship to port and claiming its cargo as a prize if it were an enemy's ship, or reimbursing the owner if it were a neutral ship. A U-boat was not large enough to put a ship in tow. During this disembarking time, the U-boat was exposed to attack by the ship in question, if they were an armed merchant ship, or by an enemy naval ship that might come to the rescue of the endangered vessel.

On April 25, 1916, the Admiralstab in Berlin ordered the commander in chief of the High Seas Fleet, Admiral Scheer, to stop the unrestricted submarine attacks. He was incensed that this weapon was being taken away form the German arsenal. Scheer was so angry about this that he did not want any of his submarines to engage in any commerce/military actions, so called them home to Germany instead. Scheer was hoping that bringing them back would cause a political backlash in Germany. Most Germans saw the unrestricted attacks as fair reprisal for the blockade that the British imposed on Germany and the whole North Sea area, which was causing mass starvation in Germany. With his submarines at home ready to be employed in some fashion, he came up with another plan for their use—they would attack their nemesis, the British fleet.

The first step of the plan was to sail a part of the German High Seas Fleet out to attack some British port in order to draw a part of the British Grand Fleet out in retaliation. The second step was for the submarines to lie in wait at the mouth of the Firth of Forth, the Moray Firth, outside of Scapa Flow, and near other British naval bases in order to attack the ships as they raced out to protect the British coast. The third step would then be a naval engagement of the surface ships where the Germans would then draw the rescuing force out farther away from the British mainland into the waiting range of the rest of the High Seas Fleet, thereby reducing the number of British ships, at a small risk to the German ships. If all went according to plan, Scheer could chip away at the preponderance of naval ships that Britain had over Germany. If this in turn could be done, then Germany could challenge Britain's domination of the North Sea, thereby winning a great battle for Germany. If it led to breaking the blockade, then the people of Germany would be able to eat again and supply much-needed foodstuffs, clothing and arms for the war effort.

The plan was set for the middle of May when the German battle cruiser, the 23,000-ton Seydlitz, would be out of dry dock; being repaired from the last battle it was involved in where it hit a mine. During the waiting period it was discovered that some of the other battleships were having condenser problems and that they would need repair as well. This postponed the start of the plan to the 23rd of May.

> Kapitan zur See, Herman Bauer, commanding the High Seas Fleet U-boat flotillas, proposed that all U-boats ready before 23 May should be sent to sea at once, so that the advance of the fleet could be preceded by a thorough

reconnaissance of the North Sea, and particularly the area in which the enemy's battlefleet was, from past observations, known to assemble whenever it was either covering a sweep of the British light forces into the Heligoland Bight or was alerted to a movement of the High Seas Fleet.[98]

Scheer agreed to allow the U-boats to leave early. This would turn out to be a tactical error that would render the submarines impotent in the upcoming battle; it would also lead Scheer into making another strategic error that would cause the American president to finally ask Congress for a declaration of war.

The condenser problems were fixed quickly, but the Seydlitz caused further delays. It was not watertight in the area where it had hit the mine and needed more work, but Scheer was not prepared to go to sea without the Seydlitz so he delayed the raid until May 29. The problem was that the U-boats could not stay out to sea beyond June 1, as they would be running low on fuel by that time and would need to come back to port. The window of opportunity was closing for Scheer's plan to work. The weather was another factor. He wanted to be able to count on air reconnaissance from the zeppelin fleet, which would need clear skies and low winds. An alternative plan was devised where he would sail into the waters off Jutland, the northern part of Denmark. (These waters are also known as Skagerrak.) The battle that was to ensue there is known as the Battle of Jutland in England and the Battle of Skagerrak in Germany. Scheer would sail in these waters, which were closer to his home port, searching for vessels to board that were bound for Britain. This, he hoped, would produce the same result as attacking the coast of Britain.

As it turned out, going to Jutland did produce the same result as attacking the British coast, but not for the reason he assumed. The British fleet would not be riding to the rescue of a ship in distress, because the British had a copy of the German Naval codes, taken in a stroke of luck by the Russians and passed on to the British. When Scheer contacted his fleet via radio, the decoders in the British Admiralty in Room 40 were listening in and passed the information to Admiral John Jellicoe, the commander in chief of the British Grand Fleet. The codes were changed slightly but not enough to stymie British intelligence. They picked up Scheer's ship-to-ship messages, and also the messages that were sent to the U-boats that were lurking in the waters off the British coast. Unfortunately for the U-boats, most of them did not receive the transmissions themselves and eight out of ten did not know when the attack was about to begin. Some sat on the bottom of the sea, positioned at their respective assignment biding time, avoiding detection, until the attack was to begin. Had they stayed in Wilhelmshaven and been sent out in close synchronization with the fleet, they might have been much more effective and might have even changed the outcome of the battle. The submarines could have truly turned it into a great day for the Germans. As it was, most of the U-boats laid impotently as the Grand Fleet put out to sea right over them racing to the battle.

The Seydlitz was finally declared seaworthy and Scheer put out to sea. The Germans had 100 warships, the British 151. These giant steel behemoths, these floating fortresses, these castles of the sea, were the reason why Britain and Germany became enemies. One hundred and one years previously, British and Prussian forces fought alongside each other to defeat France's Napoleon Bonaparte at Waterloo. Now, in 1916, Germany's High Seas Fleet threatened Britain's dominance on the sea thus posing a threat to the British Empire. Britain joined forces with its age-old enemy, France, to prevent Germany from ruling the European Continent. The British navy was going to fight the German navy for the first time in their respective histories.

An American reader may not grasp the strategic positions of Germany and Britain. This is especially true in regard to the German use of unrestricted submarine warfare. Britain had a stranglehold on Germany by blockading the North Sea. There were many things that Germany needed for its agriculture and its manufacturing base that it could not get from its own lands, or from surrounding countries. Russian Ukrainian crops, especially wheat, were a basic staple of the German diet, but Russia was now an enemy and the European breadbasket was cut off from the Germans. They also needed chemical fertilizers, many of which came from the United States, in order to enrich their own soil and produce food. Copper, chemicals for gunpowder, and rubber were other items Germany imported heavily before the war. The blockade very effectively prevented all these items from reaching Germany, as the English Channel was a simple matter for the British to close off. In the Straight of Dover, the channel is only twenty miles wide. In the North Sea there about 200 miles separating the tip of Scotland from the coast of Norway. In the era of coal- or diesel-fired ships, this was no problem to block. In essence, the German naval fleet was bottled up in the North Sea. Its greatest imperative was to break out of the North Sea and establish commercial links with the United States and other outside neutrals in order to have the food, clothing, and material they needed for their population and their war machine.

In pure Mahanian terms, Britain's geographical position provided control of the situation. Britain could close off trade to Germany and slowly starve her. This is what Britain was doing. Germany had one wild card, though, and with it they thought they could change Mahan's rules of naval warfare. Mahan had stated:

> The evidence seems to show that even for its own special ends such a mode of war (commerce destruction) is inconclusive, worrying but not deadly; it might also be said that it causes needless suffering.[99]
> It is not the taking of individual ships or convoys, be they few or many, that strikes down the money power of a nation; it is the possession of that overbearing power on

> the sea which drives the enemies flag from it, or allows it
> to appear only as a fugitive, and which, by controlling the
> great common closes the highways by which commerce
> moves to and from the enemy's shores.[100]

The submarine was still relatively new when Mahan wrote in 1890, and it seemed like the Germans were trying to rewrite the principles that Mahan had stated. There are two nagging questions about the German commerce destruction. First, they thought that it would bring Britain to its knees and end the war quickly, but the Germans had been enduring a very effective naval blockade on themselves and it did not stop their own will to fight. Even if they could inflict as much pain on Britain as Britain had inflicted on Germany, would that cause Britain to pull out of the war? Second, why were they so flagrantly uncaring about bringing another military power into the battle—the United States? Granted, in 1914, the United States fighting forces were not a match for Germany, but by 1918 they were much more than a match. The blindness of the German military leaders is astounding.

The German's use of the submarine is not as barbaric and uncivilized as it might appear at the outset—it was reprisal for the British blockade. If one is barbaric, so is the other. Of course, the sinking of a ship is more dramatic and makes greater headlines. The quiet starvation of a country does not.

> At bottom, the difference between Great Britain and
> Germany was that the injuries inflicted by the two
> belligerents upon America were of unequal magnitude:
> the British navy stopped ships and sometimes seized
> property; the German navy sank ships and sometimes
> killed people.[101]
> Before the sinking (of the Lusitania) Americans had
> been mad at Great Britain because of the blockade; it
> was likely that, over time, this resentment would have
> festered and grown worse. After the sinking of the
> Lusitania, American indignation and, ultimately, wrath,

were focused on the German submarine war, not the British blockade.[102]

When it appeared to the Americans that the submarine was being used in a military realm, it raised little concern; instead, they were aggravated by Britain's overbearing blockade. When it seemed that the Germans were engaging in an uncivilized form of warfare, pro-German sympathies disappeared. This was a propaganda coup for the British that painted their enemy as a barbaric horde. The result would have been changed remarkably if the Germans could have employed their submarines more efficiently in the Battle of Jutland.

To understand the battle that was brewing and would culminate at Jutland, one must take time to look at the antagonists. It must also be remembered that the British lived with the ghost of Nelson as both a great example of determined heroism and the curse of needing to live up to his image. He had died in the naval battle at Trafalgar, Spain, where the British had defeated the combined naval forces of Napoleon's French and Spanish fleets in 1805. Britain was the unchallenged ruler of the seas after that battle, until now. The Germans were challenging Britain's dominance of the North Sea, and if they broke out of the bottleneck they could challenge Great Britain anywhere in the world. Hence, the British Empire was challenged merely by the Germans' audacious attempt to break out of the North Sea.

The British

Admiral John Jellicoe was the Commander-in-Chief of the British Grand Fleet.

> Jellicoe's strength was his thorough professionalism, his cool analytical mind, and his iron self-control. He was neat, polite and methodical. He believed in naval traditions, procedures and decorum, among which were loyalty, scrupulous fairness, and genuine concern for the personal affairs of his officers and men. The fleet

responded to Jellicoe's transparent sincerity and obvious selflessness by giving him unreserved affection and trust. He was, said one of his Grand Fleet captains, "our beloved Commander-in-Chief, the finest character that ever was."

Jellicoe's professional experience and powers of concentration and organization were exceptional. He brought to his command an almost unparalleled technical knowledge and lifelong, deeply ingrained confidence in himself. Beyond this, Jellicoe possessed something else rare among the hundreds of conventional officers on the Navy List: he had an original mind. It was not a mind of a dreamer and genius like (First Sea Lord and the founder of the modern Royal Navy) Fisher, whose ideas ranged across the whole spectrum of naval affairs. Jellicoe's mind was the practical realistic mind of an engineer. Fisher asked Why? And Why not? Jellicoe asked How? And How much? When he found the answers, he understood, better than anyone else in the British navy, the difficulties the navy faced. He was aware of the technical achievements and rapid progress of the German Navy. He knew that the German ships were superior in amour protection and that German shells, torpedoes, and mines were more reliable than British. He was familiar with German skill in gunnery, in which he himself was an expert. As he warned Churchill on the eve of the war, it was highly dangerous to assume, as Churchill did, that British ships were superior to German as fighting machines.[103]

Jellicoe was a man who knew his own navy's strengths and weaknesses and that of his opponents as well. He was not likely to make the tragic mistake that would hand the Germans the victory that they so desperately sought, and he had the upper hand. Just as in a prize fight, it is said that for the challenger to win, he must win by a knockout. All Jellicoe had to do was to win on points, he could do that by maintaining his position. The naval build up had been the major reason for enmity between Germany and Great Britain. But it was almost two years into the war before the two navies faced off against each other. As Mahan had pointed out in his book that helped to indoctrinate Germany and the Kaiser on sea power, naval power does not rest solely on battle strength, though that is very important. It relies on being able to keep the sea lanes open, commerce coming into a country, and cutting off the commerce of the enemy.

Jellicoe's position was a defensive one. Though his countrymen may have clamored for another Trafalgar, Jellicoe could not and would not even try to deliver on that idea. The submarine, the torpedo, and the torpedo boat, as well as advances in mines, made the thought of another Trafalgar, an attack on the enemy's harbor, a contemplation of suicide. Rather, the distant blockade of the North Sea would do its quiet work of starving the German populace into submission.

David Beatty

During the Great War, Britain's best known admiral was not John Jellicoe, the Commander in Chief. It was David Beatty. The youngest admiral since Nelson, the commander of the famous Battle Cruiser Squadron, and then, succeeding Jellicoe, the Commander-in-Chief of the Grand Fleet, Beatty personified the Royal Navy to the British public. He was everything they liked to imagine in a naval hero: brave, impetuous, eager to attack, driving his ships toward the enemy at maximum speed, and then demanding that they go even faster. Beatty possessed the charisma that the calm and cautious Jellicoe lacked, and throughout the war, the younger man—Beatty, who was twelve years younger than Jellicoe—was the darling of the popular press. It was Beatty's postcard photo, not Jellicoe's that plastered every news agent's window and sold in the millions...

Beatty's aura radiated from his genuine accomplishments and in part from successful exhibitionism. He was short and trim, easy to miss in a crowd, until he made himself instantly recognizable on board ship and in photographs by turning himself into a seagoing dandy. He tilted his famous extra-wide-brimmed hat over his eyes at a jaunty, devil-may-care angle; he stuck his thumbs rakishly into the pockets of his blue uniform jacket, which his tailor had been instructed to make with six brass buttons instead of regulation eight. Like other flamboyantly egotistical warriors—George S. Patton, who wore pearl handled revolvers and high riding boots while commanding tanks, or Douglas MacArthur sloshing ashore (toward an army camera man) on a newly captured Pacific island, wearing sunglasses and a self-designed, gold-braided hat, his trademark corncob pipe clenched between his teeth—Beatty used visual imagery to capture popular fancy.[104]

It was Beatty who almost delivered the battle cruiser Squadron into the hands of the Germans, and then it was Beatty who delivered the German High Seas Fleet into Jellicoe's hands.

The Germans

Vizeadmiral Reinhard Scheer became the commander in chief of the German High Seas Fleet after Admiral von Pohl became sick and died of liver cancer in early 1916.

Entering the German navy in 1882 with the handicap of a middleclass upbringing in a country which chose most of its officers from the wealthy landowner families, Scheer found his advancement to be slow. Not until he commanded a torpedo-boat flotilla in 1900 did he make his mark, by writing a textbook on the tactical use of the torpedo. Thereafter, his worth was recognized, and by the outbreak of the war he was in command of the II Battle Squadron, comprising old pre-dreadnought battleships. He was entrusted with the command of III Battle Squadron—the newest and most powerful dreadnoughts—in December 1914. Admiral von Trotha, Scheer's chief of staff during 1916, has described him in these terms...

One could not find a better comrade. He never stood on ceremony with young officers. But he was impatient and always had to act quickly. He would expect his staff to have plans and orders for an operation worked out exactly to the last detail, and then come on the bridge and turn everything upside down. He was a very different person from me and sometimes he could not stand me. It was often very difficult for me to keep things going in accordance with the regulations...Scheer used to come on the bridge and make instant decisions. In action he was absolutely cool and clear...

It is difficult to understand why the Kaiser accepted Scheer's appointment as C-in-C, since the new commander was amongst those who, like Tirpitz, had persistently pressed for the High Sea Fleet to take the offensive: he believed that German ships were superior to that of the Royal Navy and that German officers and men were the equals of the British. However, it is precisely for these reasons that his appointment in the Fleet, which was suffering from the frustration of a year's inactivity under Pohl, was welcome. [105]

The reason why it might have seemed odd that the Kaiser had accepted Scheer is that once having built a grand navy, the Kaiser was afraid of losing it in battle. He was not the first monarch, who, having built an expensive navy became timid in its use.

Scheer's instinct for quick decisive action would confuse and astound his enemies and friends alike. Some claim that he was a genius; others say that he did not know what he was doing. His actions and his luck would help Germany in the Battle of Jutland.

Admiral Franz Hipper

Admiral Franz Hipper was a man under much stress, which temporarily took him out of action.

Physical disability had temporarily removed from command the most active German North Sea admiral,

Franz Hipper. As commander of the battle cruisers and other ships of the Scouting Groups and also as the officer responsible for their defense of the Heligoland Bight, Hipper was bending under the weight of his duties. Fatigue was compounded by sciatica. He had difficulty sleeping, and when he managed to doze off, every sound—a step on the deck above his cabin, the slapping of the halyards in the wind—reawakened him. Hipper knew that he needed a rest, but once Scheer had replaced Pohl, he decided not to ask for leave just as a new Commander-in-Chief was taking over. Two months later on March 26, Hipper feeling "terrible pain and exhaustion," applied for sick leave. The following day Scheer visited him on board Seydlitz and approved the request.[106]

Hipper took a five-week cure at Bad Neundorf, then visited a nerve specialist who listened to his complaints, examined him carefully, and announced a complete absence of any damage to Hipper's central nervous system. The admiral's symptoms, the doctor declared, were caused by stress. Relieved, Hipper returned to his new flagship, the recently commissioned Lutzow, on May 13 and resumed his command.[107]

During Hipper's absence, Scheer had tried to have Hipper replaced, but he was not allowed to do so.

"Vice Admiral Hipper no longer possesses the qualities of robustness and elasticity which...[command of the Scouting Groups] demands and it is also his view that the end of the leave will not affect a complete restoration of his abilities." Holtzendorff rejected the proposal because it seemed inappropriate for Scheer to be "coming forward with such radical suggestions so soon after assumption of command." Muller wrote on his memorandum, "I agree." There is evidence that Scheer had a certain envy of Hipper's fame and sometimes belittled him in service records, but the two men worked together for another two years at which point Hipper succeeded Scheer as Commander-in-Chief of the High Sea Fleet and Scheer became Chief of the Naval Staff in Berlin.[108]

So these are the commanders of the navies. Jellicoe was the commander in chief of the British, and Beatty, his second in command. Scheer was the commander in chief of the German forces, and Hipper, his subordinate.

After Room 40 at the Admiralty had alerted the Grand Fleet about the Germans setting sail, a serious error in communications developed. For some time there had been a rift between the civilians who worked in Room 40 and some of the naval corps. Captain Thomas Jackson, director of the Operations Division of the Admiralty, was one of those navy men who held the decoders in low esteem.

> They were in Jackson's eyes, "a party of very clever fellows who could decipher coded signals," but must never be allowed to interpret them. "Those chaps couldn't possibly understand all of the implications of interpreted signals," Jackson had said.[109]

The code-breakers were well aware of Jackson's attitude and repaid it with equal disdain; there was little communication between them.

Just past noon on May 31st, Jackson entered Room 40 and asked one simple short question. Where did the directional wireless stations place the call sign "DK?" "DK" was the call sign for Admiral Scheer's flagship, Frederick der Grosse. He was told that it was in the Jade. In other words, it seemed like Scheer's flagship had not left the Jade River after Room 40 had received transmissions indicating a large movement of ships, except that was not the case. Had Jackson bothered to question those "clever fellows" a little more they would have told him some important information. Scheer had switched his call sign to a shore wireless station at the harbor. Room 40 figured this out after the Lowestoft raid. But since Jackson seemed to have little time for the code-breakers and they for him, no more was said about Scheer's call sign. At 12:48, Admiral Jellicoe was informed that the call sign of Scheer's flagship placed it in the Jade Basin. This misinformation altered the beginning of the battle of Jutland, as Jellicoe assumed from the information that the German fleet would not be coming out to the battle. He assumed that Scheer would venture out afterward to form a cover for Admiral Hipper's return—he further assumed that any German ships that would be encountered would be a partial contingent of the High Seas Fleet. It made complete sense that Hipper would once again be running a raid out into the North Sea. Since Beatty was about seventy miles farther out and traveling a more southerly route, nearer to the German coast than Jellicoe and the rest of the British fleet, this meant that Beatty would most likely engage the enemy first.

> If Scheer and his battleships were not at sea—and he had been told that they were not—Beatty's force of six battle cruisers and four super dreadnoughts was more than adequate in speed and gun power to cope with any appearance of Hipper's battle cruisers.[110]

Jellicoe proceeded along at a leisurely fifteen knots toward a rendezvous with Beatty around 3:30 in the afternoon off the coast of Denmark. Meanwhile, around 2:30, both Hipper's and Beatty's scouting ships spotted a Danish tramp steamer, N.J. Fjord, and went over to get a better look at it. The German ship, the Elbing sent two torpedo boats, B109 and B110 over to investigate. At the same time, the light cruisers Galatea and Phaeton broke off from Beatty's turn to the north to get a better look at the lone steamer. Both pairs of ships found what they had set sail for that day—enemy ships on the horizon. The scouts on both sides sent messages back to their commanders. At 2:28 Galatea and Phaeton fired their 6-inch guns at the German torpedo boats. The Battle of Jutland had begun.

Once the German torpedo boats found themselves under attack they turned to the east with enemy shells falling in the water around them. The Elbing came to their rescue and returned fire with its 5.9-inch guns. The Galatea was struck just below the bridge, but the shell did not explode. The first hit of the battle had been scored.

As soon as Beatty had received the news of the enemy ships, he had turned east to meet them in battle. He wanted to get between the German line of ships and their home base, Horns Reef. Beatty still seethed from his lost opportunity when Hipper's ships had been able to elude him in a small previous skirmish by escaping into the fog and then safe harbors. His impetuous fly-by-the-seat-of-your-pants style would cause a problem this day. As he turned to engage the enemy, he had his flagman signal the change in direction— Rear Admiral Evan-Thomas did not see the flag signals owing to the distance between them. Evan-Thomas commanded the 5th Battle Squadron that included four Queen Elizabeth class dreadnoughts with eight 15-inch guns apiece. He was a devotee of John Jellicoe who had only been sent to be under Beatty's command ten days prior to sailing into the Battle of Jutland. He was used to taking orders and following them faithfully and dutifully; he was not used to following the flamboyant Beatty. Though Beatty had desired to have Evan-Thomas' four Queen Elizabeths in his arsenal, he never summoned Evan-Thomas over to his ship to explain tactics. When Beatty gave the order to turn north to rendezvous with Jellicoe (this first signal was received by Evan-Thomas), and then changed course to the southeast, the second signal was not received. Though Evan-Thomas could see the turn made, he did not receive any orders and continued north until there was a distance of ten miles between the ships, well out of range of assisting in the opening of the battle.

Instead of ten British capital ships against five German capital ships, the opening of the battle would be a much more even six to five.

The giant ships spent the first tense moments deploying into battle lines. There were a few shots fired by some of the smaller vessels, much like the early rounds of a long prize fight, these two behemoths of the sea snaked around and readied themselves for the battle.

Every man was closed up at his station, eagerly waiting for the signal to open fire:

> It was for everybody a moment charged with tremendous impressions when, after the breathless rush of the approach, the German and British battle cruisers, the finest and most powerful ships of both fleets deployed into a single line of battle with the majestic certainty, as certain as fate itself, waiting for the first thunder of the guns which would shatter the complete calm and the concentration of every faculty.[111]

Beatty thought for sure that this day would wipe away the lost opportunity of his and Hipper's last engagement. That was at Dogger Bank when he failed to cut off Hipper's escape. Now he had done so, and assuming, as did Jellicoe, that the rest of the German fleet was nowhere near, he felt certain that victory was in his grasp.

Both Beatty and Hipper were operating under a misconception. Each admiral thought that the small force they were about to engage in battle was the whole of the enemy ships that they would see that day. Whereas Hipper turned his ships south to make it look like he was running away again, he was actually trying to draw Beatty into the trap set by the German High Seas Fleet that was currently steaming north to meet Hipper's ships and join the battle. This was the rest of the fleet that the British thought was still sitting in the Jade River. Somewhere to the north of both forces sailed the remainder of the British Grand Fleet in all its power and glory.

When the British ships had been built by Admiral John Fisher, he built them for speed and power. Their guns ranged in size from 12 to 15 inches. The Germans on the other hand had smaller 11- to 12-inch guns. Only two of their ships had the larger 15-inch guns, but they had thicker armor. In theory, all the British had to do was to open fire at the farthest range of their guns and keep maneuvering at higher speeds than the Germans, which would keep the British out of range of the Germans as their larger, heavier projectiles rained down upon the helpless Germans. It would be like a boxer versus a brawler in a prize fight. The boxer could move around the ring throwing jabs at will at his opponent until the point that the opponent is weakened and wearied and set up for the knockout punch that would end the fight. In theory, this is how the British thought the battle should go. Theory often falls apart in practical application—in the fog of war; it is theory that is sometimes blown up. The British range finders on their guns did not keep pace with the longer range of the shells; plus, the explosive charge of their ammunition was inferior to the Germans charges. Sometimes the British shells would score a direct hit, but instead of exploding it would deflect off the ship, doing little damage. Some of the German projectiles were duds also, as the first shell that hit the Galatea was which penetrated but did not detonate. This occurred so often with the British ammunition that it became a running joke for the Germans after the fight. The British were informed of this later after the battle.

At the beginning of the Battle of Jutland, Beatty was not aware that the German ships were in his range. The German ships had a dull gray eastern sky behind them which masked their precise position; the British, on the other hand, had a bright cloudless sun-drenched western sky on this late spring day. Whereas the British rangefinders were inferior to their shooting distance, the Germans had range finders that magnified their targets at twenty-three times greater than the naked eye. They were also better marksmen than the British— add to the mix that the British had smoke blowing in front of them as the battle was about to open. The Germans were able to get the British in their sights and fired the first shots with their heavy guns. Thirty seconds later, the British line opened fire as well, but the Germans had the better luck in the opening salvos. This opening act of the Battle of Jutland is known as "The Run to the South."

The Run to the South

At 3:49 p.m., the firing had commenced. The British capital ships, the Lion, the Princess Royal, and the Tiger, had all taken hits in the opening rounds. This is not to say that the British did not land any shots; at 3:55 p.m., the Seydlitz was hit twice and at 4:00 p.m. the Lutzow was hit from a salvo fired from Beatty's flagship, the Lion.

At the same time that the Lion scored a hit on the Lutzow, the Lion almost went down in a white flash of cordite charges. The Lion was hit in the center gun turret, which

> "blew half of the roof of the turret into the air so that it fell on the upper deck with a resounding crash. It ignited the cordite charges in the loading cages, which were about to be entered into the guns. The explosion and [consequent] fire...had killed every man in the gun-house and working chamber. The igniting of the charges in the gun-house did not at once ignite other charges, which were in the loading cages a little farther down in the turret, but there must have been a good deal of smoldering material, which needed only a draft of air to burst into flame."[112]

Had it not been for the actions of Major F. J. W. Harvey, the ship might have sunk and Beatty would have gone down with it. After the initial explosion, Harvey ordered that the magazine doors be closed and the magazine flooded, preventing the fire from reaching the rest of the stored charges. His dying actions saved the ship and gained him a posthumous Victoria Cross.

The Indefatigable was not so lucky. It had been under heavy fire for about fifteen minutes when there were fierce explosions in the center and the back of the ship. The 18,500-ton steel ship disappeared from sight, the first ship sunk of the battle.

While the Germans were raining hell down on Beatty's five ships, salvation came in the form of Evan-Thomas' 5th Battle Squadron. These were the four Elizabeth class ships with the 15-inch guns that arrived at about 4:10. Though the distance was still far and the German line was shrouded in smoke,

Evan-Thomas was able to inflict pain upon the German line that relieved the pressure from Beatty's ships.

Beatty had altered his course when he realized that Evan-Thomas had joined the battle. Hipper had done the same with the result that the fleets that had been drifting apart and out of each other's line of sight came back into range and the violent battle ensued again.

Then the Queen Mary was hit.

> According to observers on board Tiger and New Zealand, three shells out of a salvo of four hit Queen Mary simultaneously. From the flying splinters and the deep red glow of fire at the moment of impact, it seemed as if the shells had failed to pierce the armour. The converse, however, must have been the case. Two further shells of the next salvo struck the ship. Again, only a little black smoke, apparently coal dust, was seen to issue from the shot holes. But then a tremendous dark red flame and large masses of black smoke belched forth amidships and the hull appeared to burst asunder, while a similar explosion forward then followed. Queen Mary broke in two, the roofs of the turrets were hurled 100 feet into the air, and in a moment the ship disappeared except for the stern with its still revolving propellers.[113]

The Tiger and New Zealand were following Queen Mary in the line of battle and barely avoided hitting the two halves that still floated. When the Princess Royal disappeared in the water spray of salvos falling all around it, Beatty was quoted as saying, "There seems to be something wrong with our ships today."[114] Then the Princess Royal reappeared from the dead.

It was at this point that Beatty sent out twelve destroyers, led by Captain Barry Bingham in Nestor to deliver a torpedo attack on Hipper's ships. They raced toward the German ships at thirty-four knots. Hipper watched as this developed sending out the light cruiser Regnesburg with fifteen destroyers to meet Bingham. Both sides fired off their torpedoes at the capital ships—only one out of twenty torpedoes the British fired found its mark. The Seydlitz was hit hard and took in hundreds of tons of water from a hole forty feet long and thirteen feet high, but it was able to retain speed and stay in line. The British ships managed to avoid all eighteen torpedoes fired at them. The destroyers battled each other in the no-man's-land between the ships. Two were sunk on either side of the battle; the Nestor and the Nomad both lost their boilers and came to a halt, then later sank. The German destroyers V-27 and V-29 also went down. During the melee of the destroyer battle, Beatty reversed course and turned north even though he still outnumbered Hipper, as his ships were taking the worst of the battle. Two of his capital ships had been sunk as well as two destroyers, while the Germans had only lost two destroyers. As Beatty was turning north, Scheer's force of the High Seas Fleet was just coming into Hipper's view. Evan-Thomas was not the only one left going in the wrong direction when the battle was first engaged. Beatty's light cruiser squadron had finally caught up with their commander and resumed their scouting position in front of the larger ships just as Beatty was changing directions again. From this vantage point they could see the German High Seas Fleet coming into view—in another ten or twenty minutes, Beatty's capital ships would have been outnumbered twenty-one to eight. If Beatty had waited any longer to turn, it is unlikely that Jellicoe could have gotten there in time to save his ships and those of Evan-Thomas; and without those ships in the British vanguard, the whole battle would have truly been a disaster for the British. Still, it is hard to conceive that the German Armada could have decisively beaten the British fleet in mass that day. In fact, that was never the point of the German attacks; it was always to draw out a portion of the British Grand Fleet, defeat them, and reduce the British numeric superiority. Once parity could be achieved, and the blockade broken, then Germany could bring Britain to the negotiating table. Beatty's turn to the north was advantageous for him and the British. His strength obviously was not in fighting Hipper in a run-and-gun duel mano-a-mano, but lay in drawing Hipper, and now Scheer, into the British trap. The tables would be turned. Beatty had thought that he was the hunter. He was shot to pieces. He turned and now Hipper and Scheer would be the hunters following the bait into a British trap. So ended the Run to the South, fifty-five minutes of violent naval fighting that saw the Germans get the best of the British. Now "The Run to the North" would begin.

The Run to the North

David Beatty's fly-by-the-seat-of-your-pants style left people lost in his wake; Evan-Thomas was one. Another commander, Commodore William Goodenough, was leading the three light cruiser squadrons and had been straining to catch up with Beatty during the whole fifty-five-minute Run to the South. Goodenough was a veteran commander and knew Beatty's style well. He knew that Beatty would try to cut off the enemy's retreat to his home base; he had no problem setting a course to the southeast after he followed Beatty's turn. When he finally resumed his proper position, forward of Beatty's capital ships, he saw an astounding sight for an English sailor—the whole of the German High Seas Fleet coming over the horizon. It was 4:35 in the afternoon. Hipper had drawn Beatty into the trap set for him and had been the bait set out to lure a portion of the British fleet into the entire German fleet. It was now up to Scheer to deliver the death blow to Beatty and his forces. Beatty, however, had an ace up his sleeve. Jellicoe was only an hour's sail to the north. With their faster ships, Beatty could turn and race to the north and lure the German fleet into a death trap set for them. Beatty had to get a closer look after he received the message from Goodenough, keeping on his southerly course until his ships were just barely at the extreme edge of the big German guns on the Konig class ships racing toward him. He began his turn having all his ships pass through the same point, while

German shells fell all around them. Luck shined on Beatty during this turn because no serious hits were scored by the Germans, no one lost power or lost speed, allowing the British to turn and run to the north.

Once again, there was confusion in the ranks. Evan-Thomas on Barnham was seven miles behind Lion doing battle with the German ships in the rear of the battle line. He could not see the message flags, nor did any of the other ships signal him by searchlight. The first that Evan-Thomas knew of the change of course was when he passed the Lion going in the opposite direction. Beatty had his signalman, Ralph Seymour, signal Evan-Thomas to inform him of his orders. The protocol in flag messaging is that the flags are put up to inform the other ships of the intended move that is to be made when the flags are pulled down; as long as the flags are up, the move has not yet commenced. Evan-Thomas, the opposite of Beatty, very by-the-books, would not have made the move until the flags were down. The message went up at 4:48 p.m. and was not hauled down until 4:54 p.m. That short, six-minute time period brought Evan-Thomas 4,000 yards, a little over two miles, closer to the Germans than Beatty was. Barnham was hit, Valiant was untouched, Warspite was hit three times, and Malaya avoided the concentrated fire by turning early instead of going to the same spot as the others for its turn.

Beatty was not out of hot water yet. He was still receiving hits from the Germans after he made his turn to the north; fortunately for him, it did not slow down his ships. At around 5:15 p.m., the action slowed and the men could try to catch their breath, but there were fires to be put out and wounded to be tended to. At 5:25 p.m., the men were at battle stations again, and at 5:43 p.m., firing was resumed.

Despite the pounding that the Germans had been giving the British, with Beatty's flagship pouring out smoke for at least an hour, the British still had their speed. Once Beatty had turned north, this left Evan-Thomas and the four Queen

Elizabeth class ships with their 15-inch guns in the rear to take a pounding and to inflict damage on the Germans with their huge 1,900-pound artillery shells.

> Barnham and Valiant were to deal with the five German battle cruisers up ahead, while Warspite and Malaya took on the four Konigs coming up behind. At the head of the German battle line, Behncke and his four formidable Konigs-Konig, Grosser Kurfust, Kronprinz Wilhelm, and Markgraf—pressed forward to the limit of their stoker's ability to shovel coal. All the while their twelve-inch guns lashed out. Barnham was the first to be struck; then she was hit again four more times.[115]

One lucky hit would have sunk any of Evan-Thomas' ships, which would then have to be left for dead; otherwise, all four of the Queen Elizabeths would have suffered heavily and been sunk. But the British guns were scoring hits on the Seydlitz, Lutzow, the Derfflinger Konig, Grosser Kurfurst, and the Markgraf. Von der Tann had all her guns silenced and became useless as a weapon, but stayed in the line in order to draw fire away from the other ships. The German guns were beginning to quiet down, and worse for them, the field of vision had changed. The Germans were now looking into a glaring setting sun, and it was the British who had a clear line of sight on their enemy.

Scheer realized that his ships would receive much damage from the Queen Elizabeths' big guns, but thought that he had a wounded enemy on the run, and that given time, one or more of the capital ships would fall prey to him and he would have his victory. What he was not aware of was that Beatty was drawing him into a trap as they neared Jellicoe's High Seas Fleet. Though beaten-up, the British ships could still outpace the German ships. If any had been hit in the engine compartments or been reduced in speed for any reason, Scheer would have had his way with the unlucky vessel and then given up the chase, having gotten his prize. The prize still eluded him, and he continued to chase Beatty hoping to catch him.

At 5:20 p.m., Scheer had signaled to give chase not knowing that the faster British ships were leading them into a trap. Beatty then altered his course from north to northeast to engage Hipper's ships again and to mask the oncoming Grand Fleet. This forced the German line to bend to the east to prevent Beatty's ships from gaining the advantage of crossing Hipper's "T." Smoke from the guns mixed with a mist to form thick dark clouds that hampered vision on the battle field. It was Hipper's job to keep the High Seas Fleet aware of changes on the battlefield. If more enemy ships appeared, he was to report it to Scheer. Because he was caught in an intense battle with Beatty and was lost in one of the cloud banks, he was not the first to spot the Grand Fleet. It was Bodicker, three miles ahead of him to the east who saw them. First he only saw a single enemy cruiser. Five minutes later, Bodicker reported British Dreadnoughts to the east; these could not be Beatty's ships, nor could they be Evan-Thomas' crew. Someone else was entering the battle. At 5:59 p.m., Bodicker saw the Grand Fleet stretched out on the horizon, 16,000 yards, within striking distance away. The Run to the North was over.

Jellicoe Rides to the Rescue

Throughout the Run to the South, Jellicoe tried to stay informed of the situation as best as he could. By adjusting his course, he ended the zigzagging picking up his speed from fifteen knots to eighteen and then twenty. That was full steam for the whole of the Grand Fleet, but he did send his three Invincibles-class ships ahead. They were seventeen-ton battle cruisers with eight 12-inch guns apiece that were led by Rear Admiral Horace Hood. These ships could steam ahead at twenty-five knots and catch up with the running battle, being screened by two light cruisers and four destroyers.

The Invincibles at first had a hard time finding the battle

in the open sea and actually appeared on the eastern side of the fight when Hood encountered Konteradmiral Friederich Bodicker's 2nd Scouting Group of light cruisers. The ships were not close enough to be recognized as friend or foe, so they continued to close in on each other. The German ships recognized the Light Cruiser Chester as British and since they knew what the British recognition signal was, flashed it, which drew Chester in even closer, to 6,000 yards. When the Germans finally opened fire, the Chester was engulfed in shells and lost its rangefinder, its communications systems, and three of its four 6-inch guns. Once again, this British ship, though ravaged with gun fire, was not slowed down. Its engines were untouched. Hood, on the Invincible, saw Chester in distress, placed his ship between it and the German light cruisers and opened fire with his 12-inch guns. The German ships fled the scene, but not before three of the four ships were hit. The Frankfurt and Pillau escaped with minimal damage, but the Wiesbaden was fatally injured, a 12-inch shell put its engine out of commission, and the ship stopped and drifted.

> To rescue the German Light cruisers, Hipper sent Regensburg and thirty-one destroyers to charge the Invincibles, but before most could launch their torpedoes, they were met by a counter charge from Hood's second light cruiser, Canterbury, and four British destroyers. In a free-swinging brawl at close quarters, the Germans somehow got the impression that many more British ships were present than was the fact; as a result, the Germans only fired twelve torpedoes, after which the thirty-one destroyers turned back.[116]

It was during this brawl that the British destroyer Shark was hit and disabled. Much of the attack became focused on either sinking it, if it was German, or saving it if it was British. At one point, the Acasta pulled up near it and the British officer asked the captain how he could help. The captain, Loftus Jones, sent him away so they both would not go down.

He then manned one of the ship's guns, when a shell hit and took his right leg off above the knee. He ordered his men to abandon ship and he died soon after in a raft from his ship.

> These small British losses were out of all proportion to the gain brought about by the surprise appearance of the 3rd Battlecruiser squadron on the starboard side of the German Battlecruisers. But for the intervention of Hood's squadron, the attack by German flotillas would have taken another direction, namely at Beatty's force, and probably would have brought the latter's encircling movement across the head of the German line to a standstill. In this case, the German Battlecruisers and battleships of the III Squadron would probably have surprised the Grand Fleet while still deploying, and would have probably succeeded in crossing the "T" (van), instead of them being placed in a tactically untenable position by Beatty's outflanking movement.[117]

When Jellicoe arrived near the battle scene, he desperately needed information, but information, accurate and precise, was the last thing that he got. One of Beatty's most important jobs, and his greatest failure, was his lack of sending messages to his commander. For over an hour and fifteen minutes, between 4:45 p.m. and 6:06 p.m., Beatty either ignored or forgot to inform his commander about the enemy's location, its battle strength, and its bearing. Jellicoe received information from Goodenough at 5:00, 5:40, and 5:50 p.m. that the enemy's battlefleet was coming north, but Jellicoe could not pin down Goodenough's precise position. This was a predicament for Jellicoe. His ships were traveling in a cruising formation, in six columns, which made them safe from submarine attack; however, in this formation, only the leading ships would be able to fire their forward guns. He had to deploy his ships into one long line of battle to bring his guns to bear on the enemy. If he deployed in the wrong direction, the Germans might cross his "T," a battle tactic where an enemy fleet goes across the foremost ship at the front of the battle line in a perpendicular fashion. They have all of their guns from all of their ships (the Germans had one hundred at the start of the fight), firing at the line of ships, raining hell down on them. The ships in the base of the "T" cannot fire because the blast might harm their own ships in front of them (friendly fire), and they might be out of range. The enemy crossing the "T" can fire at will with all his ships with minimal damage done to it, all the while inflicting heavy damage on the ships in the top of the "T." This was the situation that Jellicoe needed to avoid here. To make the correct decision he needed precise information about where the Germans were, how large a fleet it was, what direction they were traveling in, and how fast they were moving. Jellicoe got very little helpful information, especially from Beatty; part of the problem was that Beatty had lost sight of the Germans. Fortunately, at 6:06 p.m., Beatty sighted the enemy to the south of him and passed this information on to Jellicoe. Still, Jellicoe did not know how fast they were going, the exact direction they were heading, or how large a force he would be facing. Despite this lack of information, Jellicoe had to deploy. If he turned to the right, starboard, he would engage the enemy quickly, being well within gunnery range, he could also come under heavy torpedo and destroyer attack from the Germans. If he turned to the left, port, in an easterly direction, he would avoid the torpedo attacks, being 4,000 yards farther away from the German line. This move, however, would cross the Germans' "T" and put the British fleet against a dull gray sky, making them hard to see, while the Germans would be highlighted by the western sky. At first, he wanted to turn right until his methodical technician's mind calculated all the facts and he gave the order to turn to the left.

> I heard the signalman calling each word of Beatty's reply to Jellicoe's repeated demand...I then heard at once the sharp, distinctive step of the Commander-in-Chief approaching—he had steel strips on his heels. He stepped quickly onto the platform around the compasses

and looked in silence at the magnetic compass card for about twenty seconds. I watched his keen, brown, weather beaten face with tremendous interest, wondering what would he do...I realized as I watched him that he was as cool and unmoved as ever. Then he looked up and broke the silence with the order in his crisp, clear-cut voice to the Fleet Signal Officer. "Hoist equal speed pendent southeast." The officer said, "Would you make it a point to port, sir, so they will know it on the port wing column?" Jellicoe replied, "Very well, hoist equal speed pendant southeast by south." The officer then called over the bridge rail to signal the boatswain...Three flags soared up the halyards. We had not yet sighted any German vessel.[118]

It was the most important move he would ever make in his life. If he had turned to the right, Jellico would have engaged the enemy sooner and been in the thick of the action right away, but Scheer cut his teeth in torpedo boats and probably would have loved nothing more than to soften his opponent up with torpedoes and his destroyers and then come at the British with their big guns. Jellico did not give him this opportunity. In fact, Jellicoe put the Germans in peril by crossing their "T."

Fate is so cruel. Both commanders-in-chief this day would have their greatest desire appear in front of them, only to have their hopes dashed forever. Jellicoe made the perfect maneuver in order to cross the "T" of the German High Seas Fleet. Prior to that, it was Scheer who thought that he was sitting in the catbird seat. Before Jellicoe showed up, Scheer thought he had twenty Dreadnoughts, with their correspondent torpedo boats and destroyers, against Beatty's eight Dreadnoughts and retinue. Just as he was about to grab his prize, the whole of the British Grand Fleet showed up. Now that Jellicoe made the perfect move to trap the hunter, the hunter-turned-victim pulled a magnificent move himself. He made the first of his three "Gefectshekrtwendung nach steuerbord" (Battle turn to starboard).

Gefechtskehrtwendung nach Steuerbord

Scheer, in the Frederick der Grosse, was thirteenth in the long line of German warships. Even when Rear Admiral Paul Behncke on Konig was staring at six columns of the Grand Fleet, Scheer assumed that his ships where just fighting Beatty and Evan-Thomas' ships. The shock that overcame them at the sight of the most massive battlefleet put on the high seas at that point is unimaginable. Scheer refused to believe it until he got information from captured British sailors who reinforced his greatest fears.

> Scheer reacted quickly. "While the battle is progressing a leader cannot obtain a really clear picture, especially at long ranges," Scheer wrote after the war. "He acts and feels according to his impressions." Scheer saw only one way out: to order a carefully rehearsed German fleet maneuver, designed for exactly this situation: when it was necessary to break away rapidly from a stronger fleet. At 6:36 p.m., Scheer signaled Gefechtskehrtwendung nach Steuerbord. The maneuver called for each ship to make a 180 degree turn onto an opposite course.[119]

This maneuver caught Jellicoe off guard, which could only happen to a force not used to being on the defensive. For one hundred years, the British ruled the high seas, thus the thought of needing to extricate itself from a greater force was foreign to their way of thinking. The Germans, on the other hand, knew that they were the weaker force who had to be ready to escape if they were confronted by a force that they could not handle, and so they practiced escaping from that force. When they needed to, they could disappear into the mist. If it was not for the wounded Wiesbaden, and the slower ships that Scheer had mistakenly allowed to accompany him, Scheer might have escaped totally at this point with minimal damage to his ships, and the prize of having sunk two of the Grand Fleet's Dreadnoughts. There were six ships dubbed the five-minute ships by the German sailor—they were the pre-Dreadnaught ships of the 2nd squadron. They had some firepower, four 12-inch guns apiece, but they could only make eighteen knots at top speed. In pursuit of a faster enemy, they would be in the rear of the battle—in flight from a faster enemy; they were a drag on the fleet. Like the younger sibling tagging along behind their big brother's adventures, they would have to be protected from the enemy. Even though Scheer had made a great turning maneuver, and his fleet performed well in extricating itself from certain annihilation, Scheer's fleet could not outrun Jellicoe's fleet to the safety of German waters. Scheer ordered another Gefechtskehrtwendung nach Steuerbord.

Scheer's decision to turn back and engage the enemy again has been criticized by many historians. In fact, Scheer himself seemed unable to justify his actions after the fact. In his report to the Kaiser he claimed:

> "It was as yet too early to assume night cruising order. The enemy could have compelled us to fight before dark, he could have prevented our exercising our initiative, and finally he could have cut off our return to the German Bight. There was only one way of avoiding this: to inflict a second blow on the enemy by advancing again regardless of cost, and to bring all the destroyers forcibly to attack. Such a maneuver would surprise the enemy, upset his plans for the rest of the day and, if the blow fell really heavily, make easier a night escape. It also offered the possibility of a last attempt to help the hard-pressed Wiesbaden, or at least the rescue of her crew."[120]

At 6:55 p.m., Scheer ordered the second 'Gefechtskehrtwendung nach Steuerbord' sending the German High Seas Fleet straight at the full force of the British High Seas Fleet. This move did surprise the British, but the gamble did not pay off for the Germans. The British could see the German ships very clearly, yet the sun was blinding the sight of the German gunners. They could make out the flashes of the British guns, but not the ships. Without a good target to aim for, the Germans were like sitting ducks waiting for the British hunters to blast them out of the water.

"Hercules fired on Seydlitz; Colossus and Revenge on Derflinger; Neptune and St. Vincent on Derflinger and Moltke, Marlborough, ignoring her torpedo injury, fired fourteen salvos in six minutes and saw four of them hit. Monarch, Iron Duke, Centurion, Royal Oak, King George V, Temeraire, Superb, Neptune—all reported scoring hits."[121]

The German ships were being slaughtered and could not see well enough to try to hit back. During the whole time that the British were ravaging the German ships, the Germans only landed two shots, both on the Colossus.

Ten minutes of this withering attack was all that Scheer could stand. He would have to extricate his ships again. One more time he would have to execute a "Gefechtskehrtwendung nach Steuerbord." This move would be different. Before, his ships were not subjected to withering fire from the enemy, now they were a little more beat up, and closer to the enemy line than before. Scheer would send his battle cruisers and his torpedo boat flotillas in to attack the enemy's battleships, and leave a smoke screen to shield the retreat of the battleships. The signal flags went up stating: "'Schlachtkreuzer ran an den Feind, voll einsetzen!' 'Battle cruisers at the enemy. Give it everything!'"[122]

Death Ride of the Battle Cruisers

The Derflinger with eight 12-inch guns, the Seydlitz with ten 11-inch guns, the Moltke with its ten 11-inch guns, and the Von der Tann with eight 11-inch guns would have to shield the German fleet from the whole of the British fleet, which would have scores of 12-, 13-, and 15-inch shells raining down upon them. This part of the battle action is known as the Death Ride of the Battle Cruisers. While these four battle cruisers were facing down the 140-strong British battle line, the other

German ships were trying to make another 180-degree turn as they had twice before; now there was damage to some of the ships, which made them harder to control. During the ten-minute bombardment by the British, the German battle line had become bunched together, which made tight maneuvering more difficult, if not close to impossible. Scheer had turned to port instead of starboard to make room for other ships to be able to turn to the right without any problems; some of these ships had almost collided as they attempted to turn, filled with confusion, and not the precision that the first turn had exhibited. Nevertheless, all the ships managed to change their directions while the battle cruisers went on their death rides. The battle cruisers were followed by the torpedo boat flotillas. Their job was to lay down a line of torpedoes to cover for the escape of the High Seas Fleet. Hopefully (for the Germans), they would sink some of the British ships. This they failed to do, but the secondary result of their attack helped to save the German ships. The British used a turn away tactic that was common at this time by most navies. Upon seeing the track of an enemy torpedo, the captain would turn the ship away from it and outrace it. While the ship was in battle line, the full length of the ship was exposed to a possible torpedo attack. For instance, the Queen Elizabeth Class ships are 640 feet long and 90 feet wide. By turning away from the torpedo they reduced the target by about 85 percent. Add to this that the ship would now be traveling away from the torpedo and it could actually outrun it. Many torpedoes would run out of fuel before they hit using this method. Of course, when a ship takes this precautionary tactic, it takes itself out of the line of battle. So even if the torpedo does not hit or sink the ship, it has done its job by removing an enemy ship from the attack. Many such torpedoes can render an attacking line impotent, which is what happened here. There were thirty-one torpedoes fired at the British line, none of them hit their targets, but by forcing the British to turn out of their line, they changed the outcome of the battle.

The German official history comments:

> Although none of the torpedoes found their marks, the tactical effect of the massed attack of the German torpedo boats was, nonetheless, extraordinary. The twice repeated turn-away from the enemy and the movements of individual ships to avoid torpedoes...brought the British fleet into a state of complete disorder at a moment when victory seemed almost within its grasp...for the British lost complete touch with the German battleships.[123]

Once again, the battle seesawed. At one time Beatty figured that he had victory in his hand when he thought that his ten capital ships were facing Hipper's five. Then Hipper got the best of the battle and was about to deliver Beatty's banged-up force to Scheer's High Seas Fleet. The odds were now two to one against Beatty. Then Beatty high-tailed it to the safety of Jellicoe and the Grand Fleet, and the odds improved for the British to 150 to 100, three to two, against the Germans with the British having the bigger guns. Scheer left the fight, came back to fight, got clobbered, and left the fight again. Jellicoe (like a boxer who has victory in his grasp) while trying to deliver the knockout punch, ducked some lethal counter-blows only to come back around to fight some more only to hear the bell ending the round. He had to go back to his neutral corner while his enemy escaped again.

> Had Jellicoe turned toward the torpedoes and pursued, rather than turning away, he might have lost some ships—so the argument goes—but he would have inflicted further heavy damage on the Germans and perhaps even brought about their total destruction. Instead, time and range were sacrificed—seventeen minutes and over 3,000 yards—and Scheer made good his escape. Jellicoe, by this decision, was said to have forsaken the Royal Navy's chance for a new Trafalgar.
> This view would hover over Jellicoe's reputation for the rest of his life.[124]

The ghost of Nelson would haunt Jellicoe. But to be fair to the commander, turning away from a torpedo attack was accepted practice of the day.

> Long before, in his letter to the Admiralty of October 30,1914, he had made his intensions clear. He had explained that he meant to assume the defensive against all enemy underwater weapons while attempting to conserve his ships for offensive action with their more numerous, heavier guns. If the Germans attempted to retreat or escape from a Fleet action, he was determined not to pursue; if he were confronted by a concentrated torpedo attack, he would turn away. The Admiralty approved, expressing "full confidence in your contemplated conduct of the fleet in action." On May 31, 1916, therefore, John Jellicoe simply did what he said he intended to do.[125]

In WWII, the ships would turn toward the torpedoes, bow first, but that was not the case in WWI. Maybe it was the criticism that Jellicoe had to live with that made commanders rethink the action. Jellicoe was not looking for a new Trafalgar. He wanted to defeat the Germans and thought that he had the chance, but he was not going to deliver men and ships to Davey Jones' locker for vainglory. Anyway, he was between the German High Seas Fleet and their path home. The Germans would have to cross the British line to find safe harbor or run out of fuel in the North Sea. As far as Jellicoe was concerned, they would do battle again at daybreak.

Scheer had extricated his fleet from imminent disaster for a second time, yet he still had a problem, one for which he was prepared. He had to take his battered ships and do one of two things. Sail north to the tip of Denmark sail through the Kattegat, the body of water between Denmark and Sweden and then into German territory on the Baltic Sea. This was too far and some of his crippled ships would never survive the sail. The other choice was to sail to Horns Reef off the Denmark coast where the Germans had a clear lane to their home base in the Jade River about one hundred miles to the south. This lane by the Horns Reef was saturated with mines and only a precise knowledge of how to sail through there safely would get a ship to the harbor. Once the German ships had made it to Horns Reef, they were home free. The last thing Jellicoe was going to do was sail through German waters with mines, torpedo boats, and submarines lying around to inflict damage, not to mention the danger from shore batteries. Jellicoe had to deliver the death blow to Scheer's fleet before they reached Horns Reef. This did not seem like it would be much of a problem since the British Fleet stood between the German fleet and Horns Reef. Scheer had an ace left up his sleeve. The Germans were practiced at night battles, the British were not. Jellicoe fully expected that there would be some sort of night action, especially from the destroyers. But daylight would come early in this northerly section of the earth. Sunrise was around 3:00 a.m.; Jellicoe went to get some much-needed sleep in order to be ready for the morning's action.

The British commander had his doubts about the information that came from the Admiralty since the message he had received at noon telling him that the High Seas Fleet was still in the Jade. Jellicoe weighed the information that he received from the Admiralty against the information that he received from his ships, giving greater import to what his ships told him than what was sent to him by the Admiralty. His officers had either seen or engaged the enemy and certainly would have a better idea of what was happening than someone in a room hundreds of miles away. Jellicoe's disdain of information from the Admiralty was compounded when Room 40 informed him that the High Seas Fleet was ten miles to the southwest of Iron Duke. He knew for a fact that the German fleet was to his northwest, not southwest. When the Admiralty informed him that they had received information that German destroyers had been ordered to attack during the night, this came as no surprise, and added nothing new to his intelligence. At 10:41 p.m., Jellicoe was informed that the High Seas Fleet was ordered home. This information, which was true, did not sway Jellicoe. If it had, he would have realized that Scheer would be trying to cross his path sometime during the night, and he could have taken action to prevent Scheer's penetration. One piece of information that did not reach Jellicoe was Scheer's request for Zeppelin reconnaissance at Horns Reef at dawn. That piece of information, put together with the direction set for Horns Reef, might have convinced Jellicoe of Scheer's intentions. As it was, the news about the airships was not sent to Jellicoe. More crucial evidence of where the Germans were heading was squelched as well, a message ordering all the destroyer flotillas to rendezvous at Horns Reef by 2:00 a.m. was not passed onto Jellicoe either.

> Captain Admiral Jackson—he of great contempt of cryptographers and signals intelligence—was not present in the War Room that night. Admiral Oliver Stone, the Chief of Staff, charged with approving Admiralty messages sent to the Commander-in-Chief, "had left the War Room for some much needed rest and had left in charge an officer who had no experience of German operational signals." Seeing no special significance in these decoded messages, this officer carefully placed them in an Admiralty file.[126]

While the Admiralty was receiving and sitting on information, the Germans started to cross the rear of the British line. This caused many small ferocious battles at close quarters. One happened at 10:15 p.m. as four British light cruisers met five German light cruisers. In the dark it was hard to identify the ships. Commodore Goodenough on the Southampton could stand it no longer and fired a shot at the unidentified ships. They returned fire in a barrage of shells deluging the Southampton. Though much damage was done to the British ship, it was still able to fire a torpedo which hit and sunk the light cruiser Frauenlob.

The British seemed reluctant to engage or even to disclose their positions at night. Because of this fear, two of Scheer's Dreadnoughts were allowed to pass through the British lines unmolested. The Moltke had been sighted by the Thunderer, and the Seydlitz had been seen from Agincourt, Marlborough, and Revenge. Both ships were heavily damaged and were ripe for attack, but both were allowed to sail to freedom.

The Gunnery Officer aboard the Marlborough, Lieutenant-Commander Guy Royle, recorded that:

> "I missed the chance of a lifetime on this occasion. I saw the dim outline of this ship from the top and had the main armament trained on it and put a range of 4,000 yards on the sights and a deflection of 24 right, then asked the Captain [George Ross], who was in the conning tower, for permission to open fire. He replied 'No' as he thought it was one of our own ships. Of course what I should have done was to have opened fire and blown the ship out of the water and then said 'Sorry.'"[127]

At about midnight, the 4th Flotilla of destroyer escorts who were keeping station with the 5th Battle Squadron converged with the van of the German High Seas Fleet. The Tipperary was leading the twelve destroyers when it signaled the unknown ships to the starboard when they were about 1,000 yards away. Searchlights and a barrage of 5.9- and 3.5-inch shells turned Tipperary into a blazing hulk. Spitfire, which was behind Tipperary, had to maneuver to avoid hitting the burning ship. As it did so, it encountered the German battleship, Nassau, coming at it from the other direction. Nassau altered its course straight for Spitfire and the two ships collided port bow to port bow and then screeched by each other. The Nassau's 11-inch guns were fired at the smaller ship. Though the projectiles went clear over the top of the destroyer, the blast still wrecked the bridge, the foremost funnel, and the mast. Spitfire was able to limp away, but it was damaged and useless for the battle.

Confusion in the German line caused a collision between Elbing and Posen. The two collided with each other putting a hole under the waterline in Elbing which put its engines out of commission.

The command ship of the destroyer fleet, the Tipperary, was on fire and out of action so the leadership changed hands and once again a British captain was reluctant to fire first and paid the price. Commander Allen on the destroyer Broke signaled an unidentified ship and was met by a hailstorm of blinding lights and shells. In under a minute, Broke was decimated and spun out of control. It ran into the next ship in the British line, the Sparrowhawk. Contest who was next in line rammed the Sparrowhawk and took off thirty feet of its stern. Broke and Contest were able to pull out of the mess, limping out of action. The Sparrowhawk floated around until the next day when it was scuttled by its crew.

The German Light Cruiser Rostock was hit by a torpedo and took in 930 tons of water and still was able to follow the German ships slowly and from a distance.

In the 4th Flotilla, command passed to Commander Hutchinson of Achates. He was followed by Ambuscade, Ardent, Fortune, Porpoise, and Garland. It was Fortune whose luck would run out this night. Hutchinson wanted to reconnect with the British line and steered a course merging with the lead of the German line. Westfalen and Rhineland opened fire on the British destroyer. It took less than a minute to send Fortune into a watery grave.

Achates and Ambuscade thought that they were being chased by a German cruiser. It was not; it was one of their own, Black Prince, an armored cruiser. It had fallen behind the British line because of damage to its engines when it caught up to the German line of Battleships. Soon after 1:00 a.m., both Nassau and Thüringen sighted the ship, which did not reply to signals and turned away to port. Thüringen opened fire on Black Prince. All its shots from the medium and light caliber shells were direct hits owing to the fact that the ships were only 1,000 yards apart. While it was a blazing inferno, Nassau, Ostfriesland, and Frederick der Grosse piled on with their own shots. It finally blew up and sank into the North Sea.

The Ardent was the final destroyer of the 4th Flotilla to meet the German line, be illuminated by the searchlights, and destroyed by a hailstorm of small caliber shell. None of the British destroyers had bothered to radio Commander-in-Chief Jellicoe about the action with the German Dreadnoughts. Had they done so, they might have altered the course of the battle and their comrades would not have died in vain. This battle of destroyers versus the Dreadnoughts was a mismatched fight from the start and turned into a massacre. And all the while, Jellicoe had no idea that Scheer was successfully cutting across the rear guard of his ships and making good his escape.

In the confusion of the night raids, four British destroyer units teamed up, making one flotilla of thirteen ships. Commander Goldsmith led the flotilla and though some of his ships had almost been hit by the misses from the previous engagements from the Germans, he mistakenly thought that it was friendly fire coming from British ships. He also mistook the line of German battleships to be British and set a course to position himself in front vanguard of the ships. Also, he was not aware of how many destroyers he now had behind him. Although he thought he was leading five ships, he had twelve behind him. Goldsmith increased his speed to thirty knots and led his destroyers to take up their position ahead of what he thought was Evan-Thomas' 5th Battle Squadron. This move would have worked had it not been for the length of the flotilla. Eleven of the thirteen ships passed to the starboard (right) side of the German battleships. The twelfth, Petard, was almost rammed by Westfalen, but it took evasive maneuvers and turned to fire its torpedoes at the ships from point blank range, unable to miss its mark, but it was out of torpedoes. It then had to turn its back on the Westfalen and run as fast as it could as the battleship opened up with all of its small caliber guns. It took many severe hits and a few casualties, but survived the close encounter. Turbulent was not so lucky. Turbulent found its way blocked by Westfalen and Rhineland, turned parallel to the ships to race around the bow of the leading ship, Westfalen, and join up with the flotilla. But the Westfalen spotted it and blew the destroyer out of the water with twenty-nine 6-inch guns and sixteen 3 ½- inch guns.

Turbulent was the last ship sunk in battle between the two fleets. It was between 1:45 a.m. and 2:00 a.m. Daybreak would not occur for another hour. Sheer's fleet had passed through the rear of the British fleet, though it was not home free yet. There would still be some minor skirmishes and one of the German destroyers would soon be sunk by a mine. There were still ships, such as the German ships Lutzow, Elbing, and Rostock that had to be abandoned and sunk. The major fighting was over now. German torpedo boats, which were highly trained for night attack, never found their enemy, so they did not figure in the night action. They had a standing order to return to Kiel (on the Baltic Sea) around the Skaw. They did not find the enemy and they returned home going north, instead of south. Obviously that drew them away from the whole battle scene.

Three hours later at 5:15 a.m., German time, Jellicoe learned that the High Sea Fleet had escaped.

The battle was over. He had lost his opportunity to destroy the German fleet. It was time for the two combatants to go home and lick their wounds. It was only upon turning back toward Britain that Beatty got around to telling Jellicoe of the loss of battle cruisers Queen Mary and Indefatigable. Jellicoe was shocked to hear this news, especially when he learned that they had been lost early in the battle and that his battleship commander failed to keep him informed of such a devastating loss to the British navy. It might have changed Jellicoe's attitude of pursuit and engagement in order to seek revenge for the losses. It was one of the frustrations on the British side in this battle.

Who was the Victor?

The Germans claimed the battle as a great victory for them. And in a sense it was. Very few people would have given the German fleet a fighting chance against the British. The naval battles of the war up to this point had gone very poorly for the Germans. Britain reigned supreme on the oceans and everyone thought it would remain so. In thirty years, the German navy had gone from being nonexistent to audaciously challenging the reigning king. And the Germans beat the British if one counts the number of ships that were sunk by each side. The Germans sank fourteen British ships and the British sank eleven German ships. Also the German newspapers were screaming that Trafalgar was undone. The naval world had been turned upside down, according to their propaganda; it especially seemed so when the first accounts came in. The Germans got to their home base sooner than the British so they had a relatively good idea of which ships had survived and which had not. The British, on the other hand, had to wait for the fleet to sail back across the North Sea, and then wait for the wounded stragglers to limp home. So the Germans were able to get their propaganda out sooner than the British did. The Germans were crowing about their great feat while Britain silently, dejectedly waited.

> To the British public, unaware that a sea battle had even taken place, it came as a bombshell. Within an hour, London newsboys were on the streets shouting, "Great Naval Disaster!" "Five British Battleships Lost!" Flags were lowered to half staff, stock exchanges closed, theaters darkened. Overseas, on breakfast tables in New York, Chicago, and San Francisco, the headlines read, "Britain Defeated at Sea!" "British Losses Great" "British Fleet Almost Annihilated!"[128]

Did the Battle of Jutland overturn Trafalgar? Yes, in a limited sense. Obviously, Britain had not wiped out the German Fleet. Far from it, the Germans gave as good as they got, and then some. But judging the battle on a mere physical count of lost ships and men misses the point. The British still maintained a great numerical superiority in ships over the Germans. And they were building new ships faster than Germany was. So, even though the Queen Mary and Indefatigable had been lost, there were already ships to take their place. Also there was no change in position of the two navies. Germany was still stuck in their corner of the North Sea and Britain still blocked their exit or commerce from coming into them. After the Britons got over the initial shock, they were able to see clearly.

> Will the shouting, flag wagging [German] people get any more of the copper, rubber, and cotton their government so sorely needs? Not a pound. Will meat and butter be cheaper in Berlin? Not by a pfennig. There is one test and only one, of victory. Who held the field of battle at the end of the fight?[129]

Even Scheer had lost much hope in the ability of the High Seas Fleet to make an impact on the war. In a confidential report to the Kaiser he stated his opinions about the naval war.

> With the exception of Derflinger, and Seydlitz, the High Seas Fleet will be ready by the middle of August for further strikes against the enemy...Should these future operations take favorable courses, we should be able to inflict serious damage on the enemy. Nevertheless, there can be no doubt that even the most successful outcome of a fleet action in this war will not force England to make peace. The disadvantages of our military-geographical position in relation to that of the British Isles, the enemy's great material superiority, cannot be compensated [for] by our Fleet to the extent where we shall be able to overcome the blockade or the British

Isles themselves—not even if the U-boats are made fully available for purely naval operations...A victorious end to the war within a reasonable time can only be achieved through defeat of the British economic life—that is, by using U-boats against British trade...[130]

So Scheer took a realistic look at the battle he had overseen and drew his conclusion, that the German navy could not defeat the British navy. Not only that, but he did not see that the Germans could bring an end to the blockade. He did not think they could do this even if the submarines were put to an effective use against British military ships. Still, in the Battle of Jutland, the submarines stood out as a total failure. Why Scheer did not see their failure, either before or after the action as something that could be remedied, is curious. Then he drew an odd conclusion. He stated that the U-boats could bring British economic life to a halt, thereby defeating the British as a whole. But if the submarines could not be used effectively against 150 ships stationed at a handful of ports throughout Britain, how would the U-boats destroy the commerce of tens of thousands of boats in a multitude of ports? Scheer's conclusion that Germany had to use unrestricted U-boat action against Britain ensured that Germany would lose. It was the one thing that would bring the United States into the war. The German admirals always seemed to be oblivious to the political implications of their actions.

There were some Germans who feared bringing the United States into the war. But after Russia had fallen in the winter of 1917, the Germans had no fear of America entering the battle. They thought they would be lounging in Paris when the Americans arrived. The Germans were close to being correct. The American General John J. Pershing had visited France before his troops arrived and spoke to an old friend from Kansas, a writer named Dorothy Canfield Fisher, who had been living in France for a few years. "There is a limit to what flesh and blood...can stand...and the French have just about reached that limit."[131]

This dose of gloom became acute when Pershing visited General Henri Philippe Petain, the acting commander of the French army, at his headquarters outside Paris. Petain gave him the details of General Neville's failed offensive in April. Neville had claimed to have a formula for smashing through the German army in forty-eight hours. Instead, the Germans, forewarned of his attack, had inflicted 120,000 casualties on the massed French infantry before they even reached the main defensive line. Whereupon the French army not only stopped fighting, it mutinied. One division attempted to march on Paris to overthrow the government. "Down with war!" they shouted. The rebellion swept swiftly through sixteen army corps until there were only two divisions that showed any readiness to fight...

Petain had raced up and down the battle line, arresting some of the more outspoken mutineers, placating the others by promising better food, more leaves, and an absolute end to mass attacks. "We must wait for the Americans," he said. If Wilson had not declared war on April 2, a German victory would have been inevitable. Instead, the mirage of a vast American army on its way enabled Petain to stabilize the situation, though he admitted to Pershing that many divisions were still mutinous and the whole army could be described in a state of "collective indiscipline."[132]

This was the situation to which the German military staff was blind. That even the hope of the United States riding to the rescue could give the beleaguered French and British armies the will to fight on. Of course, it had to be more than just a dream, and it was reality because on April 2nd President Wilson asked Congress for a declaration of war. They gave it to him by 80 percent margins because the Germans resumed unrestricted warfare, just what Scheer had claimed would end the war. After the German troops were freed up from the eastern front, the generals sided with the admirals in support of the U-boat attacks. Gottlieb von Jagow, the pro-American foreign minister was forced out; the ambassador to the United

States, Count Johann von Bernstorff, and the Chancellor Theobald von Bethmann-Hollweg were now isolated fighting the generals and the Admiralty in trying to persuade the Kaiser against antagonizing the United States. The diplomats lost the argument and Germany lost the war.

The situation changed drastically from May 1916 to the summer of 1918. The German army had held their ground until the Americans showed up. In the summer of 1918, the German juggernaut turned into a porous sieve. They were giving ground by the mile. The German sailors had been inactive after Jutland, except for the U-boats, and were infected by Communist propaganda. German sailors mutinied in 1918. The German navy had plans for one last offensive through the English Channel set for October 30, 1918. Admirals Scheer and Hipper "hoped that, in addition to salvaging the honor of the German navy, 'a tactical success might reverse the military position and avert surrender.'"[133]

But the military situation was not to be changed through this operation. The German sailors could read the tea leaves and see that the war was coming to an end. They jumped ship, and they refused to perform their duties by the hundreds. There was no hope for them as there had been for the French and British. The Americans had already joined the fight against them. Where the French could hold out for salvation from across the ocean, the Germans could not. There was nothing to convince the sailors to go back to stoking the engines. There was nothing to convince a German soldier to continue the fight in the face of Allied tanks and fresh troops. It became easier to surrender. When German troops in mass surrendered, it opened up huge holes in the front lines that made it possible for the allies to turn the flanks of their enemy and made it impossible for other German troops to hold their ground.

But this all goes back to Scheer's decision to resume unrestricted submarine warfare. If Scheer had not advised the Kaiser to take this step, it is very likely that Wilson would have dithered until it was too late. Even if some of the pro-Entente politicians and newspapers were clamoring for the United States to go to war, how could Wilson have convinced a disinterested Congress to send American boys to die for Europe, if there was no threat to the United States? By resuming the unrestricted submarine warfare, American shipping, especially on the East Coast, was in danger. But Germany had threatened the Southwest of the United States as well; these Americans were now directly affected. The combination of these two threats directly affected everyone in the country. It could literally be called the political blunder of the century. If the Germans had honored American thoughts about freedom of the seas (which Bernstorff, Bethmann-Hollweg, and Jagow had wanted to do) even to their own detriment, how could Wilson have asked for a declaration of war? If America had not joined the war, Petain's words would have been empty propaganda that the French troops would have seen right through. They might have marched on Paris and forced surrender.

What would have happened if Scheer had not sent out his U-boats so early in mid May of 1916? What if they had gone out just a day or two earlier than the ships so that they could take their positions outside of the British naval ports? There would have been no problem in missing the signal as there was before the Battle of Jutland. What would have happened to Beatty's forces if Jellicoe had been delayed by one hour because of successful U-boat attacks that day? Or what if Beatty's ships had been hindered and slowed? And if the U-boats were aware that the battle had been engaged, might they have been ready for the returning wounded ships and made an easy prey of them?

These are impossible questions to answer, because it did not happen. What did happen was that the German navy put up a valiant fight against a superior British navy but could not beat them. It seemed like Scheer gave up the fight because of one bitter outcome. He resorted to a form of warfare that in strict Mahanian terms was worrisome but not effective in defeating an enemy. It antagonized a neutral, the United States of America, and brought it into the war. The army had no concern for the results with which they would ultimately have to deal—that is, giving hope to almost defeated armies and then fighting the fresh armies of the Americans. By threatening the United States through U-boat warfare and by threatening its sovereignty over the southwest, Germany brought in a new enemy that it need not to have antagonized. The Germans were on the verge of winning the war, and they threw it away.

As a result of the Kaiser allowing the U-boat activity to resume, he lost the war. He was forced to abdicate; the Weimar Republic was set up by the Entente powers and lasted only as long as the German people put up with a government that was not their own. This and the Treaty of Versailles allowed the evil Adolf Hitler to come to power. The outcome of WWI set the stage for all the events of the twentieth century. And the most important thing that this book is looking at, it established one fact. That is the British Empire alone could not settle Europe's affairs. The United States, like it or not, had become entangled with the state of European affairs. Could the United States have lived with a German-dominated Europe? It probably could. Britain could not. Because the German generals and admirals underestimated the ability and the effect of the United States' entry into the war, they threw caution to the wind and set the course for the century. It has been called the American Century. One might also call it the first century of the United States of Empire.

Chapter Seven
Propaganda

The British won the First World War in the opening hours after they declared war on Germany. They did so without firing a shot. There was no overwhelming cannonade to soften up the target, no machine gun nests set up, no new prototype tanks, no submarine attack, and no mustard gas drifting across enemy lines. No, on August 5, 1914, the British dispatched a working vessel into the North Sea. It was a cable ship sent out to the Dutch coastline. Its job was to sever the transatlantic cables that connected Germany with the outside world. There was "one to Brest in France, another to Vigo, in Spain, a third to Tenerife, in North Africa, and two to New York."[134]

This cut Germany off from the world outside of Europe.

What was the purpose of cutting these lines? How would this action aid the Entente cause in the war? One thing it did was to allow Britain to win the propaganda war from the very first day it entered the conflict. Germany never caught up with Britain in this aspect of the war. Germany fought Britain and France to a stalemate on French territory, forced Russia into a separate peace, and drew even with the British in the North Sea. But they never even came close to Britain in its ability to present its case to the outside world, especially the United States.

In the early years, Britain did not want actual military help from the United States. That would have been an admission that the empire was not strong enough to handle the war effort on its own. They did want to keep the flow of arms, material, food, and clothing coming into the Entente powers. And Britain certainly wanted to block these same items from reaching Germany. The blockade of the North Sea cut off the flow of goods to Germany and other surrounding countries. But severing the cables could easily have been missed or ignored as an important factor of the war. Yet, this was singly important.

Early in the war, the Germans were accused of atrocities in Belgium. These atrocity stories were released right after a German submarine sank the Cunard Lines Lusitania, a civilian ocean liner. It must be noted that this ship was impressed by the British Admiralty.

> Her (the Lusitania) armament was installed on September 17 (1914), and she entered the Admiralty fleet as an armed auxiliary cruiser, and was so entered on the Cunard Ledgers. The Lusitania was ready for war.[135]

Over 1,000 people were killed including 128 Americans in the icy waters of the North Atlantic when the Lusitania was sunk. The actual sinking of the Cunard Lines cruiser helped to confirm the propaganda, and it increased the intensity of the sinking. It was an easy jump to go from the sinking of the Lusitania to the false accusations from the war zone. The Germans were accused of systematic destruction of hospitals, of torturing prisoners, of raping and killing nuns, of killing or maiming children, even of tossing babies from bayonet to bayonet for sport. The truth of the matter was that they did execute snipers, or if the sniper could not be found in the vicinity of the attack, there were instances of the Germans randomly picking a man to be executed if the sniper was not handed over. But as for the rest, it was pure propaganda issued to make it look like Germany was destroying all of Western Civilization, and for the most part, it was believed. Throughout the war, this propaganda did its job and convinced the world, especially the United States, of the barbarism of the "Huns." It was only after the conclusion of the war that the truth came out showing that the world and especially the United States had been lied to about German savagery. This would haunt Britain twenty years later when they again needed help from their former colonists. But once bitten, twice shy, the United States proved very hard to be swayed until it was physically attacked on its own territory.

In WWI, the propaganda war affected the war at sea as well. According to international law, it was legal to blockade a city during a war, but not the whole country. And that blockade was not supposed to be imposed upon neutral countries. Yet Britain imposed a blockade upon the whole North Sea. Though the blockade was illegal, it was effective. It helped to starve the German populous. Just as with any siege, if the people were starved long enough, it would weaken their ability and will to fight.

United States Secretary of State William Jennings Bryan, the most politically influential Democrat after the president, wanted the United States to be truly neutral. As such, the country would have to insist that Britain end its blockade of the North Sea. His undersecretary, Robert Lansing, had other ideas.

> "In dealing with the British government there was always in my mind the conviction that we would ultimately become an ally of Great Britain, and that it would not do, therefore, to let our controversies reach a point where diplomatic correspondence gave place to action," Lansing said.[136]

Lansing's sympathy lay with Britain and the Entente powers. He did not want to see Germany win, nor draw even.

As such, he had a very pro-British attitude as opposed to his superior, Secretary Bryan. Lansing constantly undercut Bryan, which is the main reason Bryan resigned his post in June 1915. He did so because he was being ignored by the president who took the advice of Bryan's underling while the secretary proposed strict neutrality. The break came over the sinking of the Lusitania. Before its sinking, the Germans had complained to Bryan that the British were using civilian commercial liners to transport troops and war material to the front. This, if true, would have been a serious violation of international maritime law. It also forced the Germans into a no win position in the propaganda war. They could allow the boats to pass safely, thus giving the Entente powers unlimited supplies to go to the front, or attack the ocean liners as well as merchant ships and endure the wrath of the neutral countries. So Bryan passed the German protests to the president who did not act on the information. This situation had occurred before the Lusitania had sailed on its doomed cruise.

After the Lusitania was sunk, Lansing sent a communiqué to the German ambassador concerning the ship. The Germans had told the undersecretary of state that the Lusitania was an armed merchant vessel carrying war material. Lansing denied this in his statement.

> Of the facts alleged in your Excellency's note, if true, the government of the United States would have been bound to have taken official cognizance. Performing its duties as a neutral power and enforcing its national laws, it was its duty to see to it that the Lusitania was not armed for offensive action, that she was not serving as a transport, that she did not carry cargo prohibited by the statutes of the United States, and if in fact she was a naval vessel of Great Britain, she should not receive clearance as a merchantman. It performed this duty. It enforced its statutes with scrupulous vigilance through its regularly constituted officials and it is able therefore to assure the Imperial German Government that it has been misinformed.[137]

Bryan refused to sign the document because he knew that it was a lie. The Lusitania had been pressed into the service of the British navy from the beginning of the war. Her sister ship, the Mauretania, had just delivered Canadian troops bound for the front. The Lusitania was carrying war material also bound for the front, in direct contravention of international law for a civilian liner. And the most damning of all, the president made no attempt to investigate the allegations from the Germans that the ship was carrying munitions. The president ignored the warnings and allowed 128 Americans and over 1,000 other passengers to sail to their deaths.

> Wilson, while he privately agreed with Bryan, in his reply expressed worry over Lansing's point that if American citizens were to be warned, the administration should have done so at the time it issued its note to Germany holding that country to "strict accountability." To issue such a warning now would be a direct admission that the government failed in its duty.[138]

Now, even though it was known that Britain was illegally imposing its blockade, this information did not affect them negatively. Britain never received much bad press because of it. On the other hand, Germany was lambasted in the European and American press. They were castigated for overrunning the tiny, free, and democratic Belgians (though Belgians enjoyed as much democracy as Germans did). The Germans were falsely accused of atrocities as bad as the Belgians had committed in the Congo a decade earlier. They were depicted as modern-day Vikings in their entire cruel wrath. Of course, Kaiser Wilhelm's statement back in 1900 about the German army being feared as greatly as Attila the Hun did not help Germany's image. But just because the kaiser had a bombastic mouth did not mean that the German army was not pursing its military goals in a professional manner.

It did not matter that the Germans were or were not committing atrocities in Belgium. What mattered was what the British press said was happening. The American press picked up on the "Germans as Huns" theme and ran with it. It is hard to illicit sympathy for a nation's cause if people think that the country is a barbaric baby killer. Recent United States history can show the effects of bad publicity about troops. In the Vietnam War, United States troops were wrongly blamed as baby killers and the slaughterers of whole villages. The pictures from one such incident at Mai Lai painted an entire army for decades. Negative publicity like that increased the lack of support for the war. United States troops pulled out, and South Vietnam was crushed by the Communist North Vietnamese. A similar thing happened with Germany. From the outset of the war they were pictured as the baby-killing destroyers of Europe. They were never able to change that image. As such they were never able to get the help they needed to break the blockade to bring in the goods they needed for their population and the war effort. Their people starved as the troops slogged on in the battlefields. They were never able to win the propaganda war. They were never able to win the hearts and minds of people in the United States, and it was the United States that was supplying Britain and France with war material and food for their efforts.

Some would say that the submarine attacks by the Germans showed that they were barbaric baby killers. Yes, they sank ocean liners as well as military vessels. But the Germans knew that Britain and the Entente powers were using civilian liners to transport troops and war material.

Now how could any modern Christian nation engage in the wholesale murder of innocents as they crossed the ocean? The question can be reversed. How could Britain hide behind women and children as they transported war material? How was it that Britain could impose the slow death of Germans with their blockade? The answer is simple: because they could, because it was effective, and this was war. War is not pretty, war is not neat. There will always be civilian casualties in war whenever it occurs. The way Germany, including its populous, saw the submarine attacks, it was fair reprisal for the blockade. And they were under the misguided idea that it would help them win the war.

The German U-boat attacks of Britain's waterborne commerce were self-destructive; it galvanized the British people to see the war as an attack on the whole of the British nation, rather than a foreign fight in the land of an ancient foe, France. It reaffirmed the most dire fears stated by the warrior class that the British Isles themselves would come under attack if the Germans won the war. So it redoubled the war effort in Britain. People could do without coffee or tea or sugar. They could conserve on whatever necessities were in short supply and do without the luxury items. It turned out that the British were a hardier stock than the Germans had thought. One other curious note is this: if the British blockade of the North Sea did not bring the German war machine to a screeching halt, then why did the Germans think that a similar action against the British would stop their war machine? Maybe it was because the submarine was a new weapon and the Germans thought they could revolutionize warfare and rewrite Mahan's book on sea warfare. As it turned out, the unrestricted submarine warfare only underscored Mahan's ideas.

> It is not the taking of individual ships or convoys, be they few or many, that strikes down the power of a nation; it is the possession of the overbearing power on the sea which drives the enemies flag from it; or allows it to appear only as a fugitive; and which, by controlling the great common, closes the highways by which commerce moves to and from the enemy's shores.[139]

Some people are drawn into the idea that Germany's unrestricted submarine warfare did negate Mahan's idea about commerce destruction. It is true that the monthly amount of tonnage sunk by the Germans had risen to 800,000 tons in the spring of 1917. The Germans had assumed that six months in a row above the 600,000-ton mark would break England. Those who argue this point seem oblivious to two facts: one, the submarine attacks were sure to, and did, bring the United States into the war; two, the convoy system, which the Americans had to convince the British to implement, provided great safety for the transport ships and made things much more dangerous for the U-boats. Then the German U-boats were chased out of the oceans by the greater naval power of the combined United States and Great Britain, just as Mahan had written. The attacks made sea travel more dangerous, but it did not win the war.

There is another question about the submarine warfare that must be looked at. Should not the submarine have been used against the military ships that were imposing the blockade? Well they were, but they had a mixed effect. In September 1914, three old armored cruisers were sunk as they patrolled along the Dutch Coast. Again, not long afterward, two British ships were sunk as they were escorting a Norwegian coal shipment. These attacks came early in the war. The accompanying ships had gone to the aid of their distressed comrades thinking that they had hit a mine. So they were attacked as they tried to help pull the sailors out of the water.

Now these attacks did not raise widespread claims of barbaric Huns on the prowl. Yes, these are sneaky attacks, especially when one ship is going to the aid of the other wounded ship. But these are warrior ships, fully armed and intent on sinking and killing the submarine if they get the chance. Sneak attacks are the essence of military action. The only time an army or navy wants to telegraph its actions is when they know they are vastly superior and want to intimidate an enemy into submission without losing any of their own men or equipment. So just because the submarine is sneaky or hidden by nature of its function, it will not bring an uproar. In fact, First Sea Lord Jackie Fisher extolled the use of the submarine to the shock of many a British admiral who did not like the sneaky "un-British" attacks.

But the submarines were not as successful in finding enemy military targets as they were in finding civilian ones. At the Battle of Jutland, the only major sea battle in the WWI, the submarines failed at their mission. Ten German submarines had been sent to wait for the attack by the British High Seas Fleet. The submarines did not hear the radio messages informing them that the battle was soon to be engaged because they were hiding deep under the North Sea's surface. So the British ships were able to leave port unmolested soon after radio message tipped off the attack. Since the action of the Battle of Jutland took place on May 31st and June 1st, at the end of the fuel allotment for the submarines, the subs were already leaving from their locations as the British ships were limping back into port after the battle. Two U-boats fired on British ships, but the ships were able to take evasive action and avoid the torpedoes. Also, destroyers had been sent out to screen for the ships as they came back to port. So even during the greatest sea battle of WWI, the submarines turned out to be out of time and ineffective.

This should not have blinded the German Admiralty to their potential use, but it did. They still could have used the submarine in a strictly military use, naval ship to naval ship, but the German admirals were hell-bent on inflicting as much damage on Britain as a whole, to demoralize and starve the British people into defeat, just as Britain was doing to them with the blockade.

From a propaganda standpoint, the unrestricted U-boat warfare lost the war for Germany. From the perspective of people in the United States, the U-boat attacks verified everything that was being said about the evil Huns. And there were many in the United States that wanted the country to enter the war from the first day it started. Former presidents Theodore Roosevelt and William Howard Taft were two of the warriors clamoring for the United States to get involved to fight the Germans. In fact, all four of Roosevelt's sons joined the fight in the British military long before the United States declared war. The U-boat attacks against civilian liners just gave the Anglophiles and the Francophiles more ammunition to use to support their cause.

At the same time, there were representatives from the Northern Neutrals who were complaining to President Wilson about the illegality of the British blockade. Not to mention that the blockade was also impeding United States trade with those same neutrals, causing many businesses to lose money. German sympathizers could point to the fact that it was Britain who was limiting the freedom of the sea. This could have been a strong propaganda point in favor of the Germans—especially since the War of 1812 was fought against Britain because of the idea of freedom of the seas. But the pictures of survivors and especially pictures of the coffins from doomed ocean liners screamed louder than stories of shortages during wartime, even when those shortages led to slow death in Germany.

Still, even with the knowledge of the submarine warfare, the United States was not ready to get into the war. It would take much more because Wilson was not willing to fight for freedom of the seas. A different president, Roosevelt or Taft, would have claimed that as sufficient reason for going to war. But any president would have had to get approval from the United States Congress, and they might not have voted for it any earlier than it did in 1917.

There were millions of German-Americans who did not want to fight against Germany. Then there were people of Irish descent, who had been forced out of their homeland by the actions of the British government; they saw the Great War as a fight to preserve the British Empire. In fact, when the United States entered the war, Irish newspapers in the United States had to be censored because of their anti-British slant. Another claim of the anti-war people was that if the United States went to war, it would only be to aid John Pierpont Morgan and his business interests. There was no great grassroots clamor for war before 1917. Also, the war was not an issue that would affect the far west much. But for Anglophiles, Francophiles, or those doing business with Europe, the war meant a great deal.

At the beginning of the war, the German troops had moved quickly across Belgium into France. In the confusion, some of the news reporters had found themselves in the no-man's-land. They reported and filed stories free of any censorship by the British or French. They reported huge losses by the Entente powers. They wrote of blistering, thunderous, artillery barrages by the Germans decimating Belgian strongholds. They reported the truth about the war. So the British and the French had to put a stop to it.

> The American Irwin Cobb saw the destruction at Maubeuge (Fort), and reported on the phenomenal power of the new German heavy guns (ironically, much of the damage was done by the heavy Minenwerfer of the Pioniere, but the big guns grabbed the imagination). The English reporter Fyfe reported accurately—that the BEF (British Expeditionary Force) had been routed in the field and was in full retreat. It was the last serious reporting of the war. Reported or no, the bad news continued. By the end of August (1914) the news of the capitulation of the Belgian forts had spread, and the leveling of the Maubeuge Fort created sort of a panic. The whole line of fortification along the frontier simply unraveled.[140]

If the public in the United States had been given the truth about Germany's stunning early victories, would they have thought differently about the war? Would they have decided to accept a German dominated Europe? Would they have been shocked into aiding the Entente powers sooner, rather than later?

The British propaganda with the United States actually began with the rapprochement of the United Kingdom and the United States in the 1890s. Up to that point, the United States and Britain had rubbed against each other in disputes along the Canadian/United States border and in South America as well. There was also a lively competition that included the French over who was going to be the first to build the Panama Canal. But it was a South American border dispute that almost brought the United States and Britain to blows.

In the summer of 1895, British Prime Minister Salisbury was contemplating a communiqué from President Grover Cleveland, described as a "Twenty-one inch gun note." The communiqué demanded that the United Kingdom via their colony British Guiana and Venezuela accept the arbitration of the United States over their border dispute. The communiqué went further, stating that Britain was in violation of the Monroe Doctrine. Of course this was a document that no European power took seriously.

> "For a few days, war with Britain seemed possible," a young Winston Churchill recalled as he was traveling through the United States. "I was returning from a visit to Cuba via America at this time and remember vividly looking at the ships off the English coast and wondering which one would be our transport to Canada. But the first patriotic outburst in America soon gave way to more sober feelings. In Britain opinion reacted less violently. At the height of the crisis news arrived of the Kaiser's telegram to President Kruger in South Africa, congratulating him on the repulse of the Jameson Raid...British wrath turned against Germany rather than the United States.[141]

Public reaction in Britain to the kaiser's telegram dwarfed the reaction to the threat from the United States over Venezuela and British Guiana. According to Churchill, the British and the United States government started working together instead of against each other from that point forward. Germany, apparently, was a much more imminent threat to Britain than the United States was. This is an interesting point, because both countries went on a naval building program to rival Britain and both were expanding their territories throughout the world. But it was Germany that posed a threat to Britain.

In May of 1901, three months after he had taken office as a member of Parliament, Churchill spoke to his fellow members about Anglo-American relationships. "Evil would be the counselors, dark would be the day when we embarked on that most foolish, futile, and fatal of all wars—a war with the United States."[142]

This is the same Churchill who once had mused about which ship he would be sailing on to go do battle with the United States. But that was five years previous. He had since been a prisoner of war, escaped, fought in South Africa, and toured the United States on a speaking tour. He quit thinking about doing battle with the United States but instead looked at the possible greatness of what could be done together. Of course, Churchill was half American; his mother was American, his father English nobility. It is curious that Churchill became a leading proponent of building strong relations with the United States before, during, and after the two world wars, basically for his whole political life.

One of the concrete steps taken by Britain to build good relations with the United States occurred when France failed at its attempt to build a canal across the Panama isthmus. Britain bowed out of the competition and released the United States from the Clayton-Bulwer Treaty of 1850 to which both had agreed. This treaty prevented one from building a canal without the agreement of the other. When it was enacted it was good for the United States; it prevented Britain from building the canal and gaining a foothold in Panama (at that time a part of Columbia). By 1900, the treaty was a limitation on President Roosevelt's ideas of American power and expansion.

> By 1900 the positions were reversed; this reversal is what provoked Roosevelt's remarks during the period about unilateral abrogation if the British didn't bow out gracefully. But the British did, in keeping with their budding hands-across-the-Atlantic campaign.[143]

This is more than just propaganda. Great Britain had realized that the era of "Splendid Isolation" was over.

On May 13, 1898, he (Joseph Chamberlain, the British
Colonial Minister) spoke in Birmingham Town Hall:
"Since the Crimean War nearly fifty years ago, the policy
of this country has been strict isolation. We had no allies.
I am afraid we had no friends...We stand alone."[144]

The British saw that they were going to need friends in the
times to come. Some in the British government, including
Chamberlain, wanted to reach out to Germany and befriend
them. And when the kaiser was most amenable toward
developing good strong relations with Britain, his ministers
advised him against it. They stated that time was on Germany's
side, and that Britain would have nowhere to go. Many in the
German government thought that Britain and France would
never be able to patch things up and ally themselves together;
they thought the same about Britain and Russia. So the kaiser
was advised to stay aloof when he should have been drawing
close.

The German ambassador to England, Count Paul von
Hatzfeldt, sent a message to Frederick von Holstein, the
First Counselor of the Foreign Affairs, about Chamberlain's
overtures to German friendship.

"You and I are entirely in agreement that the idea of
an alliance is premature," Hatzfeldt had begun his
message to Holstein, knowing how Chamberlain's ideas
were viewed in the Wilhelmstrasse (from where foreign
policy was directed.) The German view continues to be
that Germany could afford to wait; as time passed and
Britain's difficulties increased, she would pay more for
the security of a German alliance.[145]

It was Germany that would pay for playing hard to get.
Its friendship with Britain drifted off. Its relations with the
United States were sometimes contentious. The United States
and Germany almost engaged in a naval battle in a fight off
of the Samoan Islands in the South Pacific in 1889 until a
huge storm drove the armed ships apart. There was no overt

reaching out as there had been between Britain and the United States.

During the First World War, Germany made a huge mistake dealing with the American people. The military staff had become convinced that unrestricted submarine warfare would bring Britain to its knees and end the war in six months. At the risk of being redundant, one needs to consider this idea with extreme incredulousness. Britain had been enforcing a blockade on Germany for almost three years, yet Germany was still fighting very well. Britain had a much larger maritime fleet than Germany had submarines. The generals and the admirals all knew that unrestricted submarine attacks were the one thing that could bring the United States into the war. They did not care because they thought the war would be over in six months, and it would be too late for the United States to take any action. Of course, they had been saying this since August of 1914. Opposed to the military was the diplomatic core, the ambassador to the United States, Johann Count von Bernstorff, Foreign Minister Gottlieb von Jagow, and Chancellor Theobald von Bethmann-Hollweg. They saw the folly of attacking the commerce, especially of the United States, and they tried their best to stop Germany from using this tactic. This was the one thing that could force Wilson's hand into joining the war, and they saw this as doom for Germany. But once the war in the east was finished, the generals had no fear. Now, with 800,000 fresh veteran troops coming from the eastern front, it looked like Germany could finally win. The military had won the day, or so they thought. They would have their extra troops and the United States could do as they wished, the generals did not care.

On January 31, 1917, Count von Bernstorff, the German ambassador to the United States, had to inform Secretary of State Lansing that unrestricted submarine warfare would resume; he was shaken to the core. He knew that this would mean that the United States would enter the war soon thereafter and he regretted the decision that his superiors had made and regretted that he had to deliver it. Von Jagow was replaced by Arthur Zimmermann as foreign minister. It was his infamous telegram that turned the tide in the United States. In Zimmermann's telegram sent to Mexico, he informed the Mexican government that Germany would support it financially if, upon the entry of the United States into the European war, Mexico would invade the United States. This arrangement was nothing new for Europe. Britain and France had paid other countries to fight to advance their own cause. But to the people of the United States, this was backstabbing treachery. This telegram, if true, would change the outlook of the war for the country. They were now being threatened at home. Mexico was being baited to attack the United States. The fears this generated were real. Much of the southwestern part of the United States was once Mexican territory. Texas had fought its own war of independence from Mexico in 1836. The states of California, Arizona, New Mexico, Utah, and Nevada had been a part of Mexico that the United States annexed in the Mexican-American War of 1846-1848. Just recently, General John J. Pershing had ended a military hunt for Pancho Villa in that went deep into northern Mexico. Villa had attacked the United States' border town of Columbus, New Mexico, burning it and killing almost two dozen people. Pershing went south of the border to try to capture him. The Americans who at one time had the least to fear if Germany had won the European war, now had a vested interest in the conflict, and in seeing to it that Germany was defeated.

The telegram was intercepted by the British and when the press first got news of it, it seemed so unbelievable that many people dismissed it as a piece of British propaganda. Zimmermann himself ended the doubt when he claimed responsibility for sending it. Any pro-German support ended that day. So the war had come home. Mexico refused to aid the Germans by invading the United States. When the unrestricted submarine warfare resumed and a couple of American ships were destroyed, President Wilson asked

Congress for a declaration of war. The opposition from the western states was gone. This was no longer a war to save J.P. Morgan's investments, nor to save the British Empire. Germany had now threatened all of the United States. The votes were overwhelming. The Senate and the House of Representatives both passed the declaration by over 80 percent majorities.

> Berlin, January 19, 1917
> On the first of February we intend to begin submarine warfare unrestricted. In spite of this, it is our intention to endeavor to keep neutral the United States of America.
> If this attempt is not successful, we propose an alliance on the following basis with Mexico: That we shall make war together and together make peace. We shall give general financial support, and it is understood that Mexico is to reconquer the lost territory in New Mexico, Texas, and Arizona. The details are left to you for settlement....
> You are instructed to inform the President of Mexico of the above in the greatest confidence as soon as it is certain that there will be an outbreak of war with the United States and suggest that the President of Mexico, on his own initiative, should communicate with Japan suggesting adherence at once to this plan; at the same time, offer to mediate between Germany and Japan.
> Please call to the attention of the President of Mexico that the employment of ruthless submarine warfare now promises to compel England to make peace in a few months.
> Zimmerman
> (Secretary of State)[146]

Von Jagow never would have sent such a telegram. He was one of the Germans who saw the potential of the United States and would not have taunted America in such a fashion. But Zimmermann did, and he was the foreign minister because generals Ludendorff and Hindenburg forced the kaiser to dismiss von Jagow.

Early in 1918, Germany almost won the war. They almost pushed into Paris. They were forty miles short of the goal.

What would the situation have been if there had not been one million fresh United States troops in France? How much thinner would the Entente's lines have been? How much more worn out? How dispirited would they have been if they knew that the United States was going to continue to sit on the sidelines and berate both sides for their mindless slaughter while making money off the war trade? Would the French armies have given up? Would the British have gone home?

Germany never cared about winning the hearts and minds of the people in the United States. They never really countered the "evil Hun" charges that the Entente had leveled at them. When the few men in the German government who respected the thoughts of the United States were jettisoned or marginalized, Germany lost the war. Germany then became, in the minds of Americans, the evil Hun that must be stopped at all costs.

When the First World War broke out, it was easy for Britain to paint itself as the protector of democracy and freedom. After all, there were many natural attachments between the United States and the United Kingdom. The American form of government was drawn directly from the British form, with slight variations. The United States was not the birth place of democracy. It was imported from Britain. Although the two countries had fought two wars against each other, the familial and commercial ties were deep. Great Britain had always been the best trading partner of the United States. Severing the transatlantic cables prevented Germany from getting its side of the story out. This was especially true about how the war was going. The British and the French were determined that they would not let the world know that they were being decimated in the battles; they did not tell the world how close the great fortress of Verdun came to falling in the first few months of the war. They would not state that they were losing up to 80 percent of their men in many campaigns. If they had, the logical assumption by the United States might have been to get on the good side of the eventual winner.

It must be remembered that despite the bluster of the kaiser, and despite the best efforts of the Entente propaganda, Germany had a parliamentary form of government. It was not as liberal as Britain's or the United States' governments. The chancellor held the most parliamentary power, the emperor held the sole control over the army, but the Reichstag had power over the spending for the military.

> The Reichstag, (lower house) elected by universal suffrage, represented a concession to the spirit of mass democracy and symbolized the unity of the Empire. It shared legislative power with the Bundesrat (upper house) as well as the right to review annually all non-military expenditure. In 1874 Bismarck grudgingly allowed the Reichstag to review army grants every seven years; in practice the effectiveness of the concession was reduced, for as the Reichstags were only triennial, only alternative Reichstags could exercise control over military expenditures, and significantly imperial ministers were not accountable to the Reichstag.[147]

Germany had universal male suffrage. Britain did not. The United States did, unless you were black and lived in the South. So Germany was not the strict authoritarian dictatorship that it was painted to be. France was a democracy, but was it a democracy worth fighting for?

The French Revolution had replaced the monarchy in 1789. This created the French Republic. It failed within years just as the Europeans had predicted that the United States would fail. The French Republic was replaced by the dictatorship under Napoleon Bonaparte. The dictatorship became an empire when Napoleon established himself as the ruler over Europe. Napoleon was beaten in imperial wars; he was deposed, came back, and was beaten again, this time for good. The monarchy then made a comeback, but the king was chased out for a republic again. Then in 1848, Louis Napoleon Bonaparte (Napoleon III), a nephew of Napoleon Bonaparte, won election as the president of the

French Republic. The presidency was a four-year term and limited to one stay in office. This restriction had been put in place by Louis' enemies to thwart what they saw as his imperial tendencies. That attempt failed when he established himself as emperor and abolished the presidency. France now became an empire again. The Prussians beat Louis' forces in 1870 in the Franco-Prussian War and Louis was forced from the throne. The empire then became a republic again.

> No French government during these years enjoyed authority or longevity. Between 1873 and 1898 the British Foreign Office had negotiated with twenty-four French Foreign Ministers and twelve French Ambassadors in London. During one five year span, 1881-1886, ten French governments rose and fell. Although the years 1898 to 1905 saw six more French governments come and go, the Ministry of Foreign Affairs remained in the hands of a single man, Theophile Declasse.[148]

The only thing that held the government together was the foreign minister. It was Declasse's goal to form an alliance with the British to help save France in the eventuality of another war with Germany. There is little doubt that the French would have fallen as quickly as it did in 1870, if the British troops had not supplied the extra men in the battles of WWI. The same point can be made about the probability that Germany would have won the war if the United States had not entered it in 1917.

What good did it do for the United States to step in and help end the war in Europe? Was the United States duped into preserving the status quo in Europe by joining the war effort? Was the United States fighting to defend democracy in France? Well, Germany was a parliamentary monarchy as was Great Britain. All of Germany was behind the war until the very end. The German populous even supported the unrestricted submarine warfare because they knew first hand that Britain was trying to starve them out of the war. Which French government was the United States supporting?

It is often stated that the United States owed a debt of gratitude to the French for its aid to the fledgling country in the American Revolution. But Louis XVI did not help the fledgling United States because he believed in the rule of democracy. Far from it; he was a ruling monarch. He did so to damage his enemy, Great Britain. He wanted to pry off a part of the English Empire, just as Britain had peeled off Canada from France. And if the United States had waited for France to win a decisive battle, as France did with the Continental Army, before committing to the war effort, then Germany would have won the European conflict. (It was the victory at Saratoga, New York, led by General Benedict Arnold, before he became a traitor, which swung Louis XVI into the American war.) The king was helping a strong contender, not propping up a dying image. It may be that there was a debt of gratitude owed from the American Revolution. But an undeclared war during John Adams' presidency between the United States and France cleared that debt. The Treaty of Paris signed in 1798 at the end of this war exonerated our old war debt. Then in 1803, President Thomas Jefferson paid an enormous amount of money, $15 million, to France for the Louisiana Purchase. That money went to Napoleon Bonaparte and helped cover the costs of his battles on the Continent. Did that money help to cover the debt of gratitude? Besides, nations do not go to war for sentimental reasons. The reason must be based in real-world politics, or the lives lost will have been wasted. If the United States and Britain were propping up a weak and dying nation, then it stands to reason that they would have to do it again. This was the case with France. It had to be propped up in 1917 and again in 1941.

As for Great Britain, it went to war to preserve its empire, which after two world wars, faded fast. In one aspect it faded because of its own propaganda. After fighting in two wars to save the world for democracy, it would be very hypocritical of them to deny full democracy to its empire. If the German empire had grown, there might have been colonial wars between Great Britain and Germany, as there had been with France throughout the years. But if WWI had ended early with a German victory, Europe might have avoided the slaughter of millions. France's foreign empire probably would have been carved up. But the British Empire could have survived. By bringing the United States into the war, the propaganda had to emphasize that this was a war to help democracy, not empire. But it was always about the empire. As First Sea Lord Jackie Fisher stated, the empire rested upon the British navy. Any navy that could threaten the British navy could in turn threaten the Empire.

> "On the British fleet rests the British Empire," Fisher said, "and only a congenital idiot with criminal tendencies would permit any tampering with the maintenance of our supremacy."[149]

Germany was building a navy that could rival the British navy. That meant that it could rival the British Empire. Fisher was not going to wait for the day that Germany had actual parity or was attacking the British Isles or Australia. He was going to take the threat out before it became too big. Also, this helps to explain why Britain could not call an end to the war once it bogged down in France. Why allow the slaughter of hundreds of thousands of young men to go on for years? It was because Germany had held onto all of Belgium and parts of northern France since the second month of the war. Britain was not going to allow Germany to be able to base itself out of Antwerp and be able to attack Britain from there. Also, if Germany's territory included all of the land that it occupied from October 1914 through July 1918, Britain would have faced a European colossus that stretched from well beyond the Baltic States and Ukraine to Antwerp on the North Sea near the English Channel. The economic and military might of such a populous, productive, military nation would have overwhelmed Britain by its mere existence. Britain could not allow it to be birthed, it had to be aborted. In the process of aborting this German colossus, the British Empire was badly wounded. And the seeds were sown for a second more evil war that would destroy Europe, Germany, and the British Empire.

It is not hard to understand how many in the United States had come to the idea between the two world wars that Uncle Sam was really Uncle Sap. It had been drawn into a war to prop up a weak and dying nation, France, and to preserve the status quo of the British Empire.

> These war moves were of profound interest to the American people. There was a general feeling that our well-intentioned entry into the First World War had been ill-advised, that none of the grandiose moral objectives had been achieved, that all the talk about ending war forever and bringing a reign of peace through the League (of Nations) had been a ghastly failure, that our allies had taunted us for making money out of the war, asked for cancellation of the war debts and called us Uncle Shylock. There was a feeling that we had been drawn into the war through ill-considered day-to-day decisions made by the administration then in power and that we had been lured in by permitting ourselves to tap the resources of war as an opportunity for business prosperity.[150]

This war to save democracy only preserved the status quo for twenty years. Since the United States had been the deciding factor in the Great War, there is no way that it could refrain from joining the next. But this idea was lost when it was needed the most, when Germany started to rearm itself for another major war.

Chapter Eight
The United States Enters the War

As the war bogged down in Western Europe, the Entente powers did everything possible to bring in other combatants to keep Germany distracted so they couldn't strike the decisive blow on the Entente forces. They bribed Romania and Italy to their side with either monetary payments or the promise of territory at the end of the war. Italy had initially been a part of the German-Austrian-Italian Triple Alliance, but refused to be dragged into the war in 1914. The alliance had been a defensive one and Italy did not consider the Austrian retaliation for the murder of Archduke Ferdinand a defensive action. So they bowed out of the alliance. They were never a strong part of the alliance, distrustful of Austria as the two of them had fought over bordering territories for centuries. Also, Italy feared Britain's naval strength. Their extensive coastline along the whole peninsula made them venerable to a seaborne attack. Now, with the hopes of being on the winning side, they dreamed of attaining even more Austrian territory.

The Austrian army was nowhere as well prepared for war as the Germans were and it turned out they needed much help.

In almost every campaign they entered into alone, they lost. They were hard pressed by Russia, and even Serbia handily beat them. The country that bears the onus for starting the war was not up to its part in the challenge. Austria did not see many victories until Italy joined the fight. This changed Austria's losing streak into a winning one. The combination of German, Austrian, and Bulgarian troops (Bulgaria joined the Germanic side) started becoming victorious in the East. At the beginning of the war, the Russians had some good success, but the Teutonic armies were able to turn the tide. Meanwhile, the war bogged down in the West. As Germany began winning the East, especially after the early battle of Tannenberg in 1914, which buoyed the careers of Ludendorff and Hiddenburg, Germany tried to get Russia to declare a separate armistice. They would not, not even when Czar Nicholas abdicated and his brother Grand Duke Michael Alexanderovitch briefly took the reins of power.

When Czar Nicholas abdicated, the Duma became the main power before the revolution disposed of it. Nicholas' brother, Czar Michael, called for universal male suffrage and a plebiscite of the people to determine the direction of Russia. The abdication of Nicholas was the result of a split in Russia between a pro-German ministerial faction and the pro-Slavic Duma faction. But before the abdications took place, the Russian army started to have huge failures on the eastern front. Czar Nicholas could not make up his mind whether to sue for an individual peace with Germany or continue the fighting and defeat the Germans. His mind was made up for him when the pro-Slavic army backed those calling for the Czar to abdicate. The pro-Slavic forces wanted to redouble the war effort and crush Germany. But the army reflected the Russian political instability. It may have been a huge country with huge resources, but it was in a state of turmoil.

The provisional government that followed Czar Nicholas' and Czar Michael's abdications was led by the Socialist

Alexander Kerensky which, in retrospect, served only as a bridge between the Czarist tyranny and the Soviet tyranny. Kerensky oversaw the Duma, which wanted to continue the war. The Bolsheviks (radical Communists) wanted to get Russia out no matter the cost. They wanted to trade war for bread, a slogan that won over many who were war weary. So within Russia there was turmoil and a struggle. This produced mixed results in the army. One of the last offenses by General Aleksei Brusilov was very illustrative. He had great success crashing through the Austrian defenses over a 200-mile stretch. It went westward into the Rumanian frontier. This success encouraged the Rumanians to declare war against Germany, at the wrong time, because the Brusilov offense was running out of gas. Hiddenburg rushed every division that could be spared from the Western front. It was hardly enough, but Brusilov's army was spent.

> Then in the end, motion died because men, gutted of supply, fighting with bare hands, could do no more. The figures from this campaign are appalling. The Teutonic armies lost 600,000 men, some 400,000 Austrians passing into captivity. But for that, Brusilov paid an exorbitant price. One million Russians were lost, the best and most loyal soldiers in the army were now gone, and the demoralized remnants were ripe for revolution.[151]
> In November 1917 the Bolsheviks came to power. The Supreme Command in Germany played a part in this revolution inasmuch as it had arranged for (Vladimir) Lenin and his associates to travel back to Russia in the spring of 1917. They lived up to their expectations, overthrowing the Kerensky government, and immediately took Russia out of the war.[152]

The arrangements for Lenin's return to Russia are sometimes held in elaborate mystery. There was nothing mysterious about it. Lenin was living in Switzerland and following the events in Russia very closely. He was constantly sending his propaganda out of Switzerland to Russia and throughout Europe. When he saw the chance to return, he had the secretary of the Swiss Socialist Party send an intermediary, Dr. Alexander Helphand, to contact the German High Command to give him transport to Russia. Once he was given permission for transport, Lenin then made further demands.

> His must be a special train, with guaranteed extra-territorial rights, no inspection of baggage, or examination of passports. German officials would not board the train; members of the party would not step from it while in transit. The Germans conceded every point, and that is how the legend of the "sealed train" came to flower.[153]

Kerensky could have had the train stopped before it came in through Finland. But he did not. He thought that Lenin would be so discredited by coming in on a special German train that he would be as tainted as the pro-German ministers in the national government had been. Kerensky was wrong. Lenin was cheered as a returning hero by the Bolsheviks and proceeded to foment trouble and work to bring the government down. He traveled to Saint Petersburg on April 16, 1917, and by December, he was in charge of the government and was talking peace terms to the Germans. It is here that Ludendorff committed one of his strategic errors that helped cause the defeat of the Germans. Ludendorff was not satisfied with just running the army. He held sway over the negotiations and pressed for the annexations of conquered Polish territory as well as the annexations of the Baltic territories. Baron Richard von Kuhlmann was the new German foreign secretary representing his government at the Russian/German peace treaty at Brest Litovsk. He wanted a conciliatory peace that would bring a quick resolution of war in the East and would not alarm the western forces watching from a distance. But Ludendorff did not budge on the annexed territories. At a meeting of the Crown Council, the Kaiser Wilhelm, Hindenburg, Ludendorff,

Kuhlmann, and the ancient chancellor, Count George von Hurtling, were present.

> Ludendorff wouldn't yield an inch on the partition of Poland and the annexation of Russia's Baltic provinces. Kuhlmann doggedly reiterated his arguments for conciliation. The kaiser fluttered back and forth between these two extremes, unable to make up his mind. Ludendorff was outraged that Kuhlmann sought to cross him. Hindenburg became awake for a few minutes when Kuhlmann asked him the blunt question: 'Why do you want the Baltic territories?' He answered: For the basing of my left wing in the next war,' and again closed his eyes.[154]

The council came to no clear decision. Later, when the Russians were finally told about the annexations, the peace conference broke down. The war in the East resumed with the German army penetrating even further into Russian territory. Ukraine also wanted its independence from Russia with the promise of German protections. All this led to an extension of the eastern front and burdened Germany with the problems faced by an occupying force.

> The kinds of victories foreseen by the German military and civil planners before 1914 demanded an enemy government not only willing to conclude peace, but also able to enforce it as well. Lacking that, the Germans in any theater were all too likely to conquer themselves to destruction, dispersing their forces as they occupied and controlled Russian territory...The general staff's encouragement of revolution in Russia, culminating in the famous "trainload of plague germs," reflected three years of failure to secure any kind of peace in the east, whether by victory or negotiation.[155]

Why Ludendorff was so blind to what his demands meant for a continuation of the war is stupefying. In one fell swoop he could have ended war in the East, and he could have released soldiers for the Western front. This could have been done while, at the same time, giving hope to those who wanted to come to a negotiated end of the war with the Germans, that the central powers were reasonable people with whom one could deal. Ludendorff threw that idea out the window slamming shut his chances for a negotiated peace in the West.

> The Bolsheviks had come to power on the slogan "Down with the war!" Now they redeemed their pledge to the Russian people-at a cost. By the terms of this treaty, "Russia lost 34% of her population, 32% of her agricultural land, 85% of her beet-sugar land, 54% of her industrial undertakings, and 89% of her coal mines. This was a German peace. Exasperation at the Bolshevik tactics and propaganda had brought out the worst in the German character—its harshness and its hypocrisy."[156]

The Soviets did not give up all this land easily. How could a worker's government give up so much productive agricultural and industrial land? Ludendorff wasted time, energy, and men in an effort to wring extreme concessions out of the Bolsheviks. This meant that more troops had to be tied down in the East instead of freeing them up to go to the western front. Hindenburg claimed that he wanted forward positions for the next war, though he still needed to win the current one. This caused a great diplomatic problem beyond Russia and Germany. The people in the West looked at the Brest Litovsk Treaty and saw that there was no reasoning with the Germans. That if they were to sue for peace with the Teutonic warlords, Ludendorff would call for outrageous demands that would make the loss of Alsace-Lorraine look miniscule. The Brest-Litovsk Treaty steeled the resolve of many in the West to continue the fight. Also, part of the forces that were left in the East was the cavalry corps. It is true that the trench warfare and the machine gun had changed much of the way in which wars were now being fought. The cavalry sweep was now a thing of the past, but there were times when cavalry, whether on horseback or on motorcycles or even bicycles, was badly needed. That came into play when the Germans had British or French troops in full retreat. There were a couple of points in the early offenses of 1918 where a cavalry charge would have turned a retreat into a rout. And considering that the great offensives of 1918 stopped forty miles short of the goal of defeating the Entente forces, cavalry or motorized forces could have delivered the knockout punch before the American forces had arrived in significant numbers to change the situation.

> But Germany's cavalry divisions were in the Ukraine and the Baltic states, supporting grandiose and senseless dreams of power. And so it came about that the German Great General Staff launched what it envisioned as the decisive battle of the war in an area which, Ludendorff admits, 'seemed to lack any definite limit', with no mobile arm for exploitation at all. It hardly seems credible, yet it was so. This attack would go as far as the German infantryman's legs would carry him, no further. As Sir John Wheeler-Bennett has said, it was Ludendorff the politician who defeated Ludendorff the soldier.[157]
> It was a crowning mercy that they had no cavalry. How many times during the retreat did we thank Heaven for this! The sight of a few mounted men in the distance would at once start a ripple of anxiety, the word "Cavalry" being whispered and passed from mouth to mouth down the firing line. Men looked apprehensively over their shoulders, fearful lest horsemen might be already behind them. Cavalry was the one factor which would have smashed the morale of the defense in a twinkling.[158]

Ludendorff strengthened the hand of the Entente by forcing a stringent treaty of annexation with Russia. They gave time for the hardcore fighters to hope for an American intervention and killed the possibility that moderates, looking for a quick end to the war, might sway the Entente, especially French powers.

On April 2, 1917, President Woodrow Wilson asked

Congress for a declaration of war. They gave it to him by overwhelming majorities. The Senate voted for it 82 to 6. The House of Representatives passed the declaration by a vote of 373 to 50. So if the vote was so overwhelming for war, why did America wait for three years before entering it? The answer is simple. Before the year 1917, most Americans did not view this war as any of their business. They adhered to President George Washington's admonitions not to get entangled with the wars of Europe. There were two things that drove America into the arms of the Entente. They were the reinstallation of unrestricted submarine warfare and the Zimmermann telegram.

Senator George W. Norris expressed his opposition to the war.

> We have loaned many hundreds of millions of dollars to the Allies in this controversy. While such action was legal and countenanced by international law, there is no doubt in my mind but the enormous amount of money loaned to the allies in this country has been instrumental in bringing about a public sentiment in favor of our country taking a course that would make every bond worth a hundred cents on the dollar and making payment of every debt certain and sure. Through this instrumentality and also through the instrumentality of others who have not only made millions out of the war in the manufacture of munitions, etc., and who would expect to make millions more if our country can be drawn into the catastrophe, a large number of great newspapers and news agencies of the country have been controlled and enlisted in the greatest propaganda that the world has ever known to manufacture sentiment in favor of the war.[159]

Senator Robert La Follette was probably the most famous and most eloquent anti-war Socialist in Congress. In his speech to the Senate he stated that though there was an overwhelming majority in the government about to vote for the war, the American populous still did not want it. He went on to question the basic assumptions of the war.

> When we cooperate with those governments (the Entente powers), we endorse the international violations of law by Great Britain; we endorse the shameful methods of warfare against which we have again and again protested in this war; we endorse her purpose to wreak upon the German people the animosities which for years her people have been taught to cherish against Germany; finally, when the end comes, whatever it may be, we find ourselves in cooperation with our ally Great Britain, and if we cannot resist now the pressure she is exerting to carry us into the war, how can we hope to resist, then, the thousand fold greater pressure she will exert to bend us to her purposes and compel compliance with her demands.
>
> We do not know what they are. We do not know what is in the minds of those who have made the compact, but we are to subscribe to it. We are irrevocably, by our votes here, to marry ourselves to a nondivorcable proposition veiled from us for now. Once enlisted, once in the copartnership, we will be carried through with the purposes, whatever they may be, of which we know nothing.
>
> But the President proposes an alliance with Great Britain, which however liberty-loving its people, is a hereditary monarchy, with a hereditary ruler, with a hereditary House of Lords, with a hereditary landed system, with limited and restricted suffrage for one class and a multiplied suffrage power for another, and with grinding industrial conditions for all the wageworkers. The President has not suggested of Great Britain conditional to her granting home rule to Ireland, or Egypt, or India. We rejoice in the establishment of a democracy in Russia, but it will hardly be contended that if Russia was still an autocratic government, we would not be asked to enter this alliance with her just the same.
>
> Italy and the lesser powers of Europe, Japan in the Orient; in fact all the countries with whom we are to enter into alliance, except France, and newly revolutionized Russia, are still of the old order—and it will be generally

> conceded that no one of them had done so much for
> its people in the solution of municipal problems and in
> securing social and industrial reforms as Germany.[160]

Eloquent speeches being put aside, the Congress voted for war with Germany. The pacifist nation was now a warrior. Germany had sealed its fate. The hammer was coming to pound out the European war upon the German anvil.

Now there is no great need here to detail the many battles fought throughout 1917 and 1918. This book does not mean to slight the memories, valor, and sacrifice paid by the many men in the First World War. But the war was sealed when the German generals decided to cast their vote for unrestricted submarine warfare. The German victory depended upon a quick victory in the west. There were no provisions made for how to handle the United States when it arrived in France. The few American troops (as the generals hoped)that made it to the Continent were supposed to become cannon fodder as the Germans rolled up the flank of the Entente forces. The Germans were repeating a short-sighted mistake that it had made in 1914.

> The size of the British Expeditionary Force—four or six
> divisions—was well known; should the English choose to
> place these men in the path of the German juggernaut,
> they would be ground under along with any Frenchman
> or Belgians who got in the way. "The more English the
> better," Moltke said to Tirpitz, meaning that if the British
> army were disposed of in Belgium, he wouldn't have to
> worry about it turning up elsewhere.[161]

Of course, this short-sighted way of thinking helped to stop the German advance. Moltke thought little of the BEF and then later paid for his arrogance when he could not achieve his goal of a quick victory in the West. Hiddenburg and Ludendorff repeated Moltke's colossal error. They minimized the impact the Americans would have on the war. They foresaw a quick end to the war while bringing in a giant populous combatant who could churn out a great industrial war machine.

It was not only the generals who were looking forward to a quick end of the war.

> Early in April a German soldier in the 371st Infantry Regiment wrote in his diary: "Near Lille we were resting from our enterprises, also to be re-equipped for the great push to come, which was supposed to take us to the English Channel. Many familiar faces had gone to be replaced by new faces to become soon familiar and then suddenly to vanish. The army had struck lately quite successfully against the French and the British. Our superiors and newspapers assured us that big events were approaching. As far as we were told there were only 30,000 Americans [in reality over 400,000], most of them inexperienced soldiers. There were more Americans to come, but then we had hundreds of submarines that controlled the seas. Now that the whole eastern army had been transferred to the west, a million strong, it seemed to us imminent that the next offensive would bring victory and peace."[162]

The German commanders had lied to themselves and to their troops. They had both planned for a quick end. The generals had always planned for the quick end, but for years it had not come. When the "great final push" failed, it must have been disheartening for the German troops, for they would soon start surrendering by the thousands. But to see the reaction of the Entente forces, it is obvious that the addition of fresh American troops gave them real hope for victory.

> The sight of these magnificent youths from over the seas, of those clean shaven lads in their twenties, brimming over with vigor and health under their new equipment, produced a prodigious effect. What a striking contrast they made with our own regiments, clad in garments soiled and worn out by so many years of war, the men of which, haggard, their hollow eyes lit up by somber fires,

> were no more than bundles of nerves held together by a
> will-power of heroism and sacrifice. All felt that they were
> to be witness of the magical operation of a transfusion
> of blood. Life was arriving in floods to reanimate the
> mangled body of France bleeding to death from four
> years of innumerable wounds.[163]

If the German generals had not supported the unrestricted submarine warfare, if the pro-American Germans who had Wilhelm's ear had not been swept into a corner of the government, this transfusion may never have taken place. France might well have bled to death. Again, this is speculation. What is known for certain is that the Germans gambled on the quick victory. After America joined the war, things changed for the Entente powers. They now could hang on desperately to the territory they had and could allow Germany to expend and bleed itself to defeat. And this they did. The Entente held on, prevented the Germans from winning the decisive battle on the Western Front and the Americans brought in the fresh troops that helped to turn the tide against the "evil Hun."

There is one other important factor that turned the war against the Germans. There was a virus from the East that came into the Western front with the troops who were fighting Russia. This was a virus of the German's own making. It was Communism. The Germans had sent Vladimir Lenin into Russia to bring down the fledgling Russian democracy by forming a Communist government there and to get Russia out of the war. When that was accomplished, the troops were free to be brought to the Western Front to help push for the final victory. The Socialist converts in the German army did not see themselves as German, but as members of the international working class. The war to them was a great capitalist endeavor to create a rich, powerful war machine. This war machine was built by the worker, and the war was fought by the worker for the advancement of the politicians who were beholden to the capitalists. To the Socialists, it did not matter if Germany won, or France, or Britain, or the United States. They were all capitalist governments using and exploiting the worker. This was a dangerous virus that sapped the morale of the German military machine when the war turned against them.

When the German offenses started to run out of gas in the summer of 1918, Ludendorff had a nervous breakdown. He lost contact with reality. He refused to allow his troops to retreat into defensive positions lest it look as if they were losing the war after getting within forty miles of Paris. Because of this, the German forces lost battles that they could have won. These losses could have been avoided, the troops saved, if Ludendorff had allowed for a retreat. It was during this time where many Germans started to surrender en masse. This caused two problems: one, the loss of men and material; two, those troops that remained out in the field suddenly had an exposed flank, because a group or battalion was gone. This is what caused a stalled offensive to turn into a cascading rout. Could Germany have retreated from forward positions and fought a defensive battle and have checked any advancement of the Entente powers once they lost the momentum in 1918? Could they have forced a more favorable peace treaty than the one they had signed in Versailles? Could the existing government of Germany, the Hohenzollern monarchy, have remained in power if there had been a gradual defended retreat? It probably could have. They were hundreds of miles away from German territory. They could have made the Entente pay dearly for every foot of ground they reclaimed as the German army slowly retreated from the land that they had occupied for four years.

> The Americans there (the Argonne Forest) beat against fire and wilderness, bravely but not cleverly. The Germans there defended not only adroitly, but determinedly, with greater savagery than is known to savages. That was the irony visited on Imperial Germany toward the end. The German soldier stayed so much more steadfast than Ludendorff's opinion of him. How could he have had a true reckoning? He had long since departed the combat

army. He was a big wheel, making imperial policy, in touch with the fighting men only in that vague way peculiar to VIP's who thumb through reams of typed analyses and really think that they know what is going on.[164]

It was the generals who were being disloyal and cowardly, not the troops. That would mean that their generals would have to remain levelheaded and not look at retreat as the same as surrender.

> The other funeral directors gathered at Spa, ironically in the Hotel Britannique. By way of prologue, Ludendorff fell apart in front of his staff on September 28. The act began as a routine review of the situation, phased quickly into a lachrymose self-justification, and concluded with a tirade against everyone else. He damned his military assistants for disloyalty, flayed the kaiser for weakness, accused the German people of mass cowardice, and blasted the Imperial Navy for treacherously undercutting the U-boat campaign.
>
> His shocked listeners watched the rage mount, the fists tighten, the neck thicken, and the face grow livid, as the words became blurred. Then the First Quartermaster stopped, foamed at the mouth, and toppled, hitting the floor in a convulsive fit. That night, still trembling and in shock, Ludendorff called on Hiddenburg. Germany was done, he said; there was no alternative but to yield all conquered territory in the West and try to negotiate a peace on the base of President Wilson's Fourteen Points. Hindenburg listened to his master's voice, and agreed completely.[165]

The generals had lied to their troops about the strength of the American forces. The generals had blundered their way into the position where they had to retreat. Is it any wonder that Ludendorff had a nervous breakdown when the "great push" failed to reach its goals?

Ludendorff, after the strain of the August reverses, was

now a sick man and undergoing psychiatric treatment. He suffered a severe setback when news reached him of America's army attack on the St. Mihiel salient. The salient had been held by the Germans since September 1914 and threatened the entire region between Verdun and Nancy as well as blocking the main railway line from Paris to the east.[166]

It is easy to imagine how close the First World War came to being over before the Americans came into the battle. The Germans had held onto French and Belgium territory since 1914. The Entente powers could not budge them. Russia was defeated. Italy was defeated. If the German generals had been diplomatic enough to avoid antagonizing the United States, Petain would not have had a hope upon which to pin a future victory. If the kaiser had the discipline of will to hold his generals in check, he might have remained the kaiser through the rest of his life. It must be remembered that his father, Frederick, who was himself a war hero might have been able to stand up to his generals, where the crippled son, who never saw any action whatsoever, was bowled over by stronger personalities. But none of these scenarios happened.

If the United States had remained neutral, there may have been mass desertions in the French army, Germany may have rolled up the French army, and Britain would have been forced to the peace table. Germany and Britain then would have divided the French imperial colonies. Belgium would have had to become neutral again though it could have remained a German satellite. Britain would have feared invasion by Germany from the lowlands, but there is no real reason to suppose that Germany would do so. Finally, there would have been no room for Adolf Hitler to rise to power, if Germany had won World War I and the kaiser had remained on the throne.

This was not the case. The German generals blundered their way into a larger war because they wanted a quick end to the war at hand. They lied to themselves and their troops. Their troops lost faith in what they had to say. The troops no longer wanted to fight and die for Germany as they retreated back to Germany. Thousands of troops in the field deserted and surrendered. This left gaping holes in the front lines that made it impossible for those who were willing to fight to carry on. So the advances that the Entente powers made turned into cascading floods. The generals were no longer in control of the troops at the front. The German navy was called out for one last attack of the Lowlands to thwart the Entente's gains. It would have been a suicide run that might have changed the direction of the war. But the navy had been inactive for two years since the Battle of Jutland. The Socialist virus that was eating into the army had already eaten and rotted the German navy. The sailors refused to sail. They figured that the war was already over at this point and they did not want to die for a losing cause. The admirals tried to reestablish discipline, some of the Socialist leaders among the sailors were shot, but the admirals were in danger of retaliation from their crews. The navy would not sail. So the generals were no longer in charge of the army, and the admirals were no longer in charge of the navy.

The German army was not beaten. They surrendered while they still occupied large portions of France and Belgium. The German Navy was not beaten by the British Navy. They mutinied at the time when they had the opportunity to strike one last suicidal blow that might have prevented a humiliating defeat. The end came suddenly. The Entente powers were planning to push into German territory, France wanted to re-occupy Alsace-Lorraine, something they had not done since 1870. A new chancellor was brought into the German government to deal with surrender terms for the Germans. He was Prince Max of Baden. He contacted President Wilson and asked for peace, according to his fourteen points that he had introduced months before. Wilson agreed. This ended the fighting for the United States, which amounted to a separate peace treaty. Britain and France could not continue without the United States so they were forced to the bargaining table before they had their revenge. They would get their revenge in the negotiations at Versailles.

Still, it must be remembered that it was the German commanders who caved in to the pressure, not the troops. This is important to keep in mind. This is one of the reasons why Adolf Hitler was able to convince Germany to go to war again twenty years later. Germany had fought the world's four greatest powers and almost won. A different strategy here, a different tactic there, and Germany would have been victorious. Hitler infamously blamed the loss on the Jewish saboteurs, not German generals. This is ridiculous on its face and ridiculous when one looks at the facts. But it was an idea that carried at a time when Germans needed to blame someone or something for their loss and humiliation. Germany's downfall was their admirals' and generals' belief in unrestricted submarine warfare, and a lack of concern about bringing the United States into the war. This is what caused the Germans to lose the war.

The problem was that the kaiser and the generals had forgotten a couple of important things about fighting a successful war. Limit the amount of enemies that you are fighting in any given battle. Do not draw in others to the fight if you can avoid it. And straight from Mahan's book, commerce destruction alone can not win wars. The German High Command had neglected these basic ideas, brought in a new colossal army, and lost the First World War. But its basic underlying strength was still there. It would rise again in twenty years. The world would once again fight on the European Continent.

The status quo had been held together through WWI. The British Empire still ruled the world and the oceans. France still had its imperial holdings. Germany had lost what little overseas colonies it had prior to the war. The United States was still an up and coming power after flexing its muscles in the Great War. But the status quo was shaky. The next major conflict would change everything.

The conclusion of WWI laid the groundwork for the second. The Allies would not negotiate with the kaiser, or with his son, nor the generals. So they forced not only Kaiser Wilhelm to abdicate, but the whole government. The Weimar Republic stepped into this vacuum. Germany narrowly escaped a Bolshevik-style revolution, but the Weimar Republic was a government that had little respect from the German populous and it was hated by many. The thing that delegitimized it the most in the eyes of the German public was that it signed onto the Versailles Treaty, not the kaiser, not Ludendorff. It was not responsible for the war that had brought about this ignominious end, yet its handwriting was on the hated treaty. To hate Versailles in Germany was to hate Weimar. Also, this was not a government of the German people's doing. It was a government imposed upon it by the very people they had almost defeated. This hatred of the Versailles Treaty and the Weimar Republic was one of the things that opened the door for Hitler to come to power.

There is a postscript to Ludendorff's story. This is the most bizarre part of it. It deals with the Weimar Republic, and a frustrated general (Ludendorff) still looking for importance in his life. His side kick (Hindenburg) rose up in national politics and became President of Germany. Ludendorff became active in the Nazi party, though in a loose way, in the early 1920s. In fact, Ludendorff was in the infamous Beerhall Putsch that Hitler led and for which they were both arrested. Ludendorff marched with Hitler and was arrested along with him. It was a time of great convulsions for German politics. Nobody, not even the Boy Scouts, spoke well of the Weimar Republic. The twenties saw hyperinflation. This is inflation where the value of the mark could change daily, or multiple times within one day. In fact, Hitler paid his men— two thousand strong were to march with him on November 9, 1923—two million marks each, for a grand total of three dollars per marcher. In the early 1920s, the Nazis were only

one group of paramilitary organizations that did battle in the
streets and voting booths of Germany.

> The Steel Helmets, ostensibly just a veterans' association,
> left no doubt in their paramilitary functions when they
> paraded through the streets or engaged in brawls with
> other groups.[167]

The Nationalists also had their own "Fighting Leagues."
The Social Democrats founded the Reichbanner Black-
Red-Gold, and the Communists had the Red Front-Fighters
League.

> On the far right there were other, smaller "Combat
> Leagues," shading off into illegal conspiratorial
> groups such as the "Organization Escherich," closely
> associated with the Steel Helmets, and the "Organization
> Consul," which belonged to a murky world of political
> assassination and revenge killings. Bands of uniformed
> men marching through the streets and clashing with
> each other in brutally physical encounters became a
> commonplace sight in the Weimar Republic, adding to
> the general atmosphere of violence and aggression in
> political life.[168]

So it is really a small wonder that Hitler and his Nazi
party were accepted in Germany in the twenties. There were
thousands of out of work veterans who truly felt betrayed by
the way the war ended. And the Nazis took the other Combat
Leagues off the street thereby restoring order—at a price.

So Ludendorff backed Hitler's march at a time when it
seemed like some group or another was going to pull off
a coup de tat on the Weimar Republic. They took over a
meeting at the Burgerbraukeller, a beer hall in Munich on
November eighth. The next day they were going to take over
the Munich city government and then after that, march
on Berlin. But things did not go well for the conspirators.
The city officials, who were at the initial meeting the Nazis

broke up, were able to get away and warned the police and the army about the upcoming putsch. The next day when the marchers approached the city center, they were blocked by armed police. After a tense standoff, someone fired a gun and all hell broke loose. Bullets flew, men dropped. Hitler fell, or was pushed to the ground, separating his shoulder. Herman Goring was hit in the thigh. Four policemen were killed, as were fourteen protestors. Hitler was arrested, tried in a highly favorable court, and was sentenced to five years in Landsberg am Lech. Ludendorff was acquitted. While Hitler was in jail, Ludendorff vied for leadership in the Nazi party though he was never able to gain control. When Hitler got out of jail after serving about one year of his five-year jail term, he reorganized the party with one new caveat. The party faithful had to submit themselves to Hitler as their leader. He then worked to push his most serious rivals out of the party. One was Ludendorff.

> And secondly, Hitler worked steadily to undermine the continuing prestige of Ludendorff, who was not only a serious rival but also becoming more extreme in his views. Under the influence of Mathilde von Kemnitz, whom he married in 1926, Ludendorff founded the Tannenberg League, which published conspiracy-theory literature attacking not only Jews, but Jesuits and the Catholic Church—a certain recipe for electoral disaster in Bavaria and other pious parts of southern Germany. Ludendorff's fate was sealed when he stood as a candidate for the Presidency in the 1925 elections on behalf of the Nazi party and received a derisory 1.1 per cent of the vote. There is some evidence that Hitler persuaded him to stand in the knowledge that his reputation would be irreparably harmed by the attempt. Nothing demonstrated more clearly than this the changed situation of extreme nationalism in Germany: the all powerful military dictator of the First World War had been pushed out to the margins of politics by the

upstart Nazi politician; the general had been displaced
by the corporal.[169]

There are some amazing things to consider: How much
prestige, how much influence did Hitler gain by rubbing
elbows with Ludendorff? What was the political capital of
marching side by side with the Hero of Tannenberg and
Liege? And then to surpass him in the subsequent elections
that were to arise. And there is one more aspect that would
be comical was it not for the monstrous effects that it would
have later on. When the spring offenses in 1918 finally ran
out of gas in August and Germany started to suffer reversals,
Ludendorff started to look for someone to blame. He liberally
shared the blame with everyone and anyone: Germany was
losing because the kaiser was weak, his staff was incompetent
and cowardly, the German people weak willed, and he saw
conspiracies everywhere. He blamed everyone except himself
and Hiddenburg. They allowed the unrestricted submarine
warfare to be reinstated. They replaced the pro-American
foreign minister with a bombastic fool who antagonized the
United States. They pushed for an uncompromising treaty
with the Bolsheviks. They left the cavalry in Russia when it
was needed in the West. They ignored the development of the
tank. Then when the final push did not go as planned, instead
of a planned withdrawal to fortified positions where Germany
still could have negotiated from strength, Ludendorff
collapsed from the weight of all the miscalculations and
started to blame others. This laid the groundwork for Hitler
to come in and put the blame on the Jews. The final twist
of this bizarre tragic comedy is that German Jews, who were
overrepresented in the heavy fighting of the front line in
WWI started to become scapegoats. Many Jews bravely fought
for and gave their lives for Germany in the Great War, only to
be blamed for losing it. Bitterly ironic.

Chapter Nine
The Great Depression and World War II

There is good reason for looking at these two major developments in world history and seeing how one fed into the other. Though Franklin Delano Roosevelt portrayed himself as the economic savior of the United States from the Depression, he did no such thing. The Great Depression of the 1930s was the longest depression the United States had ever faced. Other depressions or panics had been very short-lived. Compassionate but misguided attempts by both Presidents Herbert Hoover and Roosevelt to help the working man threw down anchors that hindered any sort of possibility of a recovery. Add on top of that, acrimonious cutthroat politics by F.D.R., putting the good of the government before the good of the people, ensured that help would not be coming. This created a political crisis that made the United States look weak and helpless going into the second major war of the twentieth century.

First the compassionate but misguided attempts.

This chapter may contain the most controversial ideas of this book, but there are questions that must be looked at. Roosevelt failed to bring the United States out of its worst and longest depression ever. It is inconceivable that any other president, regardless of party, would have survived four years, never mind eight years of depression and get reelected. Then he was resurrected by a major war. One thing must be realized by an American audience. WWI did not physically affect the infrastructure of the United States. Yes, there were men and women who were killed or maimed in the war effort, and this book does not try to diminish their sacrifices. But major parts of France and Belgium where destroyed in the war, and other parts were disrupted by the movement of men and materials. The drain on English manpower and commerce was dramatic; Great Britain was almost bankrupt at the end of the war. Conversely, American manufacturers benefited greatly from the war effort and were immune from most attacks. The few acts of domestic sabotage that were attempted, failed to halt the massive arms trade between the Entente powers and the United States. Even though Germany did not experience the physical damage that Belgium or France endured, they were subject to harsh reparations in the form of the Versailles Treaty, which became political fodder for Adolf Hitler. They were forced to change their form of government. It was not enough that the kaiser abdicated. The whole form of government was switched from a monarchal-dominated Parliament to a liberal Parliament. Kaiser Wilhelm had not been loved, but he was a symbol of the strength and stability of Germany/Prussia. Without the kaiser, traditionalists and conservatives lost the center of German political ideals. Germany lost Alsace-Lorraine, and the Rhineland was occupied. On top of all that they had to pay enormous indemnities. Germany, an economic powerhouse before WWI, was an economic pauper during the twenties. This would put a drain on the other countries in Europe because one of their major trading partners was financially sick. The United States had no such problems. It was free to fly high and to look down upon Europe as the old world that had caused the problems. So when the stock market crashed in 1929, the United States had further to fall than its Entente partners. But there were political and economic blunders that the United States committed that exasperated the downturn. These blunders were well meaning, but compounded a bad situation bringing things from bad to worse.

President Herbert Hoover was not a conservative Republican. In fact, his opinion that the government should help lift people up in hard times reflected Roosevelt's thinking more than it did the Republican laissez faire business way of thinking. He was a great engineer and organizer. He had turned failed gold mines in Australia, China, and Russia into richly producing enterprises. He helped to feed the people of Belgium during WWI. In the year after the stock market crashed in 1929, Hoover enacted government programs that hindered business growth. One of these programs was a tariff, the Smoot-Hawley protectionist tariff, which was meant to help the American people. Hoover signed it into law over the objection of over one thousand economists. The tariffs were supposed to "protect" American farmers and businesses to encourage their recovery. It did nothing of the sort; it hurt American businesses.

The thousand economists signed a letter in the *New York Times* in May of 1930 stating:

> We are convinced that increased restrictive duties would be a mistake.
> They would operate, in general, to increase the prices which domestic consumers would have to pay. By raising prices they would encourage concern with higher costs to undertake production, thus compelling the consumer to subsidize waste and inefficiency in industry. At the same time they would force him to pay higher rates of profit to established firms...Few people could hope to gain from such a change.[170]
> On June 17, 1930 (President) Hoover signed into law the Smoot-Hawley tariff. It raised tariffs by an average of 59 percent on more than 25,000 agricultural commodities and manufactured goods. The U.S. stock market plunged

and more than sixty countries retaliated with restrictions against whichever products would inflict the worst losses on Americans—typically products very different from those affected by the Smoot-Hawley. In this way, the tariff led to random damage to economies everywhere.[171]

As a result of the Smoot-Hawley Act, most European countries imposed their own tariffs.

In Britain, long the greatest champion for free trade and prosperity, Smoot-Hawley helped provoke a protectionist reaction that led to the Import Duties Act (1932), the country's first general tariff law in more than a century. Part II of the Import Duties bill provided 100 percent tariffs on goods from countries like the United States that penalized British goods...Spain raised tariffs on American cars by 150 percent. Italy did so by 100 percent...By 1934 France had restricted the import of more than 3,000 items with quotas.[172]

The Smoot-Hawley tariffs failed in their attempt to protect American business and attacked the businesses of other countries that then reacted in a natural defensive posture of retaliating with their own tariffs. Farmers were said to be the biggest proponent of the tariffs. Farm exports fell from $1.8 billion a year before the tariff to $590 million just four years later, a two-third's reduction in sales volume. Obviously, the tariff backfired disastrously and helped to prolong and deepen the depression. It also dragged other countries into an economic war that hurt all the participants.

Le Quotidien in Paris published an editorial entitled "Can Mr. Hoover Limit the Catastrophe Which the American Protectionists Are Preparing?" The daily went on to write that if the "Yankees: brought in a tariff, "there will be nothing for us to do but resort to reprisals, and that would mean war."[173]

Even the exchange rates were tinkered with by some countries as a means of retaliation. Of course, any time currency is curtailed between countries, business is impeded. Beyond this, many European countries retaliated with policies that attacked specific American companies, especially automobile manufacturers. This "nationalism" of manufacturing was the hallmark of the 1930s, especially Roosevelt's administration. But it started before he was elected.

Herbert Hoover was blind to the law of unintended consequences. Besides enacting a disastrous protectionist tariff, he also raised taxes to a war-time level.

> Concerned about budget deficits because of increased spending, Hoover urged Congress to enact higher taxes, and the result was the Revenue Act of 1932, one of the biggest tax increases in American history...Many wartime excise taxes were revived, sales taxes were imposed on gasoline, tires, auto, electrical energy, malt, toiletries, fur, jewelry and other articles, admission and stock transfers were increased; new taxes were levied on bank checks, bond transfers. Telephone, telegraph and radio messages, and the personal income tax was raised drastically...[174]

Hoover exhibited a war mentality and tried to marshal the government to pull the United States out of the depression that started on his watch. The problem with what he was trying to do was that it inhibited investment and growth. If people are taxed when they are losing money in business, that means they have even less to work with to try to fix their monetary problems. When higher taxes are slapped on the investment class incentive is taken away for people to put their money at risk in a venture capital concern. They put it in a company with the hope of getting a profit, a return on their money. If there is no return, or if the profit margin is not worth the risk because of confiscatory taxes, then the government has just killed the whole reason for investing. The money will dry up and there will be no growth in the business sector. That means no new jobs going to the worker that the government claims to be trying to help. Making the rich pay their fair share sure sounds good and it may generate votes, but it will not fix a failing economy. Since the stock market crash happened on Hoover's watch, none of the "feel good" social legislation would help him politically.

> Still, tax increases generally were like interest rate increases: bad news at a time when, just as Mellon (son of the Treasury Secretary), said, neither citizens nor the economy could handle it. Starting a business and hiring both became harder...Added to all this was the fact that Hoover's was not just any tax increase, but a giant one: an increase in the top rate from the mid twenty range to 63 percent. Such increases were the sort the country had heretofore thought possible only in wartime.[175]

All it did was to alienate the business sector of the Republican Party without bringing an end to the depression that had gripped the United States. Hoover, who had comfortably beaten former New York Governor Alfred E. Smith in 1928 with 56.9 percent of the vote, lost by the same amount in 1932. But FDR continued to inflict the same tortuous logic upon the American economy that Hoover had. But there was one difference. FDR never missed a chance to blame Hoover or the Republican Party, or business, as the problem. And the stigma adhered to Hoover and to the Republicans. When Roosevelt enacted his famous alphabet soup agencies, the NRA (National Recovery Act), the WPA (Works Project Act), etc., these agencies did little to pull the United States out of the Depression, but rather, kept the country mired in the problem by attacking investment and wealth.

One of the industries that Roosevelt targeted was the burgeoning delivery systems of electric energy. This new field of electric power had been pioneered by Thomas Edison and continued by Samuel Insull in Chicago and Wendell Willkie with his company, Commonwealth and Southern and Central Corporation. Roosevelt's administration attacked Insull with an unprecedented vehemence that sent him fleeing the country, and then when extradited, he was attacked in court as someone who had caused the depression. So after Hoover had burdened America's trading partners with commerce destroying tariffs, then piled on exorbitant taxes on the American public, Roosevelt added to businessmen's woes.

The second part was where cold-blooded partisan politics mattered more than the economic health of individual Americans. A banking crisis was hitting its highpoint in early 1933 between Roosevelt's first presidential election victory and his inaugural ceremony (the inauguration was still taking place in March instead of January as it is now) Roosevelt did nothing and said nothing. Millions were lost, businesses went under, jobs were lost, but Roosevelt allowed the crisis to peak until he was in the White House. That way, Hoover would forever be seen as the failure who brought on the worst of the depression, and Roosevelt could be seen as America's savior.

Hoover, concerned about the run that was taking place on the banks, notified Roosevelt, the president elect, that something must be done and done immediately. He had a plan to close the banks for a day and then reopen them as soon as they proved their solvency. But since Hoover was a lame duck president and the Democrats were in control of Congress and would not help him, he needed the consent of Roosevelt to stem the tide of the bank runs. Roosevelt, having been made aware of the situation, quietly ignored the pleas from the outgoing president.

> The next day he was in New York. On the night of February 18, the Inner Circle—an organization of New York political reporters—was staging its annual banquet and show in the grand ballroom of the Astor Hotel. Every prominent politician in New York attends this famous spectacle at which the political writers stage burlesque skits about New York politicos. After midnight, i.e. the

morning of February 19, and while the stage show was still in progress, Roosevelt, then being President elect, arrived at the dinner party with a large party. He took his seat of honor at the center of the head table. Raymond Moley, then his closest advisor, sat opposite him. The newspaper actors on the stage were going through some pretty hilarious farce and the audience was in an uproarious good humor. At this moment Roosevelt signaled to Moley and passed a slip of paper to him under the table. Moley read it. To his amazement it was from the President of the United States, Herbert Hoover, and it was in his own handwriting. Amidst the rising merriment Moley read with dismay:

"A most critical situation has arisen in this country of which I feel it is my duty to advise you confidentially."

Moley looked toward Roosevelt. His head was thrown back in a roar of laughter at the show. Then Moley read on. Hoover pointed out with complete realism the threat to the whole national banking structure, the flight of gold from the country, the rush of cash from the banks into hiding. Fear, he said, had taken control of the public mind. Hoover believed rightly that a new element had entered the situation—the appearance of terror. The air was full of rumors of inflation and going off the gold standard. This was leading to the withdrawal of gold from the banks. Hoover enumerated the forces that were causing the trouble:

"The breakdown in balancing the budget by the House (of Representatives); *the proposals for inflation of the currency and the widespread discussion of it; the publication of RFC loans (to banks) and the bank runs, hoarding and bank failures from this cause and various other events and rumors."*

These, he said, "had now culminated in a state of alarm which is rapidly reaching the proportions of crisis.

Hoover believed that Roosevelt should enter the situation. He proposed that Roosevelt issue some sort of statement to "clarify the public mind"…"It is obvious that you will shortly be in a position to make whatever policies you wish effective, you are the only one who can give these assurances." Mr. Roosevelt was in the position—the only

one who was able to calm the public mind, to make some
move or some gesture that would encourage confidence
and check the rising currents of terror.[176]

Roosevelt ignored the situation until he took office. Then
he implemented actions very similar to what Hoover had
suggested. He allowed the crisis to fester in order to paint his
political opponents as the culprits of the crisis, ensuring his
own free hand to do whatever needed to be done when he
could get all the glory for it.

> With a personal manner and confident soothing voice,
> he explained what he was doing about the banking crisis.
> The 'chat' went on for thirteen minutes and established
> Roosevelt as a masterful communicator. However
> disruptive the New Deal turned out to be, most people
> were glad that he was at least doing something, and
> keeping them informed.[177]

The something was what Hoover would have done as well
if the Democrats in Congress, or Roosevelt himself, had
allowed.

There is another concept that has been lost through the
decades. It helps to explain why the Depression lasted so
long. Roosevelt engaged in anti-capitalist practices which
smothered any possibility of a recovery. In fact, he and the
team of professors and thinkers around him did not have any
faith in the capitalist system. Many of the formative thinkers
in his administration were admirers of Joseph Stalin and
Benito Mussolini, who thought that capitalism needed the
direction and overlordship of the government to make sure
that the wealth of the nation was distributed properly.

> The New Deal was the American version of the collectivist
> trend that became fashionable around the world, so it
> perhaps shouldn't be surprising that New Deal utterances
> by FDR and his advisors sometimes sounded similar to
> fascist doctrines associated with Benito Mussolini....

Mario Palmieri's *The Philosophy of Fascism* (1936)... described ideas remarkably similar to those proposed by the New Dealers: "Economic initiatives cannot be left to the arbitrary decisions of private, individual interests. Open competition if not wisely directed and restricted, actually destroys wealth instead of creating it...The proper function of the state in the Fascist system is that of supervising, regulating and arbitrating the relationships of capital and labor, employers and employees, individuals and associations, private interests and national interests...More important than production of wealth is its right distribution, distribution which must benefit in the best possible way all the classes of the nation, hence, the nation itself. Private wealth belongs not only to the individual, but, in a symbolic sense, to the state as well."[178]

The Modern Corporation and Private Property is a book coauthored by Adolf Berle Jr. Among Berle's other contribution to the Roosevelt administration, this book was called the "the economic Bible of the Roosevelt administration." In this book:

Berle and Means (the co-author) asserted that the top 200 corporations dominated the American economy, and they claimed that because big publicly held businesses were run by salaried managers, not the shareholders, they were inherently inefficient. Salaried managers cherished perks and didn't want to work hard, and Berle believed that the average shareholder, with comparatively few shares, was powerless. The implication, of course, was that some kind of government intervention was needed to make a capitalist economy more efficient.[179]

FDR's lack of faith in capitalism, his constant attacks on businesses, and his pursuit of "progressive" socialist answers had international political consequences. Number one, it kept the United States economically weak. Roosevelt never pulled the United States out of the Depression. Number two, this gave economic and rhetorical cover for Fascist and Socialist governments in Europe, Hitler's Germany being one and Mussolini's Italy being another. And Hitler, at the start of his governmental career, modeled his plans on Mussolini's example. This camouflage came in the form that even the United States, a stalwart of capitalism, was following the lead of Mussolini in economic terms. If the United States was following his lead, then Mussolini must be doing something right, except the United States was abandoning its pro-business attitudes. If Hoover or Roosevelt could have cut taxes, if Hoover had not signed the Smoot-Hawley Act, if Roosevelt had not made American businesses the enemy, then the United States might have been able to right its economic ship. A successful United States would have dwarfed the fascists and proved an attractive financial market. It could have shown Europe how to do things correctly. But Roosevelt did not do this. Instead, he emulated the fascist's economic policies.

> As I write, of course, Mussolini is an evil memory. But in 1933 he was a towering figure who was supposed to have discovered something worth studying and imitation by all world artificers everywhere. Such eminent persons as Dr. Nicholas Murry Butler and Mr. Sol Bloom, head of the Foreign Affairs Committee of the House, assured us that he was a great man and had something we might well look into for imitation. What they liked particularly was his corporate system. He organized each trade or industrial group into a state-supervised trade association. He called it a *corporative*. These corporatives operated under states supervision and could plan production, quality, prices, distribution, labor standards, etc. The NRA (the National Recovery Administration) provided that in America each industry should be organized into a federally supervised trade association. It was not called a corporative. It was called a code authority. These code authorities could regulate production, quality, prices, distribution methods, etc., under the supervision of the NRA. This was fascism. The anti-trust laws forbade such

organizations. Roosevelt had denounced Hoover for not
enforcing these laws sufficiently. Now he was suspending
them and compelling men to combine.[180]

The bottom line was that the government in the 1930s went
to war with the businesses of America as the enemy. Because
businesses were under siege throughout the 1930s, they could
not rebound from the depression. Unemployment averaged
17 percent from 1934 through 1940, years that Roosevelt
presided over. During his terms in office he continually
attacked American business as the source of American
problems while he enacted government policies that chased
people away from the marketplace.

Adolf Hitler came to power during the same year as Roosevelt
though for different reasons. But it must be remembered that
Hitler was a socialist. He believed that the government was
the central body in political life to which the people owed
allegiance. Germany's militaristic heritage gave credence
to this idea. The United States was a country whose main
political ideology was *laissez-faire* free trade ideas with some
protectionism thrown in. Then the protectionism had grown,
even before Roosevelt had taken office. The commonplace
history of the twentieth century is that unrestricted free market
practices and greedy stock manipulators brought about the
Great Depression. But common conjecture can often be very
far from the truth. The crash of 1929 was nothing abnormal
to the business cycle. After a long run up, which the market
had enjoyed through the twenties, a correction was due.
Some lending practices were overly speculative, especially the
discount banks, but American businesses were solid. It was the
government, after the crash, which inhibited the businesses
from growing. Roosevelt pursued a socialist policy of recovery
throughout the 1930s. His socialist policies failed except in
one regard. He had plenty of government money to dole out
to politically needy areas and groups to ensure that he was
reelected. According to Flynn, while Roosevelt authorized
the spending of billions of dollars for relief and public works

projects, a disproportionate amount of this money went, not to the poorest states such as those in the South, but to Western states where people were better off, apparently because these were "swing" states that could yield Roosevelt more votes in the next election.

The Hatch Act was passed in 1939 to prevent government officials from pressuring other government employees in how they should vote. This kind of pressure occurred often in the newly created government jobs that Roosevelt was so famous for creating. So he was bringing in the new jobs and these people manning them were expected to repay their new employer with votes.

Roosevelt's alphabet soup agencies did nothing to pull the United States out of the Depression. The economic situation fluctuated during his terms in office, but not much. When the 1938 midterm elections came around Roosevelt was in trouble. There were over 11 million people unemployed in the United States that year. This was more than were unemployed when he was first elected in 1932. In other words, the hard economic facts showed that Roosevelt's actions to pull the country out of the Depression were a failure. This was from the man who had painted himself as the savior from the Depression. But Roosevelt had two cards up his sleeve that he could play. One, the government could borrow money from which to pay for political policies. Two, prior to the passage of the Hatch Act, the department heads and the leaders could and did pressure the workers under the threat of the loss of their job if they did not fund, support or, at the very least, promise to vote for the president's chosen politicians. And he had built many political enemies, even in his own party. Even Democrats had balked at his plans to pack the Supreme Court with pro-New Deal judges who would render judgments in his favor.

Roosevelt's policies kept his focus on the problems of the United States, and not aiding Europe or China. In the early part of Roosevelt's first term he had the opportunity to work together with Britain and France at the World Economic

Conference. He could have dropped tariffs, reaffirmed a desire for the gold standard, or he could have ended the economic nationalism that was started with the Smoot-Hawley Act.

> The U.S. delegates in London were confused; one spoke out for low tariffs, another for higher tariffs. After (the presidential advisor, Raymond) Moley arrived, Roosevelt telegraphed yet a third and forth position all variants on the question of monetary arrangements, budgets, and international relations.[181]

What Roosevelt finally did push for was raising agricultural prices. The English and French were furious at Roosevelt's dealing in bad faith.

> The Europeans felt that Roosevelt had made fools of them by inviting them to negotiate and then undermining both sides with a contradictory statement. The advisers were in agony-it was as though the doctor had jerked at the dislocated shoulder but stopped short of setting it right.[182]

So the "isolationism" of the country started from the top down. In his second term, after trouncing the Republican Alfred Landon by 11 million votes in 1936, Roosevelt supposed that he had a mandate from the people to enact all of his socialist projects that had been stymied earlier. Democrats held over 75 percent of the seats in both houses of Congress. But the Supreme Court had struck down eight of ten of FDR's New Deal measures. When they did this, FDR threatened to add more judges to the court. When he pursued this "court packing" through the Senate, he met opposition from his own party.

> Indignant though many of them had been over the anti-New Deal decisions, a considerable part of the liberals viewed the court as the bulwark of American liberties. At

the very time, when European dictators were stripping populaces of their liberties, they were especially sensitive to the danger that the United States may suffer the same malign fate.[183]

So FDR was not acting very much different than the dictators of Europe though even his own party would not allow him to get away with what Mussolini or Hitler were doing economically. The United States was not a leader in a capitalist market, but a limping impotent giant from which there was little to fear.

In the late 1930's and early 1940's when U.S. economic strength might have given pause to potential aggressors in the world, our economic weakness furnished encouragement to them instead. From the standpoint then, not only of our domestic history, but also the tragic events of WWII, it has seemed to me (according to historian Gary Dean Best), that Roosevelt's failure to generate economic recovery during this critical period deserved more attention than historians have given it.[184]

The Neutrality Act prevented the United States from aiding a belligerent country during a time of war. This was a piece of legislation that was enacted in the 1930s with a retrospective and negative view toward WWI as war clouds were again spreading over Europe. It was meant to prevent the United States from getting drawn into another European war. President Roosevelt spoke in March of 1935 to a Senate committee investigating the munitions industry. In it he lamented the fact that the United States had even entered World War I and that the pacifist Williams Jennings Bryan had been right all along. So, Roosevelt pushed for the act that would limit the ability of the United States to aid or arm countries, especially in Europe. When the Spanish Civil War broke out in 1936, the president had the Neutrality Act amended to include a ban on sending aid to countries involved in a civil war as well as one that crossed international borders. The Spanish Civil War might have been a hard choice to send aid to anyway. The Popular Front, also known as the Republicans, even though they were Communists, had won Spain's election in 1936. The National Front, the Nationalists, who were comprised of monarchists, Catholics, and conservatives, had control of the army. The National Front refused to abide by the election and overthrew the communist government. The United States, Britain, and France stayed aloof from the conflict. So it became a proxy fight with the Fascists, Germany, and Italy, aiding the Nationalists and the Communist Soviet Union aiding the Republicans. When the Soviets ended their aid, the Nationalists won and installed a Fascist government under Generalissimo Francisco Franco. It is hard to say that the United States Congress would have supported the duly elected Communists or helped to overthrow them and the electoral results. But by staying neutral, to the point of not even selling arms to either side, the former Entente powers left a power vacuum that was filled by Fascists and Socialists. It made the democracies look weak and cowardly. So even though the Neutrality Act was popular in the United States, it helped pave the way for WWII by emboldening Hitler and Mussolini.

So, FDR was consumed with domestic problems that his own solutions only compounded. He had alienated old European allies. His focus was not on international affairs. He was not an international leader, either in word or deed. Although he did make small efforts to help alleviate the tensions in Europe, he only became the butt of Hitler's jokes when the German Chancellor spoke to the Reichstag. FDR's New Deal created an economic isolationism that sat comfortably with American political isolationism.

Roosevelt could not have been blind to how bad the situation was in Europe. He had been the assistant secretary of the Navy during Wilson's administration. He could have picked up the fallen standard of Wilson's internationalism. He could have used Winston Churchill's ideas about educating the electorate. He could have sent the navy out for joint exercises with the British in the North Atlantic in the middle of the decade for a show of force. He could have had high profile American military visiting France for a show of solidarity with the Entente. If steps such as these had been taken, Hitler might not have been so bold. His adversaries within Germany might have been encouraged. But none of this happened. FDR took the easy way out; he took the politically safe route.

> When Hitler marched into the Rhineland in 1936, in spite of French pleas for an American reprimand, the president said nothing. William Dodd, US ambassador to Germany at the time, had recognized Hitler for the threat he was, but when he lodged a formal protest, he was withdrawn and denied further access to the president.[185]

Western Europe and the United States were gripped by fear, pacifism, and appeasement in almost the same fashion as socialism was sweeping these same countries.

It would take a huge calamity to break the United States out of its political and economic isolationism after a whole decade spent looking inwards. FDR was not going to spend any political capital on informing the US population of the problems it would soon face. He might have sunk in popularity and it might have cost him votes. Of course, if FDR had taken an interventionist attitude during the thirties, he would have been open to attack on those grounds. But to avoid the argument while allowing the danger to grow exposed Roosevelt as a political coward. Was it really more important to assure himself of a third term rather than making a stand in international affairs when potential enemies were still small and weak?

> The truth is that the President (Franklin Delano Roosevelt) had made up his mind to go to war as early as 1940. To believe differently is to write him, our navy chiefs of staff, and all our high military and naval officers as fools. In the First World War it took a gigantic effort

to defeat Germany. Then Britain had a million men in France. France had three million men in arms. Italy and Russia were our allies. So was Japan. Italy had a million men against Germany, and Russia had four million. Yet with all this Germany was never driven out of France. She surrendered while in possession of most of what she had conquered. Does anyone believe that Roosevelt or General Marshall or any other high military leaders thought that England fighting alone could drive Hitler's armies out of France? England did not have a soldier in France. France was prostrate. Her arms factories were in Hitler's possession. Italy was against us rather than for us. So was Japan. The President knew that to drive Hitler out of France, it would be necessary to send American armies to France and to send the American navy full blast into the war. And he knew this in October 1940.[186]

Roosevelt was entrusted by the American people with four terms. This occurred despite the fact that unemployment averaged 17 percent of the working force from 1934 to 1940 during his first two terms in office. But FDR had won enough people over to his way of thinking. Blaming others, especially the rich, was always an easy thing to do politically. It worked well when Hitler used the Jews in the place of the rich for a scapegoat for Germany's problems between the wars. And Roosevelt was a master communicator. He used the new medium of the radio to have his "fireside chats" with the American people.

Gallop polls at the time had recorded that 75 percent of the population did not want to go to war. In 1940, both the Democratic and Republican parties had official platforms that declared neutrality in the war. The Republican candidate, Wendell Willkie, was an international businessman who took an anti-war stand as well. In fact, he had closed the gap on Roosevelt and looked as if he might beat him by stating that the president was secretly planning to have the United States enter the war in Europe. No politician running for president would have been elected in the fall of 1940 if he had stated that the United Sates must enter the war as a fighting force. So Roosevelt gave an anti-war speech to bolster his position in the polls with Joseph Kennedy at his side. Kennedy was a pro-German ambassador to the Court of St. James (England), and patriarch to the Kennedy clan. Roosevelt's speech, given to a mostly Irish-American audience who were historically anti-British, with the anti-British Kennedy nearby, convinced many voters that he was against the war.

> It was in Boston, with Joseph Kennedy present, that Roosevelt made a speech so convincingly isolationist that Willkie protested, "That hypocritical son of a bitch! This is going to beat me." It included Roosevelt's famous pledge "Your boys are not going to be sent into any foreign wars."[187]

FDR's modus operandi was that he got what he wanted by whatever means possible. The Constitution and tradition did not matter to him. If the assessment of John Flynn, author of *The Roosevelt Myth,* of FDR's knowledge of the war is correct, that means that FDR lied to retain his power. By running for a third term, he wiped out 140 years of tradition started by President George Washington. On top of that, it meant that he would not, or could not level with the American public about the dangers inherent in a Nazi victory in Europe. If Roosevelt's mind was on maintaining the strength of the United States and that of our allies and main trading partners, he might have confronted Hitler in some diplomatic fashion, and strengthened the backbone of Britain and France. A second-term president has the luxury of taking an unpopular stand because it is right, not because it is politically expedient. That is, if you do not plan on running again. In 1940, there was no term limit on the president. The two-term limit was a self-imposed tradition dating from George Washington de-emphasizing the role of the president. But Roosevelt's focus was always on reelection. He would not confront Hitler until Hitler confronted him. That would mean there was no way possible to lead the people into a righteous fight without duplicity. Or was the problem the duplicity of propaganda from WWI that made another war for freedom and democracy in Europe a disgusting thought to American voters? Either way, Roosevelt chose to be duplicitous, rather than to state the truth. The truth was that the United States was needed by Britain to help save Europe from the Nazi scourge.

In November of 1940, the American people believed in sending arms to Britain or China to aid their own war efforts, which was a reversal of the Neutrality Act. The Lend-Lease bill that Congress passed in 1941, and which Roosevelt signed into law, showed that Americans were willing to help in limited ways. But they did not want to become involved in another European war. The United States had over 120,000 men killed in the First World War to maintain the status quo of Europe. When the war had ended, some of the men stayed in Europe as an occupation force. They found out how badly the German people had been starved by the war. They found out that there was no German slaughter of innocent women, children, and nuns in Belgium, as they were told by British propaganda sources. They found out that the German people were, as a whole, good Christian men and women, not the barbaric evil Huns that they had been made out to be. Some people in the United States began to feel as if the country had been duped into fighting a war for Britain.

> A legend had arisen in the United States that the British had inveigled America into entering World War I. For a self confident people, Americans had a strange addiction to believe that they were likely to be suckered by smooth talking foreigners. The character of Uncle Sap was the personification of that sense of unease.[188]

If what the British had said about the Germans as evil Huns were true, it was hard to find evidence of it once the war was over. But there was the fact that the United States had joined the war and ensured that the status quo in Europe remained the same as before August of 1914. That included preserving the British Empire's dominance on the seas.

At the outset of WWII the British found themselves in an awkward predicament. They needed the help of the United States to defeat the Nazis. But the American people were not going to swallow a bunch of "lies" and be drawn into another European war. The problem was that, this time, a barbaric evil leader was truly in charge of Germany and leading them on a path to destroy Europe, at least the Jewish and Slavic populations therein. But how is a nation convinced to make the ultimate sacrifice for another far off country, when the collective memory was the failure of the previous attempt to save Europe? Why die for a sure-to-fail effort?

> All in all, Anglo-American relations were not close at the outbreak of the war. The economic outlook of the Depression and the uncertainty over the policies of appeasement and neutrality intensified the two nations' differences rather than their common interests. Popular revulsion against the excesses of death and rhetoric during the First World War made both countries turn away from facing the possibility of a second. In the weeks before Hitler's armies invaded Poland, British officials hesitated to make overtures to the American public as they continued to live down the legacy of 1914-1918.[189]
> The British themselves could not be caught spreading atrocity propaganda because of the lurid memories of WWI. They could however, assist the "small allies," such as Czechoslovakia and Poland, to tell atrocity stories on behalf of the Inter-Allied Information Committee.[190]

Now it stands to reason that if a situation is truthfully reported one time, and a similar situation arises further down the road, and a similar finding is reported, the subsequent report will be believed because of the veracity from the initial report. The problem only arises when lies have been reported the first time. Then a similar report is like the boy who cried wolf. This is the situation in which Britain found itself. If the

German atrocities of WWI were true, if there was evidence of people systematically brutalized, raped, and murdered, then the stigma would have stuck to Germany. There is no better example than that of the Holocaust of WWII. It was so terribly horrific that it could not be believed at first. Then there were numerous films of the prisoners being released from the concentration camps. The Nuremberg Trials brought out volumes of firsthand witnesses and physical evidence of the atrocities committed by the Nazis. There was so much proof of inhumanity that the name Nazi, and unfortunately, to a certain degree, the name of Germany was associated with holocaust. This was not the case after the First World War.

France had been rolled over in WWII as easily as Belgium had been penetrated in WWI. What was the point of sending more men to die in Europe again for such a weakling nation? It lost territory in 1870, in 1914, and again in 1940. Obviously, it could not defend itself, and Germany was the greater power. What is amazing is that Hitler's armies had been able to do what the German generals in WWI had failed to do. They captured Paris in a matter of weeks. To be accurate, it was not Hitler's great planning that achieved this success. Of course, he did push into the West when his high command was dead set against such a move. Hitler was aided in conquests by the undefeated German army. It had surrendered at the end the First World War. It had not been beaten into submission. At the end of WWI General Ludendorff made one last brilliant move. He called for an armistice on President Wilson's fourteen points. (Though it was Prince Max Baden who had the unfortunate job of negotiation with Wilson, it was at the behest of Ludendorff when he panicked and saw that Germany could not win the war.) It was a way of splitting the United States off from their allies and securing a peace that would allow Germany to fight again another day. It would save the German army from being decimated and save the German land from being invaded.

The Germans who wanted to preserve their army and their military cadre intact, saw an opportunity for doing that by dealing with Wilson. And Wilson, who was determined to end it, had all the cards. Or more accurately, the Allies had lost most of theirs.[191]

In WWII, the German army had learned from their past mistakes; the tank was now going to play a major role in their battles, and they had developed a fearsome air force, the Luftwaffe. So in 1940, in a matter of weeks after turning to the West, Germany had captured France, and the Vichy government became its puppet. This caused a huge problem for those who wanted the United States to enter the war. Compared to the First World War, the second would have been over as soon as it started, if Hitler had truly been a wise strategist. He was not and Winston Churchill was reborn as Britain's leader. (He had been unceremoniously forced out of his cabinet position in late 1915 when his plan for an attack on Gallipoli, Turkey, had failed miserably.) Due to poor planning and poorer execution, the invasion was a bloody waste of British and Australian manhood, and Churchill's head had to roll. He resurfaced in a position of leadership in 1940 into the prime minister's job when no one else wanted it. Many British politicians fully expected him to fail, waiting in the wings in case he, once again, fell from power. Instead, Churchill waited for two things: one, for Hitler to make a decisive blunder that would lead to his downfall, which came in the spring of 1941 when he invaded Russia; two, for the United States to enter the war.

The problem was how to get the United States involved in the European war. This was a dilemma that Roosevelt faced. He was reelected for his third term by promising the American people that he would not send American sons into a foreign war. Even if he were to go back on his word, the Congress would never allow him to send the troops. A mere political U-turn would not work here. He would need to get a declaration of war from both houses of Congress, and the country was not in the mood for war. The real problem was how to allow the country to be attacked so that either Germany or Japan drew first blood. Then the United States could enter the war, having been drawn into it against its will. There were quite a few problems with this strategy. Although German U-boats were active in the Atlantic, they were not attacking neutral shipping to the degree that they had in 1917. There was no second Lusitania. Hitler's strict orders were for the submarines to avoid conflict with American ships. On September 4, 1941, three months before Pearl Harbor, the USS Greer was on patrol from Newfoundland to Iceland. It was doing so because of one of the deals that Roosevelt had made with Churchill passed the responsibility of patrolling the waters west of Iceland to the United States. A quick look at a globe will show that the United Sates was now responsible for patrolling almost the whole Atlantic Ocean from Maine to four hundred miles off the Irish coast. The British navy needed relief from patrolling the international waters so they could concentrate on the North and Mediterranean Seas. So the Greer patrolled from Newfoundland to Iceland, out in waters that were previously international waters, but which Roosevelt had now taken the responsibility of protecting, and it came upon a German submarine. The Greer followed the submarine for three hours when it finally fired its torpedoes at the Greer. The Greer took evasive action, avoiding the submarine and then fired depth charges. This was repeated again until the warships lost contact with each other and the Greer sailed for Iceland. President Roosevelt spoke about this incident in one of his fireside chats, putting the blame on the U-boat for firing the first shots, and painting the Greer as taking defensive actions. In retrospect, it appears that the Greer was trying to bait the U-boat into taking offensive actions so that there could be a possible flash point that would stir the American public into war frenzy. Unfortunately for Roosevelt, there would be no frenzied war cry over the Greer incident. It would take much more than one lone attack on one naval ship patrolling international waters to change the American attitude about war.

Also, with the conquest of Norway, Hitler had eradicated Germany's WWI scourge. Britain could not blockade the North Sea the way it had done in the Great War. This would make the naval war harder, but Germany's navy was not as great under Hitler as under the kaiser. Neither was Japan attacking United States ships. So President Roosevelt had to put pressure on Germany and Japan to force them to attack American positions. This way, the United States could claim that it was attacked while minding its own business. Roosevelt imposed embargoes of oil, steel, and other raw materials sorely needed in both countries. In the Atlantic, the United States lent naval ships to Britain as the former colony took over British possessions. The United States took control of the Bahamas, Jamaica, Antigua, St. Lucia, Trinidad, and British Guiana, all former British holdings. This would free up the British navy to attack Nazi positions. Also, if there were Nazi U-boats in the vicinity of these previously British islands and they mistakenly fired on an American warship thinking that it was British, well that would be an act of war on Germany's part. Beyond that, the United States navy escorted convoys of war material going to Europe. All this could have brought an American ship into contact with German submarines and could have provoked an incident that could have led to war. Unfortunately for Roosevelt and Churchill, none of this came to fruition.

For Roosevelt, it looked like the war would be over before he was sworn in for his unprecedented third term. And it might have been if Hitler had not planned for and carried out his attack on Russia in the spring of 1941. Hitler had the British army and what was left of the French (under Charles de Gaulle) pinned down in the Middle East. General Erwin Rommel had requested six divisions of tanks to drive the British and French out of Egypt. If Rommel could have crushed the allied powers in the Middle East, then it would have been a deathblow to de Gaulle's forces and might have forced the British to the peace table. The Germans would have had the oil rich Arabian lands open for the picking. In fact, Iraq wanted the British out and German protection in their land. This would have guaranteed Germany oil for their war needs. It would also have enabled them to trade oil with Japan, thereby alleviating the Allied embargo on Japan. This would have negated the need for Japan to bomb Pearl Harbor. If there was no attack on Pearl Harbor, there would be no entry of the United States into the war. On top of this fact, add that the soft underbelly of Russia would have been ripe for attack at some future point through the southern Caucasus area. All this could have happened, had Hitler first dispatched with the British and the French in Egypt. He did not.

Rommel pleaded for the tanks. Hitler refused, and then grudgingly gave him one division. Hitler was hell-bent on breaking his nonaggression pact with Russia and attacking them. This was the turning point in the war, although it would rage on for four more years. Hitler added another enemy and extended his eastern front, a front that needed very little in the way of defense before he attacked Russia. He could not aid his ally, Japan, and so being pressured by the embargos, the Japanese decided to attack Pearl Harbor. When they attacked, they drew first blood against the United States. Roosevelt then had a semi-free hand to go to war. He had one more problem, however. He had already discussed the entry of the United States into the war with Prime Minister Churchill. They had decided that Hitler posed the greater threat to the world's stability than Japan did. So it was agreed that when the United States joined the war, the concentration of forces would be upon winning the European theatre first, the Pacific second. But Japan attacked the United States, not Germany. How would Roosevelt tell the American public that the majority of the troops were being sent across the Atlantic, when a Pacific power had attacked them? Hitler solved Roosevelt's short lived problem by declaring war on the United States just a few days after the Pearl Harbor attack.

As it turned out, forces throughout the war were fairly evenly divided between the European and Pacific theaters.

Why did Hitler declare war on the United Sates? It was because Germany had a treaty with Japan to do so if and when Japan went to war with America. But why would either one of them have wanted to bring the United States into the war? Japan had a much greater reason to do so than Germany. Japan's island nation is poor in ores and oil. It needed to import much of what it needed to produce its fighting machine. Part of the reason for its imperial conquest was to secure these things. But the British, the Dutch, and the United States were working in unison to keep the pressure on the Japanese. All three countries denied oil exports to Japan and so forced the island nation to take a more belligerent stand against them. All three of the countries knew the Japanese reputation for sneak attacks. They had done so against Russia in the Russo-Japanese War in 1905. The Japanese navy had wiped out the Russian navy in a surprise attack at Port Arthur.

In 1940, Lieutenant Commander Arthur H. McCollum, head of the Far East Desk of the Office of Naval Intelligence, came up with a brilliantly sneaky plan of his own. He would goad the Japanese into attempting a sneak attack on the United States, because the American population was not going to enter the European war without a major attack occurring against the country first. The population saw the war in Europe as much ado about nothing. McCollum wanted the President to "create ado." McCollum had been raised in Japan as the son of Baptist missionaries. He knew the Japanese people and government well as he had spent much time there throughout his life. He proposed eight steps to the president that would pressure Japan into striking the United States and provoking a war. They were:

A. Make an arrangement with Britain for the use of British bases in the Pacific, particularly Singapore.
B. Make an Arrangement with Holland for the use of base facilities and acquisition of supplies in the Dutch East Indies (now Indonesia.)

C. Give all possible aid to the Chinese government of Chiang Kai-shek.
D. Send a division of long-range cruisers to the Orient, Philippines, or Singapore.
E. Send two divisions of submarines to the Orient.
F. Keep the main strength of the U.S. fleet, now in the Pacific in the vicinity of the Hawaiian Islands.
G. Insist that the Dutch refuse to grant Japanese demands for undue economic concessions, particularly oil.
H. Completely embargo all trade with Japan, in collaboration with a similar embargo imposed by the British Empire.[192]

If the United States took these actions and was able to coordinate these with the British and Dutch governments, then McCollum was sure that this would pressure the Japanese military into attacking the United States. He was sure that they would attack Pearl Harbor. Once Japan had attacked the United States, America would be at war with Germany as well. That was because Germany, Italy, and Japan had signed the Tripartite Alliance in September of 1940.

> The Tripartite Pact committed the three partners to assist each other in the event of an attack on any one of them. McCollum saw the alliance as a golden opportunity. If Japan could be provoked into committing an overt act of war against the United States, then the pact's mutual assistance provisions would kick in. It was a back door approach: Germany and Italy would come to Japan's aid and thus directly involve the United States in the European War.[193]

This plan of action meant that navy personnel would have to be put in harm's way as unknowing dupes. They would be made sitting ducks while the future enemy was allowed to come in and kill them and destroy their ships. The fleet commander, Admiral James O. Richardson, rejected this plan; he specifically rejected Roosevelt's desire to base the fleet in Hawaii. He did not think that a dangerous trap needed to be laid for the Japanese, dangerous that is to American sailors. He was sure that the Japanese would make a colossal mistake first that would draw the United States into the war. But Roosevelt was not going to wait for chance. Richardson was dismissed as fleet commander on February 1, 1941. Also the fleet command was split up into a two-ocean fleet, the Atlantic and Pacific Fleets.

There were a number of good reasons why Richardson refused Hawaii as a fleet station. They were:

1. lack of fundamental training facilities,
3. lack of large scale ammunition and fuel supplies,
2. lack of support craft such as tugs and repair ships,
4. there would be morale problems with the sailors being away from their families for extended periods of time,
5. lack of overhaul facilities such as dry docking and machine shops.[194]

In short, Hawaii was not a good place for a fleet base. It was a forward position that could handle some ships, but basing the fleet there was overloading the ability of the island to function as an installation. Yet, Roosevelt got his wish, and his wish added pressure on the Japanese. Now one would think that any fleet commander based there would understand the position he was stationed in, that he was in a forward post near a potential enemy. To some extent, the new fleet commander, Admiral Kimmel did know. But he was left out of the loop concerning some very important information.

Despite fifty years of denials, it turns out that the United States had broken many more of the Japanese codes than it admitted. Also, the Japanese navy did not adhere to radio silence in the preparation for the attack on Pearl Harbor as the story has been told. Evidence of radio signals, the transmissions themselves, and the directions from which they came exposed the Japanese navy.

Rochefort (Joseph J. Rochefort cofounder of the Navy's communication intelligence section) cited radio direction finding (RDF) as an important part of communications intelligence. He explained: "By means of radio direction finders you can ascertain the geographical position of the enemy force. That's called direction finding-DF. That's part of radio intelligence."[195]

This technique had been in use since WWI.

If the direction-finding intelligence was all the navy had, it could have followed the transmissions from the Japanese fleet and seen that a large fleet was heading toward striking distance of Hawaii. But there was more to it.

During the last days of September and the first week of October 1940, a team of army and navy cryptographers solved the two principle Japanese governmental code systems: Purple, the major diplomatic code, and portions of Kaigun Ango, a series of twenty-nine separate naval operational codes used for radio contact with warships, merchant vessels, naval bases, and personnel in overseas posts, such as naval attachés. Much has been made of the Purple code, and far too little of the naval code systems.[196]

The U.S. success in solving the diplomatic and naval code systems was a closely guarded naval secret. President Roosevelt regularly received copies of the Japanese messages decoded and translated from both Purple and Kaigun Ango...Controversy surrounds the timing of the successful decryption of the four code systems of the Kaigun Ango by the American code breakers. Testimony given to previous Pearl Harbor investigations suggests that the navy codes were not solved until the spring of 1942. The author's research proves otherwise. Their solution emerged in the early fall of 1940, at about the same time the Arthur McCollum memorandum reached the oval office.[197]

This would mean that President Franklin Delano Roosevelt knowingly and premeditatedly sent over 2,000 sailors and soldiers to die at Pearl Harbor when they were unaware of the danger that faced them. He did so to get the United States involved in a war he was convinced that America had to join. It was a conviction about which he did not tell the American voters. It, in fact, made a convenient lie, or rather a half-truth. If he had the callus ability to allow men to be killed on American territory and draw the United States into a war, then the war would not be a foreign war, even if it were fought on foreign territory. So in one sense, if honesty is discarded as a useless concept, Roosevelt did not lie. But this sort of dishonesty borders on criminality.

There is also additional information about the Pearl Harbor attack in a auto-biographical book Spy Counterspy written by Dusko Popov, a double agent working for the British. He was a Yugoslavian national businessman, with a reputation as a ladies' man, who was recruited by the Germans as a spy, but his loyalties sided with a free Yugoslavia and with pro-Western democracy. He soon made contact with British intelligence to work for them as a double agent. (The British agent and future writer, Ian Flemming, was one of his colleagues in the spy world and it is claimed that Popov was the real-life prototype for the James Bond series.) Be that as it may, Popov's book adds some fuel to the idea that Roosevelt, or at least the FBI Director J. Edgar Hoover was made aware in August of 1941 of Japan's intention to attack Pearl Harbor. The information came to light when Popov was told about Germany's microdot process of delivering coded messages. This was the process of printing coded material on a piece of film no bigger than a freckle or a period in a sentence. Under a microscope it could reveal volumes of information. Popov saw the possibilities of this microdot.

> I realized only too well, you could conceal a volume the size of the Bible in your personal belongings and carry it undetected through any control. I picked one of the dots

out of the box with tweezers and placed it on the back of my hand. It wasn't even a good sized freckle.[198]

The information on the microdot was a questionnaire that he needed to get information about. Some of the information was about the Hawaiian Islands. This raised Popov's curiosity.

> I didn't have to memorize the questionnaire but I had to study and discuss it. Picking up the list of questions I glanced at it while still sipping my second glass of champagne. This time I read further. The second heading was Hawaii. The Tirppitzufer (the German spy headquarters located in Berlin) was asking for information about ammunition dumps and mine depots on the Isle of Oahu, where Pearl Harbor is located. Tirpitzufer, my foot, I swore to myself. This was linked up with Taranto. Here was the answer to the question Johnny (Jebsen) and I were wondering about. This was the Japanese target.
>
> "What's this about the Isle of Oahu," I asked (Ludovico) von Kartshoff. I'm sure we're not planning a campaign right now in the Pacific, so it must be for our Asian ally, no? Same thing as Jebsen was working on."
>
> "So one would presume," he replied.
>
> "Hawaii is a little off my beat, unless I can pick up something in Washington."
>
> "No, I have specific instructions about that. You are to go to Hawaii as soon as possible."
>
> I nodded and murmured, "Very well." The picture was developing nicely. The Tirpitzufer—or the Japanese— weren't asking an academic question. There was some urgency about it. The action wasn't for tomorrow but it was for soon. According to Baron Gronau it would be before the Japanese fleet reached the one-year point in fuel reserves. Not difficult at all to figure out.[199]

The questionnaire showed a clear interest in the military position of the American fleet in Hawaii. The inference to

Taranto was the main clue. Johnny Jebsen had been Popov's college companion, friend, and the person who brought him into the Abwehr (the German spy organization). Jebsen was German by birth and an heir to a rich Hamburg ship owner. He, as Popov's collegiate friend, had no love for the Nazis, but Jebsen remained in Germany. To avoid the German military, he was forced into the intelligence services. He also functioned on the sly as a financial dealer in black market activities making fortunes for German officials and giving him money and blackmail information for his spy activities. So he was fully aware of and compliant with Popov's double agent status and seemed to recruit him with that hope in mind.

It was Johnny who became aware of the Japanese interest in Taranto.

On a secluded observation point of the Boca de Inferno cliffs overlooking the Atlantic outside Cascais (Portugal), Johnny gave me the details of his special mission to Italy. The breakers thundered in underneath, and not a person was in sight to disturb us.

"Peculiar," Johnny mused. "The mission was for the Japanese."

"In the south of Italy?"

"At Taranto. Major naval base there."

"I remember, that's where the British fleet attacked and put half of the Italian Navy out of action. But what do the Japanese have to do with Taranto?"

"I'll start at the beginning," Johnny offered. "The Japanese Foreign Minister, a chap named Yosuke Matsuoka, came to Berlin at the end of March. He had a bevy of navy and army brass with him to hash out military aspects of the Tripartite Act. Seems that some months before coming, the Japanese put in a request for the Abwehr to get them the details about Taranto. The Abwehr does the odd jobs for their intelligence boys, you know. Places they can't go. Too easy to spot slanty eyes and yellow epidermis. Not very Aryan our allies." Johnny couldn't resist a dig at the Nazis.

"Well, the Abwehr didn't furnish them with much. Matsuoka repeated the request when he got to Berlin, and Ribbentrop rose up on his toothpick legs and started screaming at Canaris to do something. I got nominated for the job...."

Looking at the unobstructed, limitless view of the sea, I reflected on how difficult a surprise attack would be.

"But why are the Japanese so interested in Taranto?"

"Why? Because it shows how one successful attack may annihilate a large part of an enemy fleet. Cunningham, the British Admiral, sneaked his aircraft carrier, the Illustrious, to about a hundred seventy miles from Taranto. Then he put out two waves of bombers, twelve the first time, nine the second. They dropped a potpourri of torpedoes, bombs, and flares, which proved very effective. The Japanese wanted every last detail: the effectiveness of the nets protecting the anchored ships, damage done to the dockyards, the petrol installations, the workshops. Everything. Now if they're planning something similar, they've a yardstick to go by."

"It would be hell if they really attacked in strength," I figured worriedly. "Cunningham didn't use much, nineteen planes in all. Supposing somebody put up hundreds..."[200]

This was information that Popov had received prior to knowing about the microdots. Then together with the information from the questionnaire, it was obvious to Popov that Pearl Harbor was in the cross hairs. He had been given this information in the summer of 1941. The attack on Pearl Harbor occurred in December of that year. He says he did not sit on this information. He relayed this information to his superiors in British intelligence who had a direct link to Prime Minister Winston Churchill. They in turn sent him on to the United States to inform J. Edgar Hoover, the head of the Federal Bureau of Investigation. There was no foreign espionage service, no Central Intelligence Agency at the time. Hoover was the gatekeeper through whom official intelligence information passed. Popov went to the United States, established residence in New York, supposedly to do trading for the Yugoslavian government. Though Popov was vetted by valid British sources, Hoover made him wait for weeks before granting him an interview. While he was there he reacquainted himself with an old British girlfriend and went to Miami. Hoover harassed Popov while he was on his amorous rendezvous with this young British woman who had fled to the United States during the war. Popov claims that FBI agents followed him to Miami and approached him on the beach when he was with his girlfriend. Wearing business suits, the agents looked out of place at the resort. They claimed that he was in violation of the Mann Act, transporting a girl across state lines for immoral purposes, and threatened to send them both out of the country. Popov had to send the young woman away without a good excuse; he couldn't tell her he was a spy being pressured by the FBI, and he had to return to New York alone. (This moral pressure was coming from Hoover, who would later be revealed as a cross-dressing homosexual.)

Popov was convinced that American lives were in imminent danger and that he could help divert that from happening. Of course, this would push the United States closer to war, but who would dare to sit on this information? So after weeks being in New York, posing as a Yugoslavian businessman, Hoover finally gave him an audience. According to Popov:

> J. Edgar Hoover encountered me. I use the word advisedly. There was no introduction, no preliminaries, no politesse. I walked into Foxworth's office (his FBI contact), and there was Hoover sitting behind a desk looking like a sledgehammer in search of an anvil. Foxworth, dispossessed, was silently in an armchair alongside.
>
> "Sit down Popov," Hoover yelped at me, and the expression of disgust on his face indicated that I was the equivalent of a fresh dog turd which had the audacity of placing itself beneath his polished brogans. I bit my tongue and sat in the chair across the desk from him. Now, if ever, was the time for diplomacy.

"I'm running the cleanest police organization in the world," Hoover ranted. "You come from nowhere and within six weeks you install yourself in a Park Avenue Penthouse, chase film stars, break a serious law, and try to corrupt my officers. I'm telling you right now, I won't stand for it." He pounded the desk as though to nail the words into my brain.

"I don't think," I said quietly, "that a choirboy could perform my job, but if I've caused you trouble, I pray you, forgive me."

Hoover turned to look at Foxworth (the FBI agent with whom Popov was in constant contact), his face grim, not quite able to judge if I was serious or pulling his leg. From over his shoulder he gave me a long, penetrating look, turned away again, saying not to me but to Foxworth, "He may leave now."

I lit a cigarette and settled back in my chair. The moment had come to make my play.

I gave it to him straight. "Mr. Hoover, my apologies were purely an exhibition of manners meant to take the edge off your unjustified remarks."

Hoover turned purple and choked out, "What do you mean?"

"I did not come to the United States to break the law or corrupt your organization. I came here to help with the war effort. I brought a serious warning indicating exactly where, when, how, and by whom your country is going to be attacked. I brought you on a silver platter the newest and most dangerous intelligence weapon designed by the enemy, something your agents have been trying to unearth for over a year and failed. It could have done much harm if not discovered in its initial stage. But mainly I came to help organize an enemy agent system in your country, which would be under your control and orders. I think that that is quite a lot to start with."

"I can catch spies without your or anybody else's help," Hoover barked.[201]

The dispute raged on without fruition. According to Popov, he had imparted the important information about the microdots and the attack on Pearl Harbor to the head of the FBI. He assumed that from there, from this high potentate of the United States, despite Hoover's bulldog rantings, the information would reach the highest offices in the land and prevent the attack on Pearl Harbor. It did not, or at least it seemed that it did not reach its intended destination.

Months later, as Popov was on a ship sailing north from Brazil to Canada on December 7, 1941, news of Pearl Harbor broke. He was sure that the attack had been thwarted and that the United States had scored a great naval victory. After all, he had forewarned the Americans of the impending attack, even to the degree of how it would come. But it did not matter. The attack occurred. Over 2,000 service men died unaware that they were in imminent danger. Popov writes:

> Then the news started trickling in. Involuntarily I shook my head till my brain felt as though it were coming unstuck. The bulletins were simply not believable. The Japanese had scored a surprise attack on Pearl Harbor. How, I asked myself, how? We knew they were coming. We knew how they were going to come. Exactly like at Taranto. And that's how they came, combined torpedo and dive bomber attacks, exactly as employed by Admiral Cunningham against the Italians. Except that the Japanese planes should have hardly gotten off the decks. More news. The battleships West Virginia and California had been sunk at their moorings. At their moorings, I moaned. They couldn't have been at their moorings. They had to be steaming to attack the Japanese fleet. Then it was the Arizona. Blown up. Every other battleship and unit of the fleet heavily damaged. This was Orson Wells, I thought, remembering his famous scare broadcast. I couldn't credit what I was hearing. Somewhere, somehow, there had to be an explanation. In one and a half hours the mastery of the Pacific had passed from American to Japanese hands.[202]

The only ships to escape the carnage were the two modern aircraft carriers that were sent on a mission to deliver bombers to another Pacific base. All the ships that were destroyed were vintage World War I ships.

Popov absolved Franklin Delano Roosevelt from prior knowledge of the attack. The FBI has documentary proof that FDR recieved information about the microdots, but it states nothing about Pearl Harbor. It is hard to believe that a head of state would allow such an attack on his country's defenses and military personal, unless in some callused way it suited a higher purpose and goal. It is also hard to believe that someone as hardened and calculating as a double agent could fall for pretense in government officials, but Popov was human if you read to the end of his book. He exonerated FDR and placed all the blame for Pearl Harbor at Hoover's feet. But if Hoover, a mere minister serving at the behest of the president, failed in a major cataclysmic fashion, wouldn't it make sense for his head to roll? Maybe he had information he could use to blackmail FDR. There certainly is information that FDR had love interests besides his wife, and Hoover was one to find out. But after being elected for a third term, and with a war engaged, there was little fear of that. Besides, FDR had been in the naval department during WWI, before he was governor of New York. He could not have been blind to the possibilities that Japan presented.

Roosevelt had eight years to watch Hitler, and to warn the people of the United States about the danger he posed. The same arguments made against appeasement governments in Britain and France can be leveled against Roosevelt. If the former Entente allies had stood strong in solidarity against Hitler early in his career as chancellor, he might have backed down. There were certainly people in Germany who wanted him out of power, but they needed strong outside help, help that they never got. Hitler was never stood up to before the war. And, as previously noted, the American people were distrustful of British intentions anyway and may not have wanted their president to make ominous overtures against a European power, no matter how weak that European power might have been at the time. Roosevelt probably would not have been reelected for an unprecedented third term if he had taken forceful action against Hitler in any way shape or form. But what is more important? Retaining power for a later bloodbath similar to World War I, or confronting a possible danger while it was still small enough to extinguish quickly?

This put Roosevelt in a tight box. For eight years, he paid little attention to the corporal in Germany, except to imitate his and Mussolini's economic practices. In the meantime, this corporal had rebuilt Germany into a massive fighting machine. Hitler did not have the limitations that the kaiser had. The kaiser was a member of a great European Christian family who had much interest in building his country, his family, and name into something great in Europe. The kaiser was trying to build upon the work of a long line of Prussian princes. Hitler wanted a thousand-year Reich for Germany or the funeral pyre. He got the pyre. The kaiser never thought of gathering all of Germany's Jews into one place to wipe them off the face of the earth; Hitler did. The kaiser would abdicate; sacrifice his office and power before sacrificing Germany and its people. Not so Hitler. So Roosevelt and the leaders in Britain and France let this pariah live and grow until he conquered all of Europe and threatened to invade Britain. Hitler then foolishly invaded Russia on June 22, 1941, and gave the United States time to plan to enter the war.

After December 7, 1941, Roosevelt had his war.

The bigger problem is that the United States took sides in the First World War. If the United States had truly been neutral, then it would have demanded that Britain end its blockade, just as it demanded that Germany give up the unrestricted submarine warfare. But the Wilson administration had no plans to do so. It claimed neutrality while it aided one side. This caused the German public to see Wilson as a liar and their situation as desperate. Then when the United States entered the war, they claimed that it was doing so to protect democracy. It was not. If that were the case, then Great Britain would have been forced to give home rule to all its empire including Ireland and India, something that it was not about to do in 1918. Having entered the war, the United States helped a dying nation (France) avoid a mortal blow, capitulation to Germany. It also helped Great Britain retain the status quo of its worldwide empire. And Germany remained intact after the war. All the Treaty of Versailles did was to call an armistice for twenty years until the war was engaged for act two. In act two, France did capitulate, and the British Empire broke up soon afterward from the double-edged sword of being broke and needing to grant democracy to all its empire. The United States then replaced Great Britain as the leader of the free world. Before this could take place, the United States needed to enter the Second World War.

The fact that Great Britain once again needed the help of its former colony in America cannot be overlooked. For the second time in twenty years, Great Britain failed at its goal of maintaining a balance of powers on the Continent and needed the help of the United States to set things right. This underscores the weakness of the British Empire. By the end of WWII, Great Britain no longer ruled the seas. The United States did. The power was transferred from Great Britain, the United Kingdom, to the United States. Victory in World War II was the conduit for this transfer. Great Britain was no longer great. The United States was.

The United States received the mantle of empire from Great Britain. No, there was no coronation ceremony, no transfer of the crown from the Union Jack to Old Glory. But the reality of the situation and the actions and the leadership taken in succeeding years would show the world who the emperor was.

Chapter Ten
The Cold War
"A Solemn Moment for American Democracy"

On June 22, 1941, German dictator Adolf Hitler made a blunder that caused him to lose the Second World War. He invaded Russia. By invading Russia, Hitler would lead Germany to defeat and to being split into two separate countries for over forty years.

Before Hitler engaged operation Barbarossa, Germany had only one major power fighting against him and his forces. That was Great Britain. Northern Europe was defeated and France had already surrendered. By invading Russia, Hitler had given up on defeating the British and Charles de Gaulle in Egypt. If he had defeated the Allies, there he could have driven the British out of the Middle East. This victory would have opened up the oil-rich Persian Gulf area to German conquest and would have strengthened Germany's position in the Mediterranean. It would have the further benefit of putting German troops opposite the Soviet Union's oil-laden Caspian Sea area. The Germans would have been in a position to block any supplies going to Russia via the Middle East and would have made it much easier to demand concessions from

Stalin. This would also alleviate the embargo that the Allies had imposed on Japan. There would have been no need for Japan to attack the United States at Pearl Harbor. Without this attack, the American populous would not have wanted to get involved in either the European or Pacific Wars. Obviously, this is not the course that Hitler chose. He attacked Russia, gave some breathing room to British forces in the Middle East, and he was not able to aid the Japanese.

Franklin Delano Roosevelt and Winston Churchill both realized that the United States would have to enter the war to defeat the Nazis and the Japanese. When Hitler declared war on the United States just a few days after Pearl Harbor, he had three major enemies against him, one of which (the United States) was too distant for him to touch. For this reason, alone, it is obvious that he was no military genius. The man who claimed that he would lead Germany to a thousand-year Reich ensured his own demise and that of his country. He extended his forces too far and brought in new enemies when he could have defeated the one in hand. Hitler was no Frederick the Great, the founder of Prussia, though he conquered more territory than the Prussian king. The Prussian king knew when to sue for peace with former enemies. Hitler was no Bismarck. He had united a "Greater Germany" rather than Bismarck's "Lesser Germany." Hitler's Germany included Austria; Bismarck's did not. But Bismarck knew to fight small winnable wars. And when he won in his limited quest, he then consolidated his holdings and smoothed ruffled feathers to maintain a balance of power on the European stage. Hitler was not even a Kaiser Wilhelm. The kaiser had agreed to the Schlieffen Plan, which envisioned defeating the French army in six weeks by going through neutral Belgium before turning to fight Russia. The kaiser's forces fought for four years and came close to destroying the French army. Hitler was in Paris by June of 1940, in six weeks, but it was all for nought. By May 7, 1945, Hitler was dead of a suicide, then soaked in gasoline and burnt at the same time that Berlin was reduced to rubble and burned by Russian forces. The kaiser had abdicated in order to save Germany from being invaded; Hitler choose the funeral pyre for Berlin.

The Russians had gotten to Berlin first, sacrificing 400,000 men, and some women, in order to lay waste to the capital of the Wehrmacht. When the Russians arrived, they repaid Nazi atrocities of their homeland by raping and pillaging. The phrase "Frau commen heir" (Woman come here), would often precede a gang rape of women of any age. The wartime leaders, Roosevelt, Churchill, and Stalin, had already decided that the city of Berlin would be divided between them. The French were allotted a section as an afterthought, but Stalin insisted that their territory come out of the Western areas. When the Westerners arrived in Berlin, they found the Russians had already established themselves. Russian abuse of the German populous, especially the women, got so bad that in the American and British sectors the Western troops would arrest Russian troops on sight and send them back. Sometimes the Russians were beaten and then dumped back in their own sector. The Russians took anything of value and sent it back to Moscow. That included whole factories. Stalin wanted to root up all of Germany's industrial abilities and turn it into an agricultural backwater that would never threaten the Soviet Union again. The Western powers wanted to eradicate Germany's war machine, but they also wanted and needed it to regain its position as an economic dynamo on the European landscape. There was another problem. It had become apparent that the wartime allies would not remain friends for long.

Even as the three allies were fighting alongside each other, the seeds for the next war were germinating. This alliance was the perfect example of politics making strange bedfellows. Joseph Stalin's Communist regime was distrusted and even hated by many in the Capitalist West. In fact, many Americans were fully aware of what Hitler had written in his manifesto *Mein Kampf* that he wanted to take land (lebensraums) from the Soviet Union as a place to settle Germans, and approved of the Nazis fighting the Communists.

> "State boundaries are made by man and changed by man...," [204]said Hitler. He continued,

> And so we National Socialists consciously draw a line beneath the foreign policy tendency of our pre-war period (pre-WWI). We take up where we broke off six hundred years ago. We stop the endless movement to the south and west, and turn our gaze to the land in the east. At long last we break off the colonial and commercial policy of the pre-war period and shift to the policy of the future...If we speak of soil in Europe today, we can primarily have in mind only Russia and her vassal border states.[205]

Many "America Firsters" who wanted the United States to stay out of the war wanted to see Hitler and Stalin battle it out and weaken each other to the benefit of the West. The United States had sent an expeditionary force into Communist Russia in the early twenties while it was still an infant country to overthrow the Communists. They wanted to reestablish the fledgling democracy that the Communists had overthrown. This attempt failed. Churchill was an avid anti-Communist from his early days in politics. But both Britain and the United States put aside their deep political and ideological hatred of Communism to fight the Nazis alongside Stalin.

From the beginning, France and Britain were not going to allow Germany to have its Lebensraum in the East. Notwithstanding Neville Chamberlain's appeasement embrace, Britain declared war on Germany when it invaded Poland in the fall of 1939. Hitler had claimed that he wanted no part of France, Belgium, or Holland, but he conquered them quickly after they had declared war on Germany. Britain's and France's logic was simple. First, Germany invaded a sovereign country in direct violation of the Versailles Treaty. Second, if Hitler were allowed to get his "lebensraum" in the

East, if he fought Russia, while the West stood still, he might win, and then be even more powerful in the future. If he had the granaries of the Ukraine, the oil from the Caspian Sea, the population from which to draw soldiers, and the raw materials to build his war machine, he would be unstoppable. So Britain and France had to try to stop him. The problem was that they could not.

There is an American tradition that must be kept in mind that could make the United States slow to enter a European war. It is the attitude developed early in the country's history that is not limited to the first president, but he spoke of it at the end of his time in office. President Washington had warned the young country:

> Europe has a set of primary interests which to us have none or a very remote relation. Hence she must remain engaged in frequent controversies, the cause of which are essentially foreign to our concerns. Hence, therefore, it must be unwise in us to implicate ourselves by artificial ties in the ordinary vicissitude of her politics or the ordinary combinations of her friendships or enmities. Our detached and distant situation invites and enables us to pursue a different course...Why forego the advantages of so peculiar a situation? Why quit our own to stand upon foreign ground? Why, by interweaving our destiny with that of any part of Europe, entangle our peace and prosperity in the toils of European ambition, rivalship, interest, humor, or caprice.[206]

Even if the majority of people in the United States could not quote Washington's Farewell Address, many agreed with the idea represented in it. Since many viewed WWI as a waste of men and money, Washington's words could hold even more meaning. Before the Japanese attacked Pearl Harbor, gallop polls were showing that 75 to 80 percent of the country wanted the United States to stay out of the war. It took the deaths of over 2,000 men in a (supposedly) sneak attack to anger the public of the United States enough that they wanted to join the war.

During the occupation of Germany after WWI some of the allies saw a different side to the Teutonic hordes that were supposedly destroying Europe.

> In Germany, American troops had moved into the Rhineland as part of an army of occupation. The Americans and their British counterparts elsewhere in Germany swiftly realized from the gaunt faces they saw on the street that the Germans were starving to death. The British started bombarding the war office in London with horror stories. General Sir Hubert Plumer, commander of the British occupation army, said his soldiers could not stand the sight of hordes of skinny and bloated children pawing through the garbage in the British camps. Minister of War Winston Churchill issued a statement, based on evidence he had seen from officers sent to Germany by the War Office: There was grave danger of the entire collapse of the vital structure of German social life under the pressure of hunger and malnutrition.[207]

As the evidence poured in from Germany, it seemed apparent that Britain had lied to the Americans to get them into the war and effect the outcome that was most advantageous to them. This is the exact thing that President Washington had warned the young nation against. The American people felt that they had become the pawns of British strategy.

The Great Depression had much to do with the "isolationist" attitude of the United States. It was the longest-lasting and deepest depression the country had ever seen. Of course, it was a worldwide depression, but that hardly mattered to the people of the United States. It is amazing that FDR stayed in power through eight years of it. Unemployment remained around 14-17 percent throughout his whole first two terms and it was the need to feed WWII that generated the industrial capacity to put people to work, not any of the president's alphabet soup programs. But Roosevelt had so tarred Herbert Hoover, Republicans, and business, claiming that they were the cause and effect of the Depression, that this idea was hardly ever doubted. The Depression kept Washington busy taking care of (and in some cases adding to the) problems at home, rather than being concerned about foreign affairs.

All of these issues promoted a general lack of concern about what was going on in Europe or in Asia. Also, Roosevelt never bothered to inform the people about the dangers of a Nazi-led Europe. There was, naturally, no great desire on the part of the Americans to join the war effort. It took a cataclysmic event such as Pearl Harbor to bring the United States out of the doldrums of the Depression era and back into the world scene.

The United States allied itself with its former Entente partners, but the partnership, though necessary, had soured. Communist Russia was never a good fit with the Capitalist West. The discovery of thousands of executed Polish soldiers was blamed on the Nazis, but it was clear from the evidence that it was Stalin's handiwork. One of our allies was as evil as the enemy we were trying to destroy. This had to be covered up for the sake of the Allied effort. And if it weren't for the mutual enemy, the Nazis, there would be a natural conflict with the Communists in the East and the Capitalists in the West. But the enemy of my enemy is my friend.

Underneath the warmth of wartime comrades, there lurked uncertainty. That uncertainty was what Europe should look like when the war was over. Germany was not only a tough foe to defeat, it was also a lynchpin in the economic well-being of Europe. Militarily, it was they, and especially Prussia, who had held the Russian bear at bay and far off from Western Europe.

> While the allied forces took on the terrific job of salvation, officials in London turned their attention to problems that might follow the victory. They concluded that there was no real security for Britain in the post war

world without an American commitment to maintaining the peace. The United States, they believed, must be persuaded to take on international leadership, ideally based upon a partnership between the United States and Britain that would outlast the war and win the peace.[208]

The fact that Great Britain, the former ruler of the Seas, the former ruler of the world, would have to bow down and come to this conclusion shows the weakness of the empire. After two world wars fought to preserve the empire, the empire would have to share its power and prestige with one of its former colonies that was now eclipsing it in power and strength. If it were not for the United States in WWI, Germany would have been victorious and Great Britain would have had to share the world stage with it. Again, twenty years later, Great Britain was facing a Teutonic horde that the empire could not defeat alone, and again, it turned to its former colony in America. It was a dramatic change that was taking place before the world's eyes. The torch was being passed from the mentor to the student. The teacher was being eclipsed by the pupil. Elisha would get his double portion of Elijah's spirit.

So the "isolationist" attitude at the beginning of WWII had a very real and understandable reason. Now, after the "sneak" attack on Pearl Harbor, the British were concerned about getting the United States to see beyond the war to what would be its responsibilities for the post war situation. The British were not doing this for humanitarian or democratic reasons. No, this desire to have the United States share in the world power was a realization that Great Britain was no longer "Great." It was no longer up to the task at hand. If the British Empire could have dealt the death blow to the Nazis by themselves, they would have gladly done so. If they needed only some guns, some planes, and some tanks to defeat Hitler, they would have purchased those items from the United States and prosecuted the war. They needed the United States involved in the war. Not only that, but they needed to have the United States stay in Europe once the fighting was done, because ever since the English had defeated the Spanish Armada in the days of the Tudor kings, England/Great Britain had joined forces with the weaker powers of Europe to fight the major powers. The British and the Dutch fought together to defeat Spain. Later, the British and Dutch forces fought France. France, Spain, and the Dutch forces fought against the British in the American Revolution, one of its few losses, and one of the few times that Britain fought a major war by itself. Britain and Austria had teamed up to fight France. Later on, it was Britain united with Prussia to defeat Napoleon's France. Britain's main interest in European affairs was to prevent the European landscape from being conquered by any one power. If one power controlled all of Europe, then they could easily invade the British Isles. This is why Britain's navy was so important to them. It kept the invaders away. But this is also why Britain needed the United States to be concerned about Europe after the war was over. After two world wars fighting to maintain their hold on the empire, Britain and the empire were broke and beaten. And there had been a price to pay for the help from the United States. Part of it was South African gold that had been shipped over to the United States. Another part of it was pressure from the United States that Britain needed to allow all of its dominions to be self-determined. The biggest sticking point for the Americans in WWII was how Britain was treating India. Great Britain continued to deny them India democratic rights even after India had sent thousands of troops to fight and die in both world wars. It seemed obvious to Americans that, if they were fighting alongside of Britain for a second time to secure Europe for freedom and democracy, the British should practice what they preached in India. Of course, if Britain were to give up control over its dominions, then the empire would crumble and their power would disappear. Churchill hemmed and hawed on the point about democracy throughout the empire while they fought for the rights of free and democratic countries in Europe.

> So in order to commend ourselves to the United States
> public through publicity we have to demonstrate through
> grim repetition how great a contribution Britain has
> made in the fight against the common enemy. We have
> to proclaim the renaissance of Britain in the war. In this
> respect publicity can be a servant of highest value to
> policy. For if we do not correct, through publicity, the
> illusion of many Americans that this country is doomed
> to be a satellite power, a poor relation, a sort of Uncle
> James who worked hard in his day, but is now past it,
> poor old fellow, and must be pensioned off, then our
> government will have a tough time.[209]

So said Robin Cruikshank of the British Ministry of Information.

It was obvious to anyone viewing the situation that Britain would no longer be able to manage the European landscape after the war. After there was no Germanic power, whether Prussian or Austrian, without a formidable France, without a strong Britain, there was no European power to stop the Russians from taking over all of Europe. Germany was laid to waste. Austria was defeated. France was still prostrate and licking its wounds. Russia had been badly wounded in the war also, but had recovered well and still maintained its ability to fight after Berlin collapsed.

The victorious powers were having troubles coordinating the occupation once the war was over. As stated earlier, the Russians were instituting severe punishment and retribution on Germany. The Western Allies wanted Germany and its leaders punished, but also wanted to rebuild a vibrant economy. The two sides argued and debated until the West started seeing Stalin for the Communist he was.

On February 9, 1946, Stalin made a speech that exposed his Leninist Communist roots. It was his first five-year plan since the end of the war. In the speech he declared that:

> the real cause of WWII had been the demands and the

contradictions of the capitalist imperialist monopoly and that those same forces were still at work outside the Soviet Union. Stalin proclaimed that the Soviet Union must be able to guard against all eventualities and that an absolute priority would therefore be given to rearmament. "Consumer goods" Stalin directed "would wait." The speech heralded the end to any pretense of continued cooperation with the west.[210]

George Keenan, the United States ambassador to the Soviet Union, wrote a paper that became known as the "Long Telegram" in which he assessed the thinking and the strategy of the Soviet Union. In this letter he dropped all pretenses of wartime niceties.

> "Soviet Leaders,' Kennan wrote "are driven by the necessities of their own past and the present positions to put forth a dogma which pictures the outside world as evil, hostile and menacing, but as bearing within itself germs of a creeping disease and destined to be wracked with growing internal convulsions until it is given a final coup de grace by the rising power of socialism... In general, all Soviet efforts...will be negative and destructive in character, designed to tear down sources of strength beyond Soviet control." This, Kennan felt, was in keeping with a basic Soviet instinct that there can be no compromise with a rival power and that constructive work can only start when Communist power is dominant. The prescription he proposed to counter the Soviet Union was essentially a complete reversal of the foreign policy of the Roosevelt years, when compromise, understanding and cooperation were sought. It was a call to awaken to a new danger.[211]

In the first three years after the war, most of the United States army was shipped home.

> The United States Army, made up of eight million soldiers during the war, now mustered only 1.6 million,

and the high command made it clear to Congress that, in the event of a conflict it would be impossible for more than a division of troops to be committed without partial mobilization. The newly established command known as the United States Air Forces in Europe USAFE was so weak that its commander, General Curtis LeMay feared that it "would be stupid to get mixed up in anything bigger than a cat fight at a pet store." His eleven operational combat troops, totaling 275 aircraft, faced over 4,000 Soviet planes.[212]

There was one thing that tipped the scale toward the involvement of the United States in Europe. President Harry Truman recognized the Communist threat to free people and to the United States. Consider it the British experience multiplied. If Britain's fears were real, the Soviet Union would take over all of Europe. A weakened postwar Britain would be in no position to prevent an invasion that came from Germany, Holland, Belgium, France, and across the North Sea, all at the same time. If the Western trading partners of the United States were now absorbed by a new foe, the country would stand alone against Communism. Cut off from trading partners, its economy would suffer horribly, maybe even worse than the Great Depression. It would have to fight a Russian/European enemy without any First World ally. In the late twentieth century, 3,000 miles of ocean would not be hard to transverse. And if Britain fell, its navy might go with it. (Though it should be noted that British and American naval planners had already thought through the dilemma of where the British navy would go if the island nation were ever invaded and defeated. The ships would flee to the United States and fight in exile from the American continent.)

Truman had been brought on in 1944 as Roosevelt's vice president to help FDR win the southern states in his fourth election. Truman was not informed about anything important, such as the atomic bomb in the Manhattan Project, nor was he kept up to speed in the postwar conferences. After Roosevelt's death on April 12, 1945, Truman had a learning curve to which he needed to adjust. At first he rebuffed Churchill and leaned toward Stalin, but he soon learned to take the true stock of Stalin and to stand with Churchill. In dealing with Soviet expansion, he made sure to keep them out of Japan.

> "Our experience with them in Germany, Bulgaria, Romania, Hungry, and Poland was such that I decided to take no chances with a joint set up with the Russians." Truman concluded, "The Russians were planning world conquest."[213]

On March 5, 1946 Truman introduced Churchill at Westminster College, a small liberal arts school in Fulton, Missouri. It was here that Churchill first spoke to an American audience about an "Iron Curtain."

> "The United States stands at this time at the pinnacle of world power," Churchill stated. "It is a solemn moment for American Democracy," he began, going on to talk in general terms for the need for an overall concept to clarify strategic thinking. He dwelt heavily on the special relationship between Great Britain and the United States.
> Late in his oration, he turned to the shadow that has fallen upon the scene so recently lighted by allied victory, saying that nobody knew or could know, the limits of Soviet expansiveness. From Stettin (Poland) to the Baltic to Trieste (Italy) in the Adriatic, an iron curtain has descended across the Continent. Behind that line lie all the capitals of the ancient Central and Eastern Europe. Warsaw, Berlin, Prague, Budapest, Vienna, Bucharest and Sofia, Churchill rumbled, "I do not believe that Soviet Russia desires war. What they desire is the fruits of war and the infinite expansion of their power and doctrines. "The last time that I saw it all coming,' he said near the end of his speech, referring to his speeches in Parliament on the rise of Hitler, 'no one paid attention...If all British morals and material forces and convictions are joined

with your own fraternal association, the high roads of the future will be clear, not only for us, not only for our time, but for a century to come."[214]

Not everyone believed Churchill's words. Later on at Columbia University in New York, he was met by picketers calling him a warmonger. But it became obvious that Truman believed him. When the Soviets tried to pressure the Westerners out of Berlin, Parliament and Truman stood tall. The message of WWI had sent to the people of the United States into "Fortress America." The message of WWII was that the United States now had new responsibilities that it could not turn away from. There was no doubt that the Soviet Union meant to oppress Europe. The Soviet Union was an aggressive, Communist, atheistic nation antithetical to the economic and spiritual aspects of both Britain and the United States. To succumb to the Communists would mean a disruption of life similar to that of the French Revolution in France, or for that matter, revolutionary Russia. Land-owners, businessmen, priests, ministers, and nonrevolutionary politicians would be strung up or bayoneted. Also, anyone who spoke out against the mob of "comrades," who would cleanse the populous, would be put in the gallows. Europe had seen the likes of these men before. They stood aside when Hitler had risen to power. Now they, or at least Churchill and Truman, saw another like him and were determined to stop Stalin before it was too late.

Berlin was 110 miles inside the Soviet sector. The city was supposed to function as the capital of Germany, though divided and occupied, and each of the nations was to be stationed in Berlin. There was one road and one rail line that connected Berlin with the western sectors running through a thin corridor in Soviet territory. Since the Soviets were in Berlin first, they were the ones who captured it, and they proceeded to fill all the city departments with their own people. Even a defeated Berlin that lay in rubble needed officials, especially police and the fire departments, and so on, to take care of day-to-day operations. Typically, the occupiers, whether the Western allies or the Soviets, would vet the city officials to see who was a Nazi holdout and who could be trusted, or used in an official capacity. Often, the military would just put one of their own in power, and that person would have to work with the local population. This is what the Soviets did for the most part. When they did use the local populous, they were either dyed-in-the-wool Communists, or stooges who would do their bidding. But the Soviets made sure that the police department was staffed by militant Communists. These police were used to arrest people and deport them to Russia, where many were never heard from again. These disappearances in Berlin were commonplace. It could even happen in the Western sectors of the city. So the Western allies got used to stopping any police car from the Soviet sector and sending the Russians back immediately. It was safe to assume that any Soviet police officer in the Western sector was there to rape, steal, or kidnap.

> Incidents involving armed Soviet soldiers entering the western sector to loot and rape continued to be reported, and they were brought up at the Kommandatura (the military ruling body of the four victorious countries), where they were met with Soviet denials. The four powers wrangled over the issuance of postage stamps in the city, over efforts to bring the black market under control, over such arcane details as whether Germans should be allowed to have tattoos removed, and over the important issue of food. The Americans concluded that the lowest category of rations 1,248 calories per day was below subsistence level. They proposed to raise it.[215]

In arguing the proposal before the Kommandatura, Colonel Frank Howley, the deputy commandant, used a common American metaphor.

> "You can't kick a lady when she is down," he said.

> "Why, my dear Colonel Howley," replied Colonel Dalada,
> the Soviet deputy, "that is the best time to kick them."
> "You mean food is political?" Howley asked,
> unbelievingly.
> The Soviet was smiling when he responded, "Of
> course."[216]

When Berlin's political body got back on its feet again and
tried to reinstate the city *Magistrat* (the city's administrative
body) control over the police department, the Soviets would
not hear of it. If the Magistrat tried to remove a Soviet police
officer, the officer would refuse to step down and would
remain in his post.

The first city elections were a boon to the city and a bust to
the Communists, as they were in almost any Eastern European
city where elections were allowed. Wherever there were free
and open elections, the Communists lost in landslides. In
Berlin, the Communists tried all the tricks in the book to win
the election. They lied about their opponent; they portrayed
themselves as the unifiers of Berlin while they were working to
destroy it. When that did not work, they threatened retaliation
to those who voted against the party line. They also tried to
buy votes. But there was one election pamphlet that cut right
to the heart of many Berliners.

> The Berliners linked the campaign waged by the SED
> (Sozialistische Einheitspartei, the Socialist Party) to
> the 1932 campaign by the Nazis, with the same stage
> management and flamboyant appeal to mass emotion,
> but the new party received at least one dose of its own
> vituperative medicine when anonymous pamphlets
> appeared all over the city, bearing the question of
> macabre humor. "Were you raped by a Russian?" The
> pamphlets asked. "If so then vote for the SED"[217]

It was a piece of reverse psychology since the SED was
the Communists; the voters, particularly the women, were
reminded of the horrors inflicted upon them by the invading

Communists. Needless to say, a searing negative image was brought to mind for those women and the men who cared for them.

> The elections were held on October 21, 1946 and 92 percent of the eligible voters cast their ballots. It was an overwhelming defeat for the Communist SED. The Social Democrats polled 48.7 percent, the Christian Democrats 22.2, the Liberal Democrats 9.3. The SED drew only 19.2 percent citywide and only 21 percent in their own sector. It was a showing that did not even equal that of the Communists in pre-Hitler days.[218]

The Soviets retaliated by deporting thousands of East Berliners to Russia. Though the Communists had been soundly defeated at the polls, they still continued to harass, intimidate, and beat up the victors of the election to try to get their way.

Finally, Stalin came up with what he thought was a winning plan. He assumed correctly that the West was in no shape for an all out war. He also knew that he could play on their compassion. He thought that if he starved the people of Berlin and gave the West the ultimatum—leave or die—that the West would leave out of concern for the Berliners. So he cut off the lifelines to the West, the Autobahn and the one rail line, and he stopped food and coal shipments into the city from the East. The West did not dare force its way into the 110 miles of road and train lines to Berlin. This would start a war with the Soviets in which the West would technically be the instigators, and they would be overwhelmed by the massive forces that Stalin still had. But there was one available avenue that would not violate Soviet territory. There was an air corridor that had been agreed upon by the four powers. The deputy for military government was Lucius DuBignon Clay. He was answerable directly to General Dwight D. Eisenhower, still the supreme allied commander of Europe. Clay decided to use an airlift as a temporary measure to bring in supplies until a more permanent solution could be found. There were two airports in Berlin that could be used. But even as Clay thought about the idea, he knew that it would be impossible to feed and bring in enough coal to take care of a city of 2.5 million people. As Clay saw it, "even using the most modern transport aircraft available, the C-54, with its capacity of ten tons, an airlift to Berlin would mean landing 450 planes per day in the city."[219] Clay was certain that the West would need to take the chance of starting a war with Russia by forcing the roads open in order to feed Berlin.

Little did Clay know that the airlift was exactly what would be used to save Berlin.

Clay was hoping that he could convince the president or the joint chiefs of staff to run the blockade on the ground. He went back to Washington to plead his case. There were three choices, "leave, supported by many (of the top officers in the military), attempt to stay and hope for a diplomatic solution, or fight a major war with the Soviet Union."[220]

The American military leaders were shocked to learn that Parliament had voted to stay in Berlin no matter what the cost.

> At the White House on Monday, June 28, 1948, Harry S. Truman listened intently as Undersecretary of State Robert Lovett reached the possible alternatives, beginning with the abandonment of the city, Truman cut in sharply to say something that startled everybody in the room. "There is no discussion on that point. We stay in Berlin—period." Army Secretary Kenneth Royall thinking the president's reaction too swift and unconsidered protested. "Mr. President, have you thought this through?" he asked going on to point out that the United States was committing itself to a position where it might have to fight its way into the city. "We will have to deal with that situation as it develops," Truman shot back, "but the essential position is that we are in Berlin by terms of an agreement and that the Russians have no right to get us out either by direct or indirect pressure."[221]

President Harry, "the buck stops here," Truman had made up his mind that Berlin was worth the risk of war. It was a similar decision in London. The Parliament on both sides of the aisle considered Berlin worth the risk of war. They felt that giving in to Stalin in Berlin would definitely lead to a real war later down the road. Just as Berliners had the hindsight of being able to recognize that the Soviet propaganda in the 1946 election was a reoccurrence of the Nazi propaganda of 1932, London and Washington realized their earlier mistakes as well. Truman and Churchill, then Clement Attlee (Churchill's replacement as prime minister), Parliament and Congress saw that appeasing Stalin would lead to a greater war. Standing up to him at the present moment, no matter how impossible that looked, had to be done, period!

> The drone of the planes in the sky landing at a rate of one every eight minutes, was somewhat reassuring, but Andreas-Friedrich and her daughter had both heard one of the widely circulated stories in the city about Soviet plans—the parable of the wart…The story went that a German-speaking Western Intelligence officer wearing civilian clothes somehow found himself seated between two Russian officers on a bus, or subway, or in some other place.
> "The Americans seem to be making out alright in their airlift," the first Russian commented, and the second replied, "Yes, but this morning I was talking to Alexander Gregorovitch—"
> "Who?"
> "You know the General, Alexander Gregorovitch says we'll give the Americans the wart treatment."
> "What's the wart treatment?"
> "Well when you have a wart on your finger, you tie a string around it tight, and keep tightening it. Then you wait until the wart falls off."
> "As the Berliners worried what would happen next, the twin engine C-47s that LeMay and Smith had scrapped

together from all across Europe continued their flights into the city, and the larger C-54s from across the globe began to arrive at Rhein-Main. The first of the ten-ton-capacity planes landed at 9:30 on the morning of June 30. By 7:36 p.m., it had taken off with a full load of flour.[222]

So LeMay had three groups of planes, A, B, and C, ready to fly into Berlin. Group A was based at Wiesbaden. They were all C-47s. Group B was based at Rhein-Main, which also had C-47s. Group C were all C-54s, also at Rhein-Main.

The three groups operated on a block system, with the first C-47 leaving Wiesbaden at 7:00 a.m., and the 60 remaining planes of Group A following at four minute intervals. At 11:00 a.m. when the last C-47 left Wiesbaden, the first of the fifteen planes in Group B took off from Rhein-Main, with the final plane of that group off the ground by noon. The first C-54 did not take off until twenty minutes later, as the larger planes cruised at 180 miles per hour—30 miles per hour faster than the C-47s. When the last of the C-47s of group B reached Berlin, the first C-54-having made up time and closing distance on it—was only four minutes behind, maintaining the steady beat of the airlift.

By the time the last C-54 of Group C left its Rhein-Main base, the C47s of Group A had already returned to Wiesbaden, refueled, and reloaded, and the first had taken off again. Each individual mission to Berlin took eight hours, including the time on the ground in the city, and each group flew three missions each day. The aircraft crews were assigned to a schedule where they would fly two missions—a sixteen hour stretch—and then have the next sixteen off. [223]

The planes were off-loaded by German crews overseen by United States servicemen. So in this way, Berlin was fed and warmed.

In a reversal of WWII animosities, German cities bonded with the American airlift effort. The planes that once rained death, destruction, chaos, and calamity were now flying in life-giving sustenance of food and fuel to the beleaguered German capital. The apocalyptic horsemen of death and pestilence were now angels of mercy trying to break Stalin's deadly siege.

> Throughout Germany, communities held rallies to collect food to be sent to the people of Berlin. In Melsungen an old walled town in Hesse, twenty-two miles from the border of the Soviet zone and directly under the fight path of the planes flying out of Rhein Main, the citizens rose up early one day to attend a rally in the town square. They saw the local SDP leader, Ernst Spars, point to the sky and say, "Up there the American people are showing their faith in the cause of our Berlin brothers every hour of every day. Now we must act. There is not much food here for us, but let us share with those brave Berliners what little we have." The square resounded with a "Ja!" (Yes!) from the crowd. The people of Melsungen agreed to pledge four freight cars of grain, dried fish and vegetables to Berlin."[224]

The airlift provided the least possibility of an all-out war with the Soviets. So although it was the hardest supply route to accomplish, the benefits were the greatest.

The airlift was proceeding slowly in a deadly game of chicken where the Soviets were betting that the Americans would give up their effort first, and the Americans realized they had to make a stand here or see all of Europe go under the Soviet yoke. General Clay had reported to the president that the people of Berlin where bravely withstanding the privations brought on by the Soviet blockade. He assured the president that Berlin would stand if the airlift could bring in 4,500 tons of goods per day. That was on July 19th. At that date, the airlift was bringing in only 2,500 tons per day. Truman pressed the air force to do more. Then they brought in the big gun.

A sealed envelope came to General William Turner

from the Air Force chief of staff. It contained a highly classified document addressed to General Vandenberg from Army Lieutenant General Albert Wedemeyer. In it, Wedemeyer stated his belief that the airlift could either break the blockade of Berlin outright or, at the very least, sustain the city while negotiations were going on. Citing the success of the Hump airlift in Asia, Wedemeyer recommended to the Air Force chief that Turner be sent to Germany to run the Berlin operation...The man who was called "Willy the Whip" by his staff was on his way to Germany.[225]

So Turner, the man who flew supply missions over the Himalayas, would be sent to Germany to tighten up procedures and pull off the impossible. Meanwhile, there were plenty of pilots flying in and out of Berlin daily. One of them, Gail Halvorsen, went out to see what he could of Berlin. When he came to the edge of the Tempelhof airport, where he and his fellow airmen flew into, he noticed a group of German children gathered watching the planes land. He struck up a conversation with them in broken German, and they answered in school-book English. When the conversation ended, and as he was headed for his car, he thought that there was something strange about the encounter. None of the children had asked him for candy or gum, something that he was used to from kids all over the world, wherever he flew. He reached into his pocket grabbed two pieces of gum, split them in half, and handed it to some of the kids there. He promised to drop more candy out of his plane to the kids waiting at the end of the runway if they promised to share it. Of course, the children readily agreed.

> The children shouted "Jawohl!" (Yes sir!) Then one of the interpreters, a little blue-eyed girl in oversized boy's trousers asked how they would know which plane was his. "When I get overhead, I'll wiggle the wings of the big airplane back and forth several times," he responded.[226]

So he convinced two of his regular crew members into joining his plans and they gave their candy rations and dropped three packages tied with small parachutes out of the flare chute in the engineer's station. They did this a couple of times despite the fears from his two crewmates that they would get in trouble for not following procedures. Of course, the group of children grew with each candy drop.

In the meantime, in Berlin, there were two police forces vying for control of the city. The Communists who were in place before the West showed up would not step down from their posts for the duly elected magistrates to take their offices. The propaganda war continued with recriminations being lodged by Stalin's men about the actions of the West. All of this was going on with the full understanding that if the Soviet Union wanted to, they had a larger military force on hand that could be moved in overnight. The West would have to build up for months to fight to save Berlin.

Still the planes continued to bring life to the beleaguered capital. Halvorsen kept flying his planes into Tempelhof and dropping candy to the growing band of waiting German children. Then one day, his worst fear hit him. Halvorsen went to the base operations to check on a fog delay. "In the corner of the room was a large table, stacked high with what looked like mail. Curious, Halvorsen looked at it and was startled to find that the stacks were letters addressed to Onkel Wackelflugel (Uncle Wiggly Wings) and Der Schokoladen Flieger (The Chocolate Flier), Tempelhof Central Airport, Berlin."[227]

Halvorsen kept flying, he and his crew feared that they would be in big trouble. So for a couple of weeks they didn't drop their packages. But the crowd of kids kept growing. His crew was not eating their candy, so it just piled up. Finally they decided to make one last drop. They had six packages that they parachuted out of the plane. This time they were caught. The next day a jeep met Halvorsen's plane on the tarmac. He was ordered to report to the squadron commander of Colonel James R. Haun.

"Halvorsen, what in the world have you been doing?" the Colonel began.

"Flying like mad, sir," was the best that Halvorsen could muster.

"I'm not stupid. What else have you been doing?"

Halvorsen owned up to the candy drops.

"Didn't they teach you in ROTC at Utah State to keep your boss informed?" Haun whipped a copy of the newspaper Frankfurt Zeitung from under his desk and invited Halvorsen to have a look at it.

"You almost hit a reporter on the head with a candy bar in Berlin yesterday. He's spread the story all over Europe. The General called me with congratulations and I didn't know anything about it. General Turner wants to see you and there is an international press conference set up for you in Frankfurt. Fit them into your schedule. And, Lieutenant, keep flying, keep dropping and keep me informed."[228]

Several months before Halvorsen left, he had been approached at Tempelhof by a little girl clutching a tattered brown Teddy bear. The fuzz was completely worn off the bear's elbows. The girl did not know that she was talking to Uncle Wiggly Wings, the Chocolate Flyer. She had come to the airport, like so many other Berliners, to give a gift to any one of the fliers who were sustaining them. To her, Gail Halvorsen just happened to be one of those fliers, standing by his plane.

The bear, the little girl explained, had been her constant companion during the raids and during the Soviet assault on the city.

"Please take my teddy bear," she stammered, eyes filling with tears. "Good luck he will bring you and your friends on your flights to Berlin." The worn fuzzy bear was in Halverson's B-4 bag as he boarded the plane to go home.[229]

The Marshall Plan was the economic side to Truman's hard line with the Soviets. It helped to reestablish Western Europe as a viable economic bloc. But it was a tough sell to Congress.

Any country that has just completed a hard-fought war would want peace and a reduction in the wartime taxes needed to pay for the war. But this was not to be. Of course, there was grumbling about it. Roosevelt's former vice president, the socialist Henry Wallace, "denounced it as the 'Martial Plan' and saying that it was merely an anti-Soviet ploy that would breed war." Conservative Republican Senators, led by Robert Taft, grumbled that it was global New Dealism that threatened to bankrupt the United States.[230] The chairman of the Foreign Relations Committee, Republican Arthur Vandenburg was its Senate champion. In the end, it was passed by large majorities in the Congress.

The Russians saw the Marshall Plan as part of a Western conspiracy to impose capitalism throughout the world. While the Soviet Union considered it right to kidnap people and take whole factories out of their occupied territory, they would complain that the United States wanted to actually help the Germans. It was Russia's plan that Germany was to become an agricultural backwater rather than the economic dynamo that it once had been.

The Berlin Airlift was monumental in its task. It had to feed and fuel a city of 2.5 million people while its adversary, Stalin, could sit back and watch his choke hold slowly kill Berlin's inhabitants and the willpower of the West.

For over a year, American and British pilots risked their lives to feed their former enemies. The people of Berlin worked with their new allies to build new runways and off-load the cargo that would save their city from being abandoned to the Communists. Millions of tons of food and fuel were flown into the city. The "airbridge" was so successful that at its height the planes were bringing in more goods than had previously been delivered to Berlin via truck and rail line. During this heroic success, as many as sixty-five pilots lost their lives; and the effort was so great that it forced Stalin to finally end the blockade in September of 1949.

General Lucius Clay, the American military governor

of Germany during the airlift, spoke to a joint session of Congress about the people of Berlin.

> For two years the United Sates had tried desperately to make the four- power agreement work. We failed because one of the four powers had but two objectives in Germany: the one to exact the maximum in reparations and the other to establish the type and kind of government which could be controlled or at least exploited to the full by a police state. I saw in Berlin the spirit and soul of a people reborn. Two and one half million Germans had a second opportunity to choose freedom. They had foregone their first opportunity; they did not forgo their second opportunity.[231]
> The final RAF (Royal Air Force) flight that left from the base at Lubeck was the twin engine Dakota KN652. It landed at Gatow at 7:22 on September 23. One of the ground crew at Lubeck had chalked on the nose, "positively the last load from Lubeck, 73,705 tons-Psalm 21 Verse 11." To those who bothered to look it up, the biblical reference was quite appropriate. "For they intended great evil against us; they imagined a mischievous device, which they were not able to perform."[232]

It is to the great credit of the members of Parliament in London and the members of Congress in Washington that they recognized the coming threat of Stalin and stood up to him. When the Marshall Plan, the economic relief package to rebuild Europe, came before Congress, the Senate voted 69 to 17 for it (ten Senators did not vote) and the House of Representatives voted 329 to 74 for the plan. Better than 70 percent voted for it.

The fact that it passed highlights an important aspect of political history. It can truly be called a radical change in the way that the United States saw itself. And it was definitely the final nail in the coffin of President Washington's noninterventionist attitude as expressed in his farewell address. The United States government was taking the responsibility upon itself to secure the balance of power on the European Continent. It was doing what the British had hoped it would do. This was not because of the manipulation of the elites, though Britain surely had its contacts with influential Americans in high places in education and government. It was not because Truman was in the back pocket of Churchill. It was the cold, hard reality that faced the country. The Soviet Union was a hungry expansionist power leaning on Western Europe. It already had Eastern Europe as the spoils of war, and it wanted more. Someone had to stop them. Great Britain was willing to fight, but two world wars in which it needed help from the United States both times proved that Britain alone was not up to the fight. If the United States did not stand with the British against the Soviet Union in Berlin, it was clear that the United States would have to stand up to the Soviets later, when the Soviets would be even stronger, and perhaps without Britain's help.

Great Britain had fallen from power. Two successive world wars broke her bank and killed thousands upon thousands of its men. One can question whether or not there should have been an armistice in WWI after the war had bogged down, say in 1915. The kaiser was not evil incarnate, though propaganda made him out to be. From 1939-1945 Europe saw evil incarnate. The people of the United States could rightly ask in hindsight, "Why did we go to war in 1917? But the concentration camps of WWII verified the reason we went into another European war. After WWI, the evidence that was found was of British propaganda and lies. So the United States was slow to answer the call the second time. The second time was a real call of danger. Then following the Nazis, the Communist bear came stalking its prey.

But the mantle of the world's policeman had passed from Britain to the United States by the end of WWII.

When war had come in 1939, Great Britain had plentiful dollar and gold reserves, and her international debts amounted to 439 million Pounds. When the war ended, her reserves were depleted and the nation was 3.5 billion Pounds in debt.[233]

The frigid weather in the winter of 1946/47 was a body blow to the reeling British economy, and in the cabinet, debate raged as to where Britain could cut her draining overseas' commitments. In the early months of 1947, it seemed that the sun never set on Great Britain's responsibilities and expenses.[234]

Previously it was said that the sun never set on Great Britain's Empire.

Her exchequer had been drained by the cumulative effects of two world wars and the Great Depression, and the pound sterling retained its value only through massive infusions of American and Canadian dollars.[235]

Is it any wonder that Great Britain could not be in the vanguard of any fight against a formidable foe? If the United States had abandoned Berlin, if it had forsaken the Marshall Plan, Stalin might have gotten most of Europe. What he did not take physically would have been in the form of a vassal state doing his will, such as what Vichy was to Hitler. Communism and capitalism could not have mixed and there would have been a bloody conflict much like World War II. The Cold War (the period of East-West conflict from 1948-1989) boiled and cooled, then simmered, erupted, and cooled again. But there was never a major war between the two main antagonists, the United States and the Soviet Union.

In the late 1940s, the sun was setting on the British Empire. Prime Minister Ernest Bevin would have to give up Britain's control of Palestine. He handed it over to the newly formed United Nations. India would win its independence. The empire was unraveling.

As Churchill had so precisely stated in his "Iron Curtain" speech, The United States stood at the pinnacle of world power in the late 1940s. It could choose to climb down from that pinnacle, if it wanted. But that would have exposed Western

Europe to Soviet conquest, which would have led later on to war between the United States and an even larger, stronger Soviet Union. Stalin had already drawn the line at the Iron Curtain. The United States, led by Truman, would let it go no further. Berlin would be fed and warmed by the Berlin Airlift. The Cold War had begun. The United States would now fight the Soviet Union in proxy battles for world dominance to see who would become the emperor of the world.

Epilogue

A student of American history might consider this examination of the United States and its current mission as the new empire as being incomplete. One might think that because I am not going to delve into the Korean War, the Vietnam War, either Gulf Wars, or the War on Terrorism that I have fallen short of my goal of presenting the United States as an empire. Well, for one to cover the whole of the twentieth century in detail would take volumes. There is probably much that I could have added just from World War I. But my point is this: World War I was a war fought to protect the status quo of Europe. That status quo was that Britain had its empire intact. It ruled the oceans and therefore the world. France was a subordinate empire that had been thoroughly beaten by Britain, with the aid of the Prussians, and as such, no longer posed a threat to Britain's empire. Russia had a vast land empire stretching from Eastern Europe through Asia to the Pacific Ocean, but it was not an immediate threat to Britain. The United States had potential as an empire, but as of yet it was untested. Wilhelm's Germany threatened to destabilize the balance by threatening Britain's unrivaled domination of the seas and by threatening to reduce the power of France even further than it had already been diminished. Germany, the power in the middle of Western Europe, was considered a direct threat to Britain. Why it did not dawn on Jackie Fisher, the First Lord of the Admiralty, that a strong Germany held back the Russian bear from invading Europe, I do not know. Of course, Russia was no threat, even in the immediate aftermath of WWI, because it was still in the throes of the Soviet Revolution. But after WWII, the Russian bear stood and growled and no one in Europe could stop it. The old barrier of Prussia/Germany was destroyed. Austria was no more. France was beaten, and Britain was broken and beaten up. There was no one to stand up to the Russian bear, in the form of the Communist Soviet Union, except the United States. The United States had to and did step into the role previously fulfilled by Great Britain. The United States took on Britain's former role of ensuring the balance of power in Europe. It also projected its power around the globe, just like Great Britain, in varying degrees of success and sometimes failure—in Korea, Vietnam, the Middle East, Latin America, and so forth. It did so claiming, rightly, that it was advancing the cause of democracy. In 1989, the Berlin Wall came down. The Iron Curtain had become a porous sieve. Communism had been defeated, democracy and capitalism had won. Being the agent through which democracy and capitalism is spread is still an act of imperialism whether or not the United States wants to admit it. Butdemocracy imposed on another is still an imperial act. It may be a benevolent imperialism, but it is imperialism nonetheless. The same goes for free trade. Opening a country to free trade may be beneficial to all countries involved, but if it is imposed from the outside, it is still an imperial act.

But this all started when the United States entered World War I as a belligerent. If it had not, then Germany could very well have won the war. The kaiser's Germany was not the terrible hordes of barbaric Huns that Entente propaganda made them out to be. If a strong Germany had remained in Europe throughout the 1920s, it is unlikely that the Soviet Union would have ever grown to threaten or dominate Europe. Would there have been imperial clashes between Great Britain and Germany throughout the world? Probably, and what of the United States? Well we certainly would not have troops stationed in Germany. There would have been no need for NATO (North Atlantic Treaty Organization). There may have been no Korean or Vietnam wars, at least not for the United States.

So it was World War I that changed the whole of world history and set the stage for the "American Century." It was a war that we need not have joined. But we did and since then we have become:

The United States of Empire

Endnotes

Introduction

[0]1 Ferguson, Niall. Then Pity of War Explaining World War I. (New York, Basic Books, 1998), 337.

Chapter One
The Formation of German and the Franco-Prussian War.

[1] Bresler, Fenton. Napoleon III-A Life Napoleon III-A Life. (New York Carroll & Graf 1999), 339
[2] Fraser, David. Frederick The Great by David Fraser (New York, Fromm International, 2001), 15
[3] Fletcher, Richard. The Barbarian Conversion From Paganism to Christianity (New York A Marian Wood Book Henry Holt and Company 1997), 194
[4] Fraser, Frederick Great 6
[5] Ibid 7.
[6] Ibid 16.
[7] Ibid 16.
[8] Ibid 8.
[9] Ibid 21.

[10] Ibid 297.

[11] Schama, Simon.   Citizens A Chronicle of the French Revolution.   (New York, Alfred A. Knopf, 1989), 211.

[12] Fraser. Frederick Great, 56.

[13] Schama, Citizens, 25.

[14] Ibid 354

[15] Ibid 354

[16] Ibid 29

[17] Ibid 171

[18] Ibid 640

[19] Bressler Napoleon III 361

[20] Ibid 364

[21] Ibid 364

[22] Ibid 361

Chapter Two
The Boer War

[23] Packenham, Thomas . The Boer War. (New York, Random House, 1979), XIII

[24] Ibid 13

[25] Ibid XXVII

[26] Ibid 102

[27] Ibid 607

[28] Ibid 155

[29] Carter, Violet Bonham. Winston Churchill An Intimate Portrait. (New York, Harcourt, Brace and World, 1965), 33.

[30] Ibid 36

[31] Ibid 38

[32] Ibid 41

[33] Ibid 44

[34] Ibid 45

[35] Gilbert, Martin. Churchill and America. (New York, Free Press, 2005), 36

[36] Packenham, Boer War, 326

[37] Ibid 363

[38] Ibid 399

Chapter Three
Location, Location, Location

[39] Massie, Robert K.. Dreadnought Britain Germany, and the Coming of the Great War. (New York Random House, 1991), 307.

[40] Ibid 87

[41] Ibid 893

[42] Marshall, S.L.A.. World War I. (Boston Houghton Mifflin Company, 1964), 50.

[43] Philips, Kevin. The Cousin's Wars: Religion Politics and the3 Triumph of Anglo-America. (New York, Basic Books, 1999), 64.

[44] Massie, Dreadnought, 895

[45] Ibid 895

[46] Ibid 895 Attribute to someone.

[47] Ibid 896

[48] Simpson, Colin. The Lusitania. (Boston, Toronto, Little and Brown Company, 1972), 26.

[49] Ibid 38

[50] Mahan, Alfred Thayer. The Influence of Sea Power Upon history 1660-1783 (Dover, Little and Brown Company, 1987) 30

[51][52] Ibid 200

[53] Wegner, Wolfgang. The Naval Strategy of the World War, Classics of Sea Power. trans. Holger Herwig (Annapolis Maryland, Naval Institute Press, 1989), 15.

[54] Ibid 22

[55] Ibid 28

Chapter Four
The Gospel According to Mahan

[56] Almighty, God. The Bible. (Cambridge, Cambridge University Press 1621), II Chronicles 26:15

[57] Massie, Dreadnought, 478.

[58] Mahan, Influence, 225

[59] Ibid 237

[60] Massie, Dreadnought,274

[61] Churchill, Winston. The Great Republic. (New York, The Modern Library, 2001), 136

[62] Massie, Dreadnought, 192

[63] Ibid 855

[64] Kaiser Wilhelm (Sutton Publishing Phoenix Mill, United Kingdom, 1999), 6

[65] Ibid 5

[66] Massie, Dreadnought, 135

[67] Ibid 449

[68] Ibid 409

[69] Ibid 403

[70] Ibid 402

[71] Ibid 406

[72] Ibid 609

[73] Ibid 618

[74] Ibid 622

[75] Ibid 623

[76] Ibid 618

Chapter Five
The War to End All Wars.

[77] Massie, Dreadnought, 859.

[78] Ibid 859

[79] Ibid 859

[80] Fromkin, David. Europe's Last Summer. Who Started the Great War in 1914? (New York: Alfred A. Knopf, 2004), 153.

[81] Ibid 143

[82] Massie, Dreadnought, 838

[83] Ibid 839

[84] Ibid 840

[85] Ibid 863

[86] Ibid 866

[87] Ibid 867
[88] Ibid 869
[89] Ibid 874
[90] Ibid 876
[91] Ibid 898
[92] Ibid 902
[93] Ibid 903
[94] Ibid 904
[95] Ibid 905
[96] Ibid 907

Chapter Six
The Battle of Jutland

[97] Simpson, Colin, Lusitania, 92.
[98] Tarrant, V.E.. Jutland, The German Perspective. (London, Brockhampton Press 1999), 50.
[99] Mahan, Alfred Thayer, Influence of Sea Power, 136
[100] Ibid 138
[101]   Massie, Robert K. Castles of Steel Britain, Germany and the Winning of the Great War at Sea. (New York, Random House, 2003), 536
[102] Ibid 534
[103] Ibid 57
[104] Ibid 83
[105] Tarrant, Jutland, 72.
[106] Massie, Castles of Steel, 557
[107] Ibid 558
[108] Ibid 558
[109] Ibid 580
[110] Ibid 582
[111] Tarrant Jutland 72
[112] Ibid 84
[113] Ibid 90
[114] Massie, Castles of Steel, 596
[115] Ibid 602

116 Ibid 608
117 Tarrant, Jutland 120
118 Massie, Castles of Steel, 612
119 Ibid 622
120 Ibid 625
121 Ibid 626
122 Tarant, Jutland 157
123 Ibid 167
124 Massie, Castles of Steel, 631
125 Ibid 632
126 Ibid 642
127 Tarrant, Jutland, 195
128 Massie, Castles of Steel 660
129 Tarrant, Jutland, 250
130 Ibid 250
131 Flemming, Thomas. The Illusion of Victory in World War I. (New York, Basic Books, 2003), 114
132 Ibid 115
133 Massie, Castles of Steel, 775

Chapter Seven
Propaganda

134 Massie, Castles of Steel, 77
135 Simpson, Lusitania, 28
136 Ibid 55
137 Ibid 203
138 Ibid 194
139 Mahan, Influence of Sea Power, 138
140 Mosier, John. The Myth of the Great War. A New History of World War I. (New York, Harper Colins, 2001), 77
141 Churchill, Republic, 238
142 Martin, Churchill and America, (New York, London, Free Press, 2005), 45.
143 Brands, H.W.. T.R. The Last Romantic. (New York, Basic Books, 1997), 479.

[144] Massie, Dreadnought, 246.

[145] Ibid 292

[146] Arthur Zimmerman, Zimmerman Telegram, World War I Document Archive gwpda.org,.

[147] Carr, William. The History of Germany. (New York, St. Martin's Press, 1969), 126.

[148] Massie, Dreadnought, 342.

[149] Ibid 406

[150] Flynn, John. The Roosevelt Myth (San Francisco Fiftieth Anniversary Edition, 1998), 154

Chapter Eight
The United States Enters the War: The great Push to Paris Fails

[151] Marsahll, World War I, 263

[152] Carr, History of Germany, 241

[153] Marshall, World War I, 322.

[154] Ibid 329

[155] Showalter, Dennis E..Tannenberg Clash of Empires. (Washington D.C. Brassey's 2004), 346

[156] Marshall, World War I, 333

[157] Terraine, John. To win a War, The year of Victory. (London, Cassell, 2000), 39.

[158] Ibid 72

[159] Senator George W. Norris Senate speech on vote for war www.mtholyoke.edu/acad/intrel/doc19.htm

[160] Ibid Senator La Follette www.mtholyoke.edu/acad/intrel/doc19.htm

[161] Massie, Dreadnought, 896.

[162] Johnson, J.H.. 1918 The Unexpected Victory. (London, Cassell, 1997), 55

[163] Ibid 72

[164] Marshall, World War I, 437.

[165] Ibid 438

[166] Ibid 132

167 Evans Richard J.. The Coming of the Third Reich. (New York, Penguin Press, 2004), 73

168 Ibid 74

169 Ibid 202

Chapter Nine
The Great Depression and World War II

170 Shlaes, Amity. The Forgotten Man A New History of the Great Depression. (New York, Harper Collins Publishers, 2007), 96

171 Powell, Jim. FDR's Folly How Roosevelt and His Policies Prolonged the Great Depression. (New York Three Rivers Press, 2003), 43

172 Ibid 43

173 Shlaes, Forgotten Man, 97.

174 Powell, FDDR's Folly, 48

175 Shlaes Forgotten Man

176 Flynn, Roosevelt Myth, 16

177 FDR's Folly 55

178 Ibid 76

179 Ibid 14

180 Flynn, Roosevelt Myth, 39

181 Shlaes, Forgotten Man, 161

182 Ibid 163

183 Powell, FDR"s Folly 209

184 Ibid 267

185 Schlaes, Forgotten Man, 61

186 Flynn, Roosevelt Myth, 273

187 Renwick, Sir Robin. Fighting With Allies. (New York, Toronto, Time Book Random House 1996) , 39

188 John Chettle Winston Churchill in America. Smithsonian 32???? (2001): 86

189 Brewer Susan A.. To Win the Peace British Propaganda in the United states During World War II. (Ithaca and London, Cornell University Press, 1997), 30.

[190] Ibid 47

[191] Mosier, Myth of the Great War, 335

[192] Stinnett, Robert B.. The Day of Deceit. (New York, Free Press, 2000), 8

[193] Ibid 13

[194] Ibid 18

[195] Ibid 65

[196] Ibid 21

[197] Ibid 22

[198] Popov, Dusko. Spy Counterspy. (Greenwich Connecticut, Fawcett Publications, 1974), 123

[199] Ibid 124

[200] Ibid 120

[201] Ibid 140

[202] Ibid 157

Chapter Ten
The Cold War A Solemn Moment in American History

[203] Hitler, Adolf.   Mein Kampf.   Trans. Ralph Manheim (Boston, Houghton Mifflin Company, 1971), 644

[204] Ibid 653

[205] Ibid 654

[206] George Washington, Farewell Address, 1798

[207] Flemming, Illusion of Victory, 355

[208] Brewer, To Win the Peace, 2.

[209] Ibid 1

[210] Haydock, Michael D.. City Under Siege, The Berlin Blockade and Airlift, 1948-1949 (Washington and London, Brassey's 1999), 69

[211] Ibid 70

[212] Ibid 120

[213] Ibid 50

[214] Ibid 78

[215] Ibid 63

[216] Ibid 63

[217] Ibid 80

[218] Ibid 82

[219] Ibid 149

[220] Ibid 151

[221] Ibid 152

[222] Ibid 161

[223] Ibid 173

[224] Ibid 174

[225] Ibid 179

[226] Ibid 177

[227] Ibid 185

[228] Ibid 193

[229] Ibid 260

[230] Ibid 114

[231] Ibid 272

[232] Ibid 274

[233] Ibid 77

[234] Ibid 92

[235] Ibid 92

Bibliography

Gleichen,Lord Edward, editor. Chronology of the Great War 1914-1918. Greenhill Books, London, Stackpole Books Pennsylvania 2000

Bressler, Fenton Napoleon III - A Life. Carrol & Graf Publishers, New York, 1999.

Fraser,David. Frederick the Great. Fromm International, New York, 2005

Fletcher,Richard. The Barbarian Conversion - from Paganism to Christianity, published by Henry Holt and Company Inc. New York, 1997

Schama, Simon. Citizens - A Chronicle of the French Revolution. New York, Alfred A. Knopf 1989

Massie, by Robert K.. Dreadnought Britain Germany, and the coming of the Great War. Ballantine Books, New York, 1991

Massie, by Robert K.. Castles of Steel Britian Germany and the Winning of the Great War at Sea. Random House, New York, 2003.

Marshall, S.L.A.. World War I. ?????The Hough Miflin Company, Boston, 1964

Philips, Kevin. The Cousin's Wars Religion Politics and the triumph of Anglo-America. Basic Books A member of the Perseus Books Group, New York,1999.

Simpson, Colin. The Lusitania. Little and Brown Company-Boston-Toronto,   1972

Mahan,   Alfred Thayer. The Influence of Sea Power Upon History 1660-1783. Dover Publications, New York, 1987.

Wegner, Vice Admiral Wolfgang.   Classics of Sea Power: The Naval Strategy of the World War. Translated by Holger Herwig. Naval Institute Press, Annapolis Maryland, 1989.

Packenham, Thomas. The Boer War. Random House, New York, 1979.

Carter,   Violet Bonham. Winston Churchill an Intimate Portrait. Harcourt Brace and World, New York, 1965.

Gilbert, Martin. Churchill and America. New York, London, Toronto, Sydney, Free Press, 2005

Churchill, Sir Winston The Great Republic, A History of America. Modern Library Paperback Edition, New York, 2001.

Van Der Kiste, John. Kaiser Wilhelm II   Germany's Last Emperor. Phoenix Mills United Kingdom, 1999.

Fromkin, David. Europe's Last Summer   Who Started the Great War in 1914. Alfred A. Knopf, New York, 2004.

Mosier, John. The Myth of the Great War A New Military history of World War I. Harper Collins, New York 2001.

Gilbert, Martin. Churchill and America. Free Press, New York, 2005.

Brands, H.W..   T. R. The Last Romantic. Basic Books A Subsidiary of Perseus Books, New York, 1997.

Carr, William. A History of Germany. St. Martin Press New York 1969.

The Declaration of Independence.

Powell, Jim. FDR's Folly How Roosevelt and his New Deal Policies Prolonged the Great Depression. Three Rivers Press New York, 2003.

Flynn, John T.. The Roosevelt Myth. Fox and Wilkes, Fiftieth Anniversary, San Francisco Edition 1998.

Chettle, John H.. Winston Churchill In America. Smithsonian 32(2001): 80-90.

Brewer, Susan A.. To Win The Peace British Propaganda In The United States During World War II Cornell University Press Ithaca and London,1997.

Hitler, Adolf. Mein Kampf. 1925 translated by Ralph Manheim Houghton Mifflin Company, 1971.

George Washington. Farwell Address by the First President of the United States, 1798.

Fleming, Thomas. The illusion of Victory America in World War One, America in World War I. Basic Books New York, 2003.

Terraine, John. To Win a War. Cassell Military Paperbacks, 2000.

Tarrant, V.E.. Jutland, The German Perspective. Brockhampton Press, Ebbw Vale, 1995.

Preston, Diana. Lusitania An Epic Tragedy. Walker and Company New York, 2002.

MacMillan, Margaret. Paris 1919 Six Months That Changed the World. Random house, New York, 2001.

Holmes, Richard. In the Footsteps of Churchill A Study in Character. Basic Books, New York 2005.

Powell, Jim. Wilson's War . How Woodrow Wilson's Great Blunder Led to Hitler, Lenin, Stalin & World War II. Crown Forum, New York, 2005

Richie, Alexandra. Faust's Metropolis, A History of Berlin. Carroll and Graf Publishers, New York, 1998.

Middlebrook, Martin. The Kaiser's Battle. Penguin Books, New York 2000

Showalter, Dennis E.. Tannenberg Clash of Empires Brassey's Washington D.C., 2004.

Ferguson, Niall. The Pity of War. Basic Books, New York 1999.

Made in the USA
Middletown, DE
26 May 2015